Modern European History

A Garland Series of Outstanding Dissertations

MODERN EUROPEAN HISTORY

The Political Thought of Yu. F. Samarin, 1840–1864

Loren David Calder

Garland Publishing, Inc.
New York and London 1987

Library of Congress Cataloging-in-Publication Data

Calder, Loren David, 1929–
    The political thought of Yu. F. Samarin,
1840–1864.

    (Modern European history)
    Originally presented as the author's thesis
(Ph. D.—University of London, 1980)
    Bibliography: p.
    1. Samarin, IÛ. Ḟ. (IÛrĭĭ Ḟedorovich), 1819–1876—
Contributions in Political science.   2. Conservatism—
Soviet Union—History—19th century.   3. Political
participation—Soviet Union—History—19th century.
I. Title.   II. Series.
JC248.S25C34   1987   320.5′092′4   87-7546
ISBN 0-8240-8052-1 (alk. paper)

All volumes in this series are printed on acid-free,
250-year-life paper.

Printed in the United States of America

THE POLITICAL THOUGHT

OF

YU. F. SAMARIN
1840 - 1864

BY

LOREN DAVID CALDER

All quotations from Russian language sources have been translated

by the author, unless otherwise indicated

ABSTRACT

Yu. F. Samarin (1819-1876) was one of the original Slavophils.
He was the most important Slavophil statesman, making a very significant
contribution to the formulation, drafting and implementation of the
Emancipation Edict of 1861. He also served creatively in the whole
range of Zemstvo council work at both the provincial and municipal levels,
and made a substantial impact on policy as a passionate exponent of
Russian interests in Poland and the Baltic provinces.

In this dissertation Samarin's development and performance as
a political thinker is examined from his early days as a Master's student
at the University of Moscow to the completion of his work on the peasant
land reform in 1864. Chapter I provides an introductory survey of his
career. Chapter II contains an examination of the impact on his political
philosophy of his family upbringing, his Russian Orthodox religious
training, his friendships with Konstantin Aksakov and Alexander Popov, and
his study of the philosophers Hegel and Khomiakov. Chapter III contains
an examination of his analysis of the influence of Catholicism, Protestantism
and Orthodoxy on Russian history. In this chapter relationships between
Church and State, and finally the impact of Peter the Great's "Spiritual
Regulation" on Church-State relations is of special importance. Chapter IV
provides an examination of the political content of his writings during
the period 1844-1848 when he was a civil-servant working in St. Petersburg
and Riga, and Chapter V contains an examination of his work as an authority
on the peasant question.

This dissertation establishes that Samarin was a competent political theorist, who is best characterized as an "enlightened conservative." As such he was a Christian statesman. As such he believed in the organic development of society, and loved what was essential in Russia's traditional institutions, the autocratic monarchy and the Orthodox Church. As such he believed in justice for all, freedom of conscience, freedom of opinion, popular participation in decision-making processes, and the orderly evolution of political, economic and social forms of relationship.

TABLE OF CONTENTS

The general purpose of this thesis is to examine the political thought of Yu. F. Samarin as set out in his writings from 1840, when he was a student at the University of Moscow engaged in writing a Master's thesis, to 1864 when he completed his work on the Great Peasant Reform. Samarin's status as the most outstanding Slavophil statesman, his life-long preoccupation with political questions and his stellar performance as propagandist, polemicist and reformer establish his political thought as a credible subject for investigation. The fact that no book-length piece has been written on Samarin's political thought in any language, makes it a desirable subject for investigation and the fact that no full-length study of Samarin at all has been written in the English language to date gives it very real potential value for British and North American students of Russian affairs.

The specific purposes of this thesis are: (1) to complete a thorough, comprehensive and systematic summarization of Samarin's political thought; (2) to organize and to explain his political thought; (3) to establish on this basis his position on the broad spectrum of political opinion; and (4) to attempt an assessment of his stature as a political theorist. In short, this thesis is to be a systematic typological enquiry in the classical tradition.

The organizational framework of this study is chronological for two main reasons. On the one hand, Samarin's life and thought divide into neat segments on the basis of his evolving interests. On the other hand, he was not a political thinker in the tradition of great theorists like Plato, Aristotle and Hobbes who analyzed the state and

other political institutions as well as the norms and goals of political activity in the process of creating theoretical systems, but a
thinker who analyzed and wrote about current political issues as his
interests and experience dictated, scattering his political ideas
throughout the whole corpus of his work in a relatively unsystematic
way.

The chronological limitations imposed on the investigation are
both logical and desirable for the following reasons. First, the
objective of being thorough and comprehensive does not mesh well with
the scope of Samarin's political activities and the prolific output of
his pen. Second, on Samarin's own testimony his theoretical position
was firmly established by 1848,[i] and his energies were consciously
expended to implement its elements in concrete reform measures altering
age-old landlord-peasant relationships. Thus his work on the Great
Peasant Reform can be seen as a laboratory test case for his political
ideas and a suitable point at which to terminate this study of his
political thought.

The adjective "political" is a complex word. It has not had, and
does not now have a precise, narrowly definable meaning. The Shorter
Oxford Dictionary defines political as "of, belonging or pertaining
to, the state, its government and policy; public, civil; of or pertaining to the science or art of politics." For Plato, not only government, but every important relationship in society had political signi-

---

[i]See p. 233 above.

ficance.[ii] Presumably, therefore, almost any concatenation of topics focussing on societal relationships of consequence - demographic shifts, poverty, ideological strife, racial discord, class conflict, governmental structure, freedom of expression, economic equality, religious toleration, public order, law enforcement, transfer of power - identifies political issues. Aristotle argued that every political association involves "authority" or "rule", and his influence has been so pervasive that it has generally been accepted since his time that "a political relationship in some way involves authority, ruling, or power."[iii] Count Metternich, the famous Austrian Chancellor, associated politics with the relationships between states:

> Politics is the science of the vital interests of States, in its widest meaning. Since, however, an isolated State no longer exists and is found only in the annals of the heathen world ... we must always view the Society of States as the essential condition of the modern world. The great axioms of political science proceed from the knowledge of the true political interests of all States; it is upon these general interests that rests the guarantee of their existence. The establishing of international relations on the basis of reciprocity under the guarantee of respect for acquired rights ... constitutes in our time the essence of politics, of which diplomacy is merely the daily application. Between the two there is in my opinion the same difference as between science and art."[iv]

[ii]Sheldon S. Wolin, "Political Theory-Trends and Tools", International Encyclopedia of the Social Sciences, David L. Sills, ed., (New York: The Macmillan Company and The Free Press, 1968), p. 324.

[iii]Robert Dahl, Modern Political Analysis (Englewood Cliffs: N.J., Prentice-Hall, Inc., 1976), pp. 1-2.

[iv]Quoted in Harold Nicolson, The Congress of Vienna, A Study in Allied Unity, 1812-1822 (New York: The Viking Press, 1962), p. 39.

For Bernard Crick, a contemporary British political scientist, politi-

cal action is the process through which democratic societies work out

their differences:

> There is no end to the praises that can be sung of poli-
> tics. In politics, not in economics, is found the creative
> dialectic of opposites: for politics is a bold prudence, a
> diverse unity, an armed conciliation, a natural artifice, a
> creative compromise, and a serious game in which free civi-
> lization depends; it is a reforming conserver, a sceptical
> believer, and a pluralistic moralist; it is a lively so-
> briety, a complex simplicity, an untidy elegance, a rough
> civility, and an everlasting immediacy; it is conflict
> become discussion; and it sets us a humane task on a human
> scale. And there is no end to the dangers that it faces:
> there are so many reasons that sound so plausible for
> rejecting the responsibility and uncertainty of freedom ...
> political activity is best seen as only one form of power
> relationship and political rule as only one form of govern-
> ment.[v]

Harold Lasswell, an outstanding contemporary American political scien-

tist, defines "political science as an empirical discipline", which

"studies the shaping and sharing of power", and "a political act, [as]

one performed in power perspectives."[vi] Robert Dahl, another con-

temporary American political scientist, claims, reminiscent of

Aristotle, that "a political system [government, state, power, or set

of decision-making processes] is any persistent pattern of human rela-

tionships that involves to a significant degree, power, rule, or

authority."[vii] Finally, David Easton, the father of contemporary

systems analysis, says that "political life concerns all those varie-

---

[v]Bernard Crick, In Defence of Politics (Harmondsworth, Middlesex, England: Penguin Books Ltd., 1976), pp.160-161.

[vi]As quoted in Dahl, Modern Political Analysis, pp.2-3.

[vii]Ibid., p.6.

ties of activity that influence significantly the kind of authoritative policy adopted for a society and the way it is put into practice. We are said to be participating in political life when our activity relates in some way to the making and execution of policy for a society."[viii] The common elements in all of these statements refer to government, the exercise of power and the processes by which communities resolve all issues of general relevance and concern. For the purpose of this study, therefore, every Samarin thought which seems to fall between these limits will be considered to have political significance.

The word "thought" is used in this study in the very broad meaning that has been found best for examining the ideas of political theorists:

> It comprises a thinker's entire teaching on a subject (his lehre), including his description of the facts, his explanations (no matter whether religious, philosophical, or empirical), his conception of history, his value judgements, and his proposals of goals, of policy, and of principles.[ix]

The organizational framework of this thesis is chronological except for Chapter I which provides a biographical sketch highlighting

---

[viii]David Easton, The Political System: An Inquiry into the State of Political Science (New York: Alfred A. Knopf, 1965), p.128. On another occasion Easton defined "a political system as that behavior or set of interactions through which authoritative allocations (or binding decisions) are made and implemented for a society." David Easton, "Political Science", International Encyclopedia of the Social Sciences, David L. Sills, ed., (New York: the Macmillan Company and the Free Press, 1968), vol. 12, p.285.

[ix]Arnold Brecht, "Political Theory-Approaches", International Encyclopedia of the Social Sciences, vol. 12, p.307.

the main facts of Samarin's life and thought. Chapter II deals with

the development and exposition of Samarin's ideas 1840-1844 when he was

a Master's student at the University of Moscow and came under the

influence first of Hegel and then of Khomiakov. Chapter III treats the

political ideas set out by Samarin in his M.A. thesis "Stefan Yavorsky

and Feofan Prokopovich" (June 3, 1844). Chapter IV focuses on

Samarin's political thought 1844-1848 when he was a civil servant

employed primarily in drafting administrative reforms for the city of

Riga. Chapter V deals with Samarin's political thought 1848-1864 as

expressed and exemplified by his work on the emancipation problem.

The bibliography is the result of an exhaustive search for every

piece, large or small, written by Samarin during his very active career

as scholar and polemicist, as well as for every piece written about him

up to the present time. It contains a more extensive listing than any

other source presently available, and except for listing the contents

of approximately two volumes of unpublished letters in the Department

of Manuscripts of the Lenin Library in Moscow, appears to be absolutely

complete. Of course this claim could not be made if it were not for

the great contribution which Samarin's younger brother, Dmitri, made in

collecting, organizing and publishing the Sochineniya (Works) in ten

volumes between 1877 and 1896. Nor can the contribution of Peter

Samarin, a nephew, go unmentioned. He published volume twelve of the

Sochineniya, containing Samarin's correspondence 1840-1853, collected

two other volumes of correspondence for publication, and also prepared

prefaces for an eleventh volume which was to contain most of the articles listed on pages 325-326 below. Baron B.E. Nol'de deserves special mention too for the important contribution which the extensive bibliographical notes appended to his excellent study Yuriy Samarin i ego vremya (Yuri Samarin and his times) have made to Samarin scholarship. One last word, the general bibliography contains a selection of books and articles on all of the subjects which were of special interest to Samarin.

The best sources of information about Samarin are the extensive biographical and analytical prefaces to each volume of the Sochineniya. Of these the most important are in volumes five and seven. The best single volume study of Samarin's life and thought is the above-mentioned book by Baron B.E. Nol'de, Yuriy Samarin i ego vremya. The best articles on Samarin's career were written by Peter Struve ["Yuriy Samarin: Opyt Kharakteristiki i otsenki" (A characterization and evaluation)] and Paul Vinogradov ("A Prophetic Career").

Extensive use of quotations has been made in this study, because the flavour and content of the subject's thought is best transmitted in his original statements. In translating these statements, the main concern has been to render the original as accurately and clearly as possible, even when this has meant excessive literalness and awkward English syntax. Quotation marks have not been used for emphasis and therefore, usually mark words, phrases and sentences of Samarin himself. Russian words have been transliterated according to the English-style system as modified by the Slavonic and East European Review. The sole exception to this rule is to transliterate the surnames Herzen and Khomiakov in accordance with current practice.

CHAPTER I

A Biographical Sketch

Yuri Samarin belonged to the same generation of Russians as Leo Tolstoy, Fedor Dostoyevsky, Mikhail Katkov, Alexander Herzen, Nicholas Chernyshevsky, and the Tsar Alexander II. He enjoyed all the advantages of noble birth, being born in St. Petersburg on April 21, 1819 into a family that moved in the highest court circles. Enormous patrimonial estates held near Moscow, Tula and Samara were the basis of the family's affluence, and long associations with the court were the guarantee of its social and political privileges.[1]

In 1826, when Yuri was still only seven years old, his father moved his family to Moscow. In view of the depth of Yuri's future Russian patriotism, it is worth noting that his father's main reason for leaving St. Petersburg was to break his children away from the French atmosphere of its court. As an indicator of how pervasive this atmosphere was, Yuri spoke only French at this stage of his development.

The elder Samarin's main concern when he reached Moscow was to superintend the education of his children. To this end he established a very good household school, setting high standards and employing only the best teachers. Yuri Samarin obtained all of his basic education in this family school. When he entered the University of Moscow, in 1834 at the age of fifteen, he had an excellent knowledge of Russian, French and Latin, and a good grounding in Greek, German, geography and arithmetic.

On entering the university Yuri elected to study in the Faculty of Arts (slovesnoe otdelenie). His favourite subject was history and his

---

[1]Baron B.E. Nol'de, Yuri Samarin i ego vremya (Paris, 1926), pp. 8-9. This is the one full-length biography of Samarin available. It is an excellent work, rich in factual detail and penetrating analysis. Another useful work is Dmitry Samarin, "Biograficheski ocherk Yu. F. Samarina," Sochineniya Yu. F. Samarina, IX (Moscow, 1898), IX-XXIV.

favourite professor, the famous historian and exponent of "official

nationalism," M.P. Pogodin. Certainly Samarin was pushed towards

Slavophilism by Pogodin's teachings, for he said of him:

> He had an independent direction of thought...warmed by
> a deep sympathy for Russian life....He brought us to a
> completely new view of Russian history and Russian life in
> general. Western formulas were not applicable to us; in
> Russian life there was some kind of particular beginning
> foreign to other people; her development proceeded by
> another law, as yet undetermined by science. Pogodin said
> this to us fairly awkwardly, without proof, but in such a
> way that his conviction became a part of us.[2]

These ideas Samarin would express repeatedly as a mature Slavophil

politician and polemicist. He finished his course at the university in

1838 at the top of his class.[3]

It was at the university that Samarin met Konstantin Aksakov,[4]

his closest and most influential friend of the period. These two young

men, their respective courses completed, began to study for the

master's degree together. Through diligent study, writing and

discussion they gradually consolidated their views on religion, Russia

and Europe. One of the immediate consequences of this friendship for

Samarin was that it brought him into contact with literary and

progressive Moscow. Gogol and Lermontov frequented the Aksakov home,

---

[2]Yu. F. Samarin, "Iz vospominanii ob universitete 1834-1838," Rus', No. 1 (November 15, 1880), p. 19.

[3]Among his classmates was S.M. Solov'ev, the outstanding historian, and M. Katkov, the influential conservative journalist of the 1870's and 1880's. Nol'de, p. 13.

[4]Konstantin S. Aksakov (1817-60) became one of the most prominent Slavophils. A son of the writer S.T. Aksakov, he was the Slavophil historian and philologist. In his work he developed the belief that religious and moral factors determine the historical process, that the true religion was Orthodoxy, and that only on the basis of Orthodoxy could durable political and social forms be created. See K.S. Aksakov, Polnoe sobranie sochineniy, ed. I.S. Aksakov (3 vols.; Moscow, 1861-80).

as did Stankevich, Belinsky, Herzen, Bakunin and Granovsky. It was
during this period also that he and Aksakov met and joined the group of
people which later became known as the Slavophils. First among them
were Aleksey Khomiakov and Ivan Kireyevsky, the principal founders of
the Slavophil movement.[5]

In the spring of 1840 Samarin began work on his Master's thesis, a
project which had a decisive influence on his future career.[6] His
assigned topic was Stefan Yavorsky and Feofan Prokopovich, preachers
and administrators of the Russian Orthodox Church during the Petrine
era. Already convinced that religious questions were of vital
importance and finding them of absorbing interest, he decided that in
writing his thesis, he would seek to establish his position on religion
and on the religious conflicts that had rent history. On this founda-

---

[5]Alexey S. Khomiakov (1804-60) was a public-man, poet, and
philosopher-theologian. He had roots in the old aristocracy, was a
wealthy landowner, and was a founding member and leader of the
Slavophil movement. In the late thirties he began to enunciate
Slavophil doctrine. He proclaimed that Russia had a unique course of
development opposed to that of the West with its individualism and
materialism. He valued the commune (obshchina) because it embodied the
principle of brotherhood, and he was a convinced monarchist and
defender of autocracy, even while he favoured political and social
reforms. He believed in the superiority of Orthodoxy and in the
primacy of faith and religion. See A.S. Khomiakov, Polnoe sobranie
sochineniy (8 vols.; Moscow, 1900-1904).

Ivan V.Kireyevsky (1808-56) a prominent philosopher and publicist,
was also one of the founders of Slavophilism. As an active propagator
of Slavophil ideas he exercised a powerful influence on the movement.
He was convinced of the superiority of the Russian experience based on
the commune (obshchina) and Orthodoxy. He emphasized the importance of
revelation and was sceptical of rationalism. See Polnoe sobranie
sochinenii Ivana Vasil'evicha Kireyevskogo, pub. A.I. Koshelev (2
vols.; Moscow, 1861).

[6]The most detailed account of Samarin's life during this period
is to be found in D. Samarin, "Dannyya dlya biografii Yu. F.
Samarina za 1840-1845 gg.," Sochineniya, V (Moscow, 1880), XXV-XCII:
also in Russkiy biograficheskiy slovar', XVIII (St. Petersburg, 1904),
133-46.

tion his thesis took shape. In the first part, "Stefan Yavorsky and Feofan Prokopovich as Theologians," he sought to establish the place of Orthodoxy as a religious teaching. In the second part, "Stefan Yavorsky and Feofan Prokopovich as officials of the Church," he studied the relationship of the Orthodox Church to the Russian state. In the third part, "Stefan Yavorsky and Feofan Prokopovich as Preachers," he examined the literary content of their writings. This third part had little real interest for Samarin, but had to be written to satisfy university requirements.[7]

This period saw the youth pass through a crisis arising from a conflict between faith and reason. Essentially he tried to prove, using Hegel, that Orthodoxy was the only true religious doctrine. His deliberations led him into a morass of confusion and doubt from which Khomiakov extricated him by bringing him to the view that belief cannot, and should not, be demonstrated rationally. Khomiakov's strength lay in his unshakable faith in Orthodoxy and this characteristic Samarin came to share with him. Certainly the mature Samarin was distinguished by a deep and abiding faith in the Russian Orthodox Church as an institution, and as an "organism of truth and love."[8]

The second part of Samarin's thesis--a study of Church-State relationships in Russia--merits special attention for it foreshadows the direction of his future career. In this work he set himself a

[7] Sochineniya, V: Stefan Yavorsky i Feofan Prokopovich (Moscow, 1880). Part 3 was published separately by the University of Moscow as Stefan Yavorsky i Feofan Prokopovich, kak propovedniki (Moscow, 1844). Samarin's collected works were published in eleven volumes (I-X,XII) between 1877-1911.

[8] Nol'de, p. 31: see P.K. Christoff, A.S. Xomjakov (The Hague, 1961), p. 56.

political question, thus for the first time entering into a field of thought and action in which he would distinguish himself later. The privileged environment in which Samarin grew up and his family's long tradition of close relations with the court all but guaranteed that he would be a monarchist. In fact, autocracy became, for him, the foundation of Russian society. He would say as late as December, 1867:

> that it is still not time for Russia to think about a change of the existing form of government...autocracy was never so strong morally as now...at this minute no other power could inspire such faith, could dispose so easily of such voluntary, unanimous, and unqualified co-operation from the nation; I conclude from this that the historical calling of autocracy has still not been fulfilled and that it is still destined to do much for Russia.[9]

However, conservative as Samarin's belief in autocracy might seem, he revealed strong liberal tendencies early: while working on this part of his thesis he modified his monarchical principles to argue that "absolute power...must be founded on the acknowledgement of a wide sphere of freedom for the subject."[10] He also argued that a free church in a society recognizing freedom of religious conscience for every one of its members was mandatory for human fulfillment.

Samarin presented his thesis in the fall of 1843, and defended it brilliantly the following spring. He now had to decide on a direction for his future career. While his personal inclination was to pursue a life of scholarship, his father was anxious for him to enter the government service, so that Samarin, accepting his father's wishes, left for St. Petersburg and an appointment in the Ministry of Justice

---

[9]Samarin, Sochineniya, VII (Moscow, 1890), 4.

[10]Nol'de, p. 27.

(August, 1844).[11]

In all he spent two rather depressing years in St. Petersburg, moving to various governmental departments but always doing the same thing--copying and correcting reports. His response to his work and to the deadening bureaucratic atmosphere of the capital was positive, however; for we see him in a letter of this period reproaching Konstantin Aksakov for his "Moscowism," that is, for his tendency to denounce St. Petersburg, and yet make no positive contribution to the improvement of affairs. Samarin himself began a serious study of Russia's history for the purpose of gaining a clearer understanding of her present political, cultural and religious situation.[12] On this basis he would soon be active in defending Russia's traditions, and in reforming her institutions, for he was already convinced that theory must be wedded to practice. Time and again in his career he used theory based on research as an adjunct to practice, and habitually urged others to take an active line. As this period advanced there was a steady growth in his interest in social and political questions. It culminated in two events signalizing active involvement in politics. First, in May, 1846, he was posted to Riga, in the service of the Ministry of Internal Affairs, to work on a commission established to draft a plan for reform of the administrtive structure and economy of the city. Second, his article "On the opinions of 'Sovremennik' (contemporary) - historical and literary" was published in the Slavophil journal Moskvityanin (Muscovite).[13]

---

[11]D. Samarin, "Dannyya dlya biografii Yu. F. Samarina za 1840-1845 gg.," Sochineniya, V (Moscow, 1880), LXXIX-LXXXIII.

[12]Sochineniya, XII, 149-57.

[13]Nol'de, p. 35. Khomiakov and Samarin were the most active Slavophil polemicists during the 1840's. Christoff, p.85.

This article contains Samarin's first clear formulation of some basic Slavophil teachings. To summarize briefly he asserted: (1) that Western individualism leads nowhere; (2) that the idea of man in society under law does not grow out of individualism; (3) that Europe was searching for such an idea; (4) that the Russian experience was relevant because it provided such an idea in the "commune"; (5) that Christianity had brought "consciousness and freedom" to Russian life; (6) that the problem of Russia's "internal history" had been "to enlighten the national communal principle by the communal principle of the Church"; and (7) that the aim of Russia's "external history" had been "to defend and to protect" this enterprise "by the creation of a strong state structure" in harmony with it.[14]

Samarin's work in Riga involved writing a history of that city's institutions as part of a series of steps towards far-reaching administrative reforms.[15] With the scholarly thoroughness which so typified him, he examined Russia's relatons with the whole Baltic area in the process. His finished work, "an excellent, undated, historical and juridical monograph,"[16] was published by the Ministry of the

---

[14]Sochineniya, I (Moscow, 1877), 63-64.

[15]Riga, located at the mouth of the Western Dvina river, was for centuries the chief commercial and administrative centre of Livonia, the indigenous homeland of Latvians and Estonians. Russia has had a long involvement with the region, going back at least to Kievan times when Vladimir (980-1015) tried to establish his authority there. In the twelfth and thirteenth centuries, settlement and conquest under the auspices of the Livonian and Teutonic orders established political and economic power in German hands--a situation which continued under successive conquests of the region by Poles (sixteenth centruy), Swedes (seventeenth century), and Russians (eighteenth century). See A. Bilmanis, A History of Latvia (Princeton, New Jersey, 1951); and E. Uustalu, The History of the Estonian People (London, 1952).

[16]Nol'de, pp. 40-41.

Interior for distribution among the highest members of the government. As so often happened the projected reform was dropped: as for the publication, it was subsequently lost or destroyed, probably by fire.[17] His work was not barren, however, for he took a few dominant ideas from his research and experience in Riga. First, he acquired an abiding distrust of constitutionalism because of the way in which the privileged German landholding element had used constitutional guarantees to protect their narrow class interest--insofar, his faith in the virtues of a responsible monarchy were confirmed. Second, he came to an important decision concerning the peasant question, which he already considered of paramount importance in Russia. His work in Latvia convinced him that the abolition of serfdom must be engineered by the government under conditions guaranteeing peasant rights, and especially their right to land.[18]

Samarin's service in Riga ended in turmoil. By the end of it he had become so angered by the direction of Russian policy in the Baltic region that he wrote a long pamphlet, Letters from Riga, denouncing it. Something of his aim and mood is contained in the following quotation from a letter to Konstantin Aksakov (April, 1848):

> The systematic oppression of Russians by Germans is an hourly insult to Russian nationality before the eyes of many of her representatives--this is what stirs the blood in me and I work for only one thing--to bring the fact to people's attention....[19]

Even before his return to St. Petersburg, he began to circulate manuscript copies of his pamphlet. His attack on government policy,

---

[17]Sochineniya, VII, CXXXV.

[18]Nol'de, pp. 42-43.

[19]Sochineniya, XII, 200.

erupting in the hermetically sealed atmosphere of Nicholation Russia, created a small storm in court circles. Its principal effect was to provoke the powerful German party to take reprisals. Nicholas was pressed for action, and Samarin was promptly lodged in the Peter-Paul fortress. After a twenty-day imprisonment he was taken to Nicholas, who administered a sharp rebuke, accusing him of divulging state secrets and of stirring up enmity between Germans and Russians. The affair ended with what was, in effect, banishment from the capital-- first to Moscow, and later to the provinces.[20]

After a three-month stay in Moscow, Samarin was posted to Simbirsk on the Volga. From there he was shortly sent to Kiev, where he was placed at the disposal of Governor-General Bibikov. Much of this period, brief as it was, was devoted to the study of the peasant question. As indicated above, he was already convinced that a just solution to this question would have to be enforced and guaranteed by the government.

Fortuitously, Samarin's arrival in Kiev coincided with the introduction in the south-western region of inventories designed to determine the land relationships between landlords and peasants. Samarin did not play an active part in this process, but he studied it closely and wrote about it, gaining thereby a knowledge of the peasant question that he was able to turn to account during the reforms of 1857-1863.

By 1850 Samarin was in charge of Bibikov's chancellery. However, the demands of civil service work seriously impeded his new research and reform interest, so that when the need to manage the family estates

---

[20]Ibid., VII, XC ff. Samarin recorded Nicholas' rebuke verbatim.

because of his father's illness arose, he retired, settling once again in Moscow (1852).[21]

He was now convinced of the need to abolish serfdom. Characteristically he began a full-scale study of peasant-landlord relationships, village agriculture and peasant life in general.[22]   The next five years were spent in this pursuit. The summers were passed studying and working on the family estates in the Tula and Samara regions: the winters were passed in Moscow, in study and discussion with his Slavophil friends--Cherkassky,[23] Khomiakov, Koshelev,[24] and Konstantin and Ivan Aksakov.[25]

---

[21]Nol'de, pp. 59-60.

[22]V.N. Bochkarev, "Yuri Fedorovich Samarin," Velikaya reforma, V (Moscow, 1911), 94.

[23]Prince Vladimir A. Cherkassky was a politician and reformer. He played an important role in bringing the peasant reform to fruition and was a key figure in preparing the peasant reform in Poland (1864). He was elected mayor of Moscow in 1869 and was active in preparing the municipal statutes of 1870. See Kniaz' Vladimir Aleksandrovich Cherkassky. Ego stat'i, ego rechi i vospominaniya o nem (Moscow, 1879).

[24]Aleksandr I. Koshelev (1806-83) was a prominent Slavophil and publicist. He issued a number of Slavophil publications including Russkaya beseda (Russian Conversation), 1856-60. He stood for the establishment of representative institutions at the local level and the convoking of a consultative assembly. He played an active role in preparing the peasant reform and wrote extensively on political questions: see, for example, Konstitutsiya, samoderzhavie i zemskaya duma (Leipzig, 1862).

[25]Ivan S. Aksakov (1823-86) was a brother of Konstantin Aksakov, and a prominent Slavophil publicist, especially during the later stages of the movement. His strongly nationalistic political creed was expounded in the Slavophil journals which he published, namely: Den' (1862-65); Moskva (1867-68); Moskvich (1867-68); and Rus' (1880-86). Aksakov was always viewed with suspicion by the government and Den', Moskva and Moskvich were all suppressed by the censor. See I. S. Aksakov, Polnoe sobranie sochineniy (7 vols.; Moscow, 1886-87); and Ivan Sergeevich Aksakov v ego pismakh (4 vols.; Moscow-St. Petersburg, 1888-96).

The articles which he wrote during this period played a decisive role in shaping his future career. In 1853 he began to write a series of papers on the peasant question which, distributed among his friends and in highest court circles, helped to set the stage for emancipation.[26] But recognition did not come as quickly as it might have, because his Slavophilism made him suspect.[27] The situation changed when the reign of Alexander II began, and the Slavophils won permission to publish their own journal, Russkaya beseda, and later Sel'skoe blagoustroystva, devoted exclusively to peasant affairs. While Samarin gave much time to these journals including writing two articles on nationality and science, he concentrated most of his attention on the peasant question, advocating a reform programme which was moderate. His central concern was to find a way to destroy serfdom, and at the same time preserve the communal basis of Russian agriculture.[28] His connections, especially with the Grand Duchess Helen and the Grand Duke Konstantin (influential reform-oriented members of the Royal family), his literary gifts, and scholarly analysis established him as an authority on the peasant question.[29]

Samarin was first and foremost a doer. The Imperial Rescript of November 20, 1857, commanding the nobility to prepare proposals for the

---

[26]Bochkarev, V, 96-97: see M.T. Florinsky, Russia, II (New York, 1961), 885.

[27]Samarin said in a letter to K. Aksakov (1844): "We...have attracted...strong undeserved suspicion from the government side and distrust from the side of society." Sochineniya, XII, 150.

[28]Bochkarev, p. 95.

[29]See ff. 29. (over)

"improvement of peasant life" (a circumlocution for emancipation), gave

him the opportunity for which he had been waiting. Under the terms of

the Rescript, committees of landlords were formed in every province of

the empire. He was asked to represent the government on the Samara

provincial committee. With hope and enthusiasm he welcomed the opportu-

nity, and for the next five years worked, almost without interruption,

on the peasant reform. This would prove to be the most difficult, and

perhaps the most successful, period of his life.[30]

From the very beginning, the provincial committees were rent with

disputes between a large majority defending the interests of the land-

lords, and a small minority working for the well-being of the peasants.

Samarin was among the small minority. He rejected unconditionally the

proposal that every peasant should be given freedom without land. He

stood for a moderate programme of reform, maintaining communal land

ownership, and guaranteeing each peasant a land allotment sufficient to

support himself and his family. He held a key position on the Samara

committee; in fact, as a literary man and a theoretician with a clearly

---

[29]The Grand Duchess Helen Pavlovna (1806-73) was born Frederika-
Charlotte-Maria Princess of Wurtemberg. In 1823 she married the Grand
Duke Michael Pavlovich and settled in Russia where she played a
prominent role as a patron of the arts and as a creator of welfare and
educational institutions. During the Crimean War she helped to lay the
foundations for the Red Cross. In the late 1850's she was a passionate
and enlightened proponent of peasant reform.

The Grand Duke Konstantin Nikolaevich (1827-92) was a brother of
Alexander II. For many years he was commander of the fleet and
chairman of the state council. An able man with an eye for reform, he
was a key factor in bringing the peasant, judicial and censorship
reforms to fruition. After the Crimean War, he was a powerful force in
modernizing the Russian fleet and in re-establishing Russian sea power
on the Black Sea.

[30]Bochkarev, p. 98.

articulated programme, he did the bulk of the work. It is interesting
to note that relations on the committee were so strained and the
opposition of the landlords so impassioned that Samarin never went out
of the house unless he was armed and accompanied by a bodyguard.[31]

In the spring of 1859, an Editing Commission, headed by Ya. I.
Rostovtsev, was established in St. Petersburg to examine the proposals
of the various provincial committees and to draft the emancipation
statute. As an expert Samarin was invited to participate in the work
of this Commission. By mid-summer he was working in St. Petersburg,
where he quickly discovered that he was in disagreement with the basic
principles of the reform as set out by his more conservative colleagues. While he considered resigning, he was prevailed upon to stay,
and continued to serve the Commission until its work was completed in
October, 1860. He worked mainly on the question of obligations, but
also played an active part in compiling the proposals of the south-
western region. There was a brief interruption of three months in his
service because of a nervous breakdown, brought on by the heavy strain
of his work, for this was a very difficult period for the members of
the Commission--not only was there great social animosity, but the work
was very strenuous, especially for someone like Samarin whose great
writing capacity was exploited.[32]

After the preliminary drafting of the Emancipation Statute, Samarin
remained in St. Petersburg for consultation with the Grand Duke

_____

[31]Ibid., p. 100.

[32]Nol'de, pp. 112-31.

Konstantin, while it was being discussed by the Main Committee. During this period he wrote several notes refuting arguments against the proposals of the Editing Commission. He also wrote a first draft of the Emancipation Manifesto. The planning and drafting of the Emancipation Statute was over: Samarin was certainly one of its "principal authors."[33]

Samarin's work on the peasant question did not end with the publication of the Emancipation Manifesto (February 19, 1861). The reform still had to be implemented, and Samarin, even though he had some reservations about its final form, worked hard to put its measures into effect. In March, he was again in Samara, this time serving the government as a Member (chlen) on the provincial commission responsible for introducing the reform. During this period agreements were drawn up between the landlords and their peasants, fixing land allotments and obligations. Samarin's task was to verify these agreements. Because of the illiteracy of his assistants, however, a much greater volume of work fell on his shoulders. He was, in fact, a "leading executor"[34] of the reform, and his impartial and diligent service did much to improve the government office's standing among the peasants.[35]

---

[33]Nicholas V. Riasanovsky, Russia and the West in the Teaching of the Slavophils (Cambridge, Massachusetts: Harvard University Press, 1952), p. 57. V. I. Semevski, Krest'ianskii vopros v Rossii v pervoi polovine XIX veka, II (St. Petersburg, 1888), 417, credits Samarin with making a "significant" contribution to the reform.

[34]Riasanovsky, p. 57.

[35]Bochkarev, p. 103.

When most of the agreements were completed, Samarin considered his task done, and retired for a second time (summer, 1863). The nobility of Samara who had followed his career closely and had come, despite earlier differences, to value his sterling qualities, feted him.[36]

Samarin was not, however, destined to take his ease, at least not for a while yet. Revolt had broken out in Poland in January, and he was soon caught up in government attempts to deal with it. In October he was asked by Nicholas Miliutin[37] to take part in a commission being established to work out a solution for the peasant question in Poland. Miliutin, who was head of the commission and who had worked with Samarin on the Emancipation Statute, chose him because of his theoretical knowledge.[38] Samarin, who had already revealed his deep concern over the borderlands in his Riga days, accepted. Then he, Miliutin and Cherkassky, the third member of the Commission, spent six weeks in Warsaw and a few days in a lightning tour of south-western Poland. Samarin's observations and impressions were expounded in a comprehensive note to the Tsar and contributed to a new programme for the reconstruction of Polish peasant life and village government. This programme, based on the Slavophil point of view, was ratified by Alexander (February 19, 1864) and remained the government programme for Poland over the next half-century.[39]

---

[36]Nol'de, p. 145.

[37]Nicholas A. Miliutin (1818-1972), a prominent statesman of Alexander II's reign, was close to the Slavophils. He was an exponent of enlightened absolutism and played a leading role in preparing the peasant and administrative reforms of the reign.

[38]Bochkarev, p. 104.

[39]Florinsky, II, 916.

Samarin's attitude to Poland was complex. He was sympathetically inclined towards the Poles as members of a Slavic nation, but he hated Polonism which he viewed as the "armed propaganda of Latinism [Catholicism]...a sharp wedge...driven into the heart of the Slavonic world...."[40] To Polonism he opposed Eastern Slavonic Orthodoxy. While anxious to irradicate Polonism, he did not advocate Russification, including the imposition of Orthodoxy, because he believed that the Poles had a right to cultural and national self-determination, in other words, freedom of religious instruction, a national language, and independent civil government. His final aim was to achieve, through a gradual mingling of Poles and Russians, complete reconciliation in a greater Slavic unity. His method of achieving this objective was to suppress the revolt, and then to win the support of the Polish peasantry by emancipating them on favourable terms. In all fairness it should be pointed out that Samarin's programme, eschewing Russification, was implemented more harshly than he envisaged.[41]

When, at forty-five, he returned from Poland, Samarin found his health broken. However, he was far from despairing for he felt he could still look forward to useful work. In fact, he was to live another twelve years and to accomplish an outstanding amount of work in that period. These last years of his life were devoted to public and literary activity, following a uniform pattern. Almost every year he went abroad, both for reasons of health and for the publishing of his literary work. The fall usually found him on the Volga where he

---

[40]Quoted from Bochkarev, p. 105.

[41]Bochkarev, p. 105.

saw to the management of his estates and the schools which he had
founded on them. He also hunted for he was a passionate hunter. The
winters he spent in Moscow working in duma and zemstvo councils. As
this period coincided with the sterile second half of Alexander's
reign, Samarin became increasingly estranged from governmental circles.
He was remembered only once, being entrusted with the presidency of the
Samara Provincial Zemstvo conference (December, 1865).[42]

As suggested above, Samarin's public activities were concentrated
in Moscow. The laziness, the sloth, and the ignorance, which he had
encountered in the provinces after the reform of 1861 had brought him
to the point of despair, but it had been instructive. It had convinced
him that the proper task for the moment was, eschewing constitutional
reform projects like those of Koshelev and other liberals, to concentrate on creating efficient organs of local self-government, i.e., on
the Zemstvo programme.[43] It is not strange then, that from 1866
onward, he should serve as an elected representative on both the Moscow
City Duma and Moscow Provincial Zemstvo Council. He was a very active
representative and his clear, logical exposition was both impressive
and effective. He served on various commissions, frequently as chairman, and drafted many reports. His most noteworthy work went into
drafting a reform of the poll-tax. Samarin proved to be a reliable
leader and a diligent worker, accepting all manner of assignments--
whether locating cemeteries or planning for the removal of garbage, no
task was too humble. "It was a time," he said, "for stonemasons, not

---

[42]Nol'de, p. 193.

[43]Bochkarev, p. 106.

architects."[44]

Samarin's literary activity during this final twelve-year period
was impressive. To this period are related his best-known works. In
1865 he began to publish a long, hard-hitting attack on the Jesuits--
The Jesuits and their Relation to Russia[45]--which won him considerable notoriety. In 1867 he edited and published the first Russian
edition of Khomiakov's philosophical writings. For this work he wrote
a long preface evaluating the role of Khomiakov as philosopher and
theologian. It was "superb...expressing the character of the teaching
and the point of view of Khomiakov...."[46] Samarin was ambitious to
continue the philosophical work of Khomiakov (his friends, especially
Ivan Aksakov, hoped that he would), but he became convinced that he
lacked the philosophical depth required. Apropos Peter Struve has
remarked: "as distinct from Kireyevsky and Khomiakov...the mind of
Samarin was not a philosophical-constructing, but a civil-servant
arranging and regulating [one]...the mind of Samarin was the mind of a
statesman and political thinker."[47] There are two other examples
of Samarin's philosophical writing from this period: an analysis of
K.D. Kavelin's book, The Problems of Psychology, and a brief study of
Max Mueller's History of Religion.

Samarin was a great Russian publicist--some of his Russian

---

[44]Nol'de, p. 145.

[45]Samarin, Sochineniya, VI (Moscow, 1887), 1-326.

[46]Prince V. Odoevski, an outstanding Schellingist, as quoted in
Christoff, p. 37 n.

[47]Peter Struve, "Yuri Samarin. Opyt kharateristiki i otsenki,"
Vozrozhdenie, No. 376 (June 13, 1926). Sochineniya VI, XI.

contemporaries called him the greatest publicist of all times. While
this latter opinion is exaggerated, there is no doubt at all that
Samarin was among the best. His publicist work is distinguished by
scholarly analysis, precision, lucidity and power. Certainly his most
important work of this kind was Borderlands of Russia, an extensive
publication stretching into three volumes, which began to appear in
1867, and continued to appear regularly until his death in 1876. In
Borderlands, he returned to the study of Russia and the Baltic states,
which had occupied his attention during his stay in Riga twenty years
earlier. It was written to combat the autocratic, class character of
Russian policy in the 1860's, which Samarin feared would provoke a
centrifugal or separatist movement in the borderlands--in Finland, the
Baltic states, Poland, and even in the Ukraine and the Caucasus.[48]
It was published abroad as was almost everything written during this
period. The first two issues of Borderlands provoked the Tsar's
displeasure, leading Samarin to write a personal explanation of his
position. It provoked a heated debate in Germany and made the author
famous in Europe. It received a mixed response in Russia: nationlists,
who favoured a strongly pro-Russian policy, welcomed it; while less
committed Russians accused him of chauvinism. It is a measure of his
influence that his programme was adopted by Alexander III.

One of Samarin's last publications was the booklet, Revolutionary
Conservatism (Berlin, 1875). This booklet was a long letter to General
Fadeev, attacking his constitutionalism. Samarin still regarded

---

[48]Nol'de, pp. 202-204.

constitutionalism as a gentry device for the perpetuation of their

class interests. When General Fadeev, who had roots in the highest

government and court circles, appeared as the exponent of a new con-

stitutionalism and at the same time disparaged the basic foundations of

the Great Reforms, Samarin felt compelled to speak out against him.[49]

Samarin enjoyed an enormous reputation, and the signs of it took a

tangible form during these last years. Among the distinctions bestowed

on him was the creation of five scholarships bearing his name, and his

enrolment as an honorary member of both the University of Moscow and

the Moscow Ecclesiastical Academy. After his death, the University

created a special prize to be granted in his name to the best composi-

tion on peasant and Zemstvo affairs.

During this period his health was generally poor, partly because he

was troubled by a chronic nervous condition. Over the summer and fall

of 1875, however, his health seemed sound and his energy unabated, so

that his death came quite unexpectedly from a minor cause. Late in

December, he went to Berlin to have the sixth issue of Borderlands

published, as well as to study the institutions of local government and

the tax system in Prussia. Early in March, he insisted on having a

small swelling about the size of a hazelnut removed from his right arm.

As a result of this minor operation, he contracted blood poisoning and

died on March 19, 1876.

In summary, a few very basic ideas emerge as the under-pinning of

Yuri Samarin's Slavophilism. First, he believed in Christianity, and

---

[49]Bochkarev, p. 106.

especially in the superiority of the Russian Orthodox Church as a manifestation of that faith. Second, he believed that Russian autocracy was still a just and viable political institution. Third, he was a Moscovite who looked on the West with circumspection; certainly, he repudiated Western individualism in favour of collectivism as exemplified in the traditional Russian commune. Fourth, he was an enemy of arbitrariness, corruption and irresponsibility in government, and a friend of reform, his sole proviso being that reform be consistent with the national experience. Finally, he believed in religious liberty, and the freedom of thought, of press and of conscience which it implies.

Samarin ranks very high among the Slavophils. Only one or two-- Khomiakov and perhaps Kireyevsky, both theorists and older than he was--could be ranked higher. He earned this distinction by writing, and by participating in practical reform work. The volume and range of his writing made a powerful impact on his contemporaries, including government. In volume, his written work comprises fifteen heavy tomes, including four of letters. In range he wrote on many subjects -- on philosophical and religious questions (two volumes), on the peasant question (three volumes), on literary and historical questions (one volume), on nationality and borderland questions (four volumes), and on financial and educational questions (one volume). The impact of his work can be documented and has been acknowledged by authority: he was a prime mover in conditioning the government to accept peasant reform, and played a big role in drafting and implementing that reform; he was active in establishing local government under the zemstvo system; and finally, he established the basis of Russian policy towards the border-

lands in the last quarter of the nineteenth century. Samarin cer-

tainly was an important Slavophil, and without doubt he was the most

important Slavophil statesman.[50]

---

[50]Paul Vinogradov calls Samarin "...the greatest Slavophil
statesman" ("A Prophetic Career," British Review, XII [October, 1915],
3). A.D. Gradovski ("Pamati Yuriya Fedorovicha Samarina [1876 g.]," IX
[St. Petersburg, 1904], CXLVI) says: "While Kireyevsky,Khomiakov and
the Aksakovs tried to apply their principles to purely cultural
questions (religion, science, art, philosophy) it fell to Samarin to
apply them to political questions, and not only to theory, but also to
practise." Baroness Rahden describes him (1869) as "...the head and
the standard bearer of the national movement." (The Correspondence of
Iu. Samarin and Baroness Rahden 1861-1876, ed. and trans. L. Calder,
H. Cheyne and T. Scully, [Waterloo, 1974] p. 128).

CHAPTER II

Jousting With Hegel

By birth, by training and experience, Yuri Samarin was a member of the Orthodox communion. As a mature adult he became a staunch proponent of orthodoxy. As Samarin's biographer and publisher, his brother Dmitry says, "...in life, in a spontaneous religio-moral sense...Samarin was orthodox, owing to the influence of the surrounding family sphere and [his] special inborn sensitivity to the basic elements of national life. These elements had ...a great influence...on the thought of Samarin...."[51] And indeed, orthodox thinking was a heavy component in his first writings, and further, what is very relevant for this investigation, it provided the basis for his political philosophy, as shall be demonstrated in this chapter.

What seems to be the first major statement of Samarin's views appears in a long letter written in the fall of 1840 to Monsieur Mauguin, a member of the French Chamber of Deputies. At the time Monsieur Mauguin was visiting Moscow, where he made the acquaintance of Samarin and his close friend Konstantin Aksakov. Inevitably, considering the Samarin-Aksakov preoccupation with Russian nationhood and their rejection of the "Franco-German tendency" of Vissarion Belinsky and his "co-workers" in the 'Moskovskiy Nablyudatel' they proceeded to explain their view of what was essentially Russian and national.[52] Samarin reacted so forceful-ly to these discussions, that he felt compelled to write a "courteous"

---

[51]Sochineniya Yu. F. Samarina. Volume V. "Stefan Yavorsky i Feofan Prokopovich", pub. D. Samarin. (Moscow, 1880),p. XXV. This particular volume of Samarin's collected works contains a long detailed biographical account of the years 1840-1845, in which many valuable excerpts from important letters are to be found.

[52]Ibid., p. XXXVII.

"sharp" letter to Mauguin outlining his views on what he called: "...the three periods of exclusive nationality (isklyuchitel'noy natsional'nost'), imitation (podrazhaniya) and intelligent nationality (razumnoy norodnost') and the two principles of our nationality (narodnost'), orthodoxy (pravoslavie) and autocracy (samoderzhavie)."[53]

Writing with self-confessed missionary zeal[54] Samarin described the period of "exclusive nationality" as the period preceding the establishment of Peter the Great on the Russian throne at the end of the seventeenth century. During this stage of development Russian life was "national" (natsional'ny) because the Russians knew only their "fatherland" and "hostile" relations with their neighbours. This was an age of almost continuous warfare between the various Slavic tribes, on the one hand, and incursors from the outside like Pechenegs, Mongols and Poles, on the other. Throughout all of this period "Russian nationality" (narodnost') gradually "strengthened" until "at the beginning of the fifteenth century its material existence was guaranteed." From this point Russia was hard pressed "to defend her spiritual independence" and to protect herself from the "antinational civilization" of the West. By this time the Catholics were firmly established in Kiev, "the ancient cradle of Orthodoxy", and were using it as the advanced base for their conquest of

---

[53]Sochineniya Yu. F. Samarina. Volume XII. "Pis'ma, 1840-1853", pub. P. Samarin. Moscow. 1911, pp. 18-19. This quotation, and the information preceding it is taken from a letter to Konstantin Aksakov. It is followed by a request that he (Aksakov) explain to Mauguin how "the Germans through their poetry and philosophy, had saved us from the French yoke and prepared us for the period of intelligent nationalism." Defining the scope of his letter further Samarin stipulated that he would say nothing about national character, language and popular beliefs etc. knowing that you are writing about them."
[54]Ibid., p. 19.

the north. The Popes spearheaded this Western attack and were remorseless enemies encouraging the use of "weapons" at one moment and "quiet propaganda" at the next, straining "to tear Russia from her isolation" and to draw her into the main stream of Western development.[55] At this point Moscow emerged as the "heart of Russia" and the successful defender of Orthodoxy and nationality. Catholic influence was followed at once by Protestant influence from Germany which "embraced" the north, but was similarly unsuccessful in undermining Russia's faith - "...victory went to Orthodoxy and Russian nationality...which was preserved inviolate and pure...for the future."[56] Such was Russia when Peter the Great came to power: such was Samarin's perception of the period of "exclusive nationality".

With the establishment of Peter in power the second period of Russian history, which Samarin called the period of "imitation" began. During this period Russia lost sight of "her past", her "national principle (narodnoe nachalo) disappeared as it were", and led by Peter she became "blinded" by the "blessings" of "Western enlightenment."[57] She became receptive first to French and then to German "influence". Soon these "influences" "combined" to produce a concerted Western attack, not on "Russia's independence" and not on her "faith", which were secure, but on her "social structure".[58] Western "influence", Samarin said:

> ...set itself the objective of destroying our state principle - autocracy; it wanted us to believe that we languished under a yoke of tyranny and arbitrariness; it tried to instil in us its hatred

---

[55]Ibid., p. 448.

[56]Ibid., p. 449.

[57]Ibid., p. 449.

[58]Ibid., pp. 449-450.

of despotism, which was just and reasonable [as an objective]
in other lands, but made no sense [in Russia].[59]

This "fatal influence" produced two dreadful and unfortunate events: an

attempt during the reign of the Empress Anna to create an "aristrocratic

constitution", and the Decembrist "plot" concocted by a "generation" which

did not "know its fatherland, and loved the West too much." In these

crises when autocracy was threatened "the people [narod]" recalled their

past, "...repudiated the reformers, and once more our historical princi-

ple, the monarchical principle was saved, just as once the independence

and faith of Russia was saved."[60]

Characterizing thus the impact and fate of Western "influence" during

this period, Samarin acknowledged that French influence was "extended",

and "in several respects beneficial"; but he assured Mauguin that it did

not penetrate to "the people", leaving its main mark only "on language,

literature and morals."[61] In conclusion Samarin asserted that the

period of "imitation" established a "pale, lifeless cosmopolitanism" in

Russia which was "essentially-false", but which was useful to experience

because it helped Russians to a better understanding of their "nationality

(narodnost')."[62]

The third period of Russian history, that of "intelligent nationalism"

was just beginning, as Samarin saw it. In this period Russia firmly based

in her nationality and loyal to her principles would come into her own.

As he optimistically expressed it:

59Ibid., p. 450.

60Ibid., p. 450.

61Ibid.

62Ibid., p. 451.

Everything is still in the future; but this future can only be
the fruit of the past. And so, let us turn to the study of our
past. Let us extract it from the dust, let us study the embryo
of life in it, our native principles which have not been able
to achieve proper development as yet. Up to this time Russia
has played only a passive role in the world; she passed almost
ten centuries in a defensive position; up to this time her influence on the West has been purely material. The time is
coming when she will influence the West through her ideas. The
influence of the West on Russia has ended; henceforth we will
borrow only the material results of Western civilization from
her, as for example, industrialization; from now on our development will be entirely independent.[63]

Samarin, having raised the question of Russia's ambition, hastened to

allay any fears that Mauguin might have had about Russian territorial

expansionism by stating categorically that Russia had no ambition for

"bloodletting", "booty", or "conquest", and that "Providence" had no such

plans for her. Her ambitions were "boundless" he agreed, but insisted

that they were of a different order. However, feeling unable at this

point in his letter to outline them in a way which would be credible and

do them justice, he asked Mauguin to take note of the "splendid expres-

sion" of them in Khomiakov's poem: "Be proud, flatterers have said to you

(Gordis', tebe l'stetsy skazali)."[64]

---

[63]Ibid., p. 451.

[64]Ibid., p. 452. This poem was written in 1839 and appears under
the title "To Russia" in Aleksey Stepanovich Khomiakov, Polnoe Sobranie
Sochineniy (Moscow, 1900) IV., 229-230. In it Khomiakov urges Russia to
turn her back on material wealth, imperial power, and haughty pride. He
urges her, instead, "to seek the spirit of life" in "the past", to listen
"to the word of the Creator", and "to preserve great sacrifices", "pure
deeds", "brotherhood", "justice", and mercy for mankind. His final
admonishment to her is:
    Pay attention to [the spirit of life]--and all peoples
    Having embraced them with your love,
    Tell them the secret of freedom,
    The radiance of faith pour on them!

Having outlined the three periods of Russian history in this way,
Samarin proceeded "to define the component elements of Russian nationality: the religious principle and autocracy."[65]

He began by establishing the perimeters for his discussion of "the
religious principle", limiting himself to "a glance at Orthodoxy from the
historical point of view." This limitation was established partly because
he felt "an exposition of the character of Orthodox dogma" would lead too
far afield, and partly because he felt unequal to the task. Samarin then
proceeded to make the following three points: Orthodox dogma shares
neither the "aberrations" of Catholicism nor the "errors" of Protestantism; it occupies a central position between these two extremes; and it is
based on an "independent principle", which is distinctive and immune to
attack from either Catholicism or Protestantism.[66]

Continuing to define the distinguishing features of Russia's
"religious principle", Samarin made a number of important points. The
first one was that Orthodox dogma, like Catholic dogma, "acknowledges the
authority of the Church"; but that unlike Catholic dogma, it does not
invest "infallibility" and "absolute authority" in the Popes, but in
Ecumenical Councils. The second point was that the Orthodox church had
not, like the Catholic church, "expropriated for its own use" Christ's
promise of everlasting life. The third one was that the Orthodox church
had not "incarnated" in a Pope "the spiritual unity of the Church", and
the fourth was that it had not "materialized Christianity." The fifth
point was that the Orthodox church had been "deprived" of "temporal power"

---

[65]Ibid.

[66]Ibid., p. 452.

and had therefore played a "purely-moral role in Russian history": not
being distracted by "temporal power" and "interests" it had not lost sight
of its tasks and had not compromised its "principles." He concluded:

...the absence of absolute authority, constantly in the hands of
a single person, [and] the absence of temporal power - this is what
saved [Orthodoxy] from the abuses, to which Catholicism has been
subjected; this is why, after almost nine centuries of Christianity
in Russia, we do not have to separate the affairs of the Church
from the affairs of the faith....[67]

Samarin could not leave his discussion of Russia's "religious principle" without saying a few words about Protestantism; and even though he
thought it "superfluous" to discuss the differences between Orthodoxy and
Protestantism, he had a few telling points to make. In his view Protestantism was nothing more than a "series of contradictions which were born
of the abuses of Catholicism and which were necessarily and logically
bound to one another." In fact, he said: "Protestantism, itself, was not
a religion, but only the negation of Catholicism, which had been deprived
of a vital principle" and was therefore sterile. His analysis led him to
the conclusion that "only Orthodox doctrine could satisfy the needs of
mankind."[68]

"The Monarchical principle is the main accomplishment (velikoe delo)
of our history. It is nothing more than the development of this
principle."[69] Thus Samarin began the last section of his letter to
Mauguin. In developing his argument in support of this assertion, Samarin
advanced the Norman or Scandinavian theory of the origins of the Russian

---

[67]Ibid., pp. 452-3.

[68]Ibid., pp. 453-4.

[69]Ibid., p. 454.

state; that is, he stressed the crucial role which Norse Vikings played in

creating Russian unity, government and culture. However, there is a

strong nationlist element in his interpretation of the Normanist theory

which gives it a special complexion. Like the Normanists he drew his

evidence from the "ancient chronicler Nestor."[70] Like them he noted

that Russia was, at the beginning of the ninth century, a large country,

bounded by Lake Ladoga, the Ural Mountains, the Black Sea and the

Carpathians, inhabited by separate and distinct Slavic and Finnish tribes.

Like them he attached great importance to the appeal which "four tribes:

---

[70]Ibid., p. 454. This reference is to the medieval annals, which
are the earliest native sources for Russian history. Known as the
Chronicles of Nestor in Samarin's day they are now referred to as the
Primary Chronicle (Nachal'naya Letopis) or The Tale of Bygone Years
(Povest' Vremennykh let). They cover the period from 852, the traditional
date for the beginning of Russian history, to 1110. For a solid English
translation see Samuel H. Cross, The Russian Primary Chronicle,
(Cambridge: Harvard University Press, 1930). When Samarin was writing
this letter the Normanist interpretation was generally accepted. The
major Russian historians (Karamzin, Pogodin, Solov'yov, Klyuchevsky,
Milyukov) and the major Russian philologist (Shakhmatov) were all
Normanists. Since Samarin was writing in 1840 it is worth noting that it
was 1871 before the first effective challenge to the Norman theory
appeared in D. Ilovaysky's, O Mnimom Prizvanii Varyagov. See Cross,
Primary Chronicle, pp. 121-2. Current Western opinion, based on
archaeological research as well as Greek, Arab and other sources,
emphasizes the comparatively high level of cultural and economic
development among the Slav tribes of the Volkov, Lovat, Dnieper region
when the Scandinavians assumed political power in the ninth century, and
concludes that the Scandinavians did not originate the Russian state, but
made a significant contribution to its establishment at a critical stage
of its development. On this important and controversial question see
Cross, Primary Chronicle; Nora K. Chadwick, The Beginnings of Russian
history: An Enquiry Into Sources (London: Cambridge University Press,
1946); Vilhelm Thomsen, The Relations Between Ancient Russia and
Scandinavia and The Origin of the Russian State (London, 1877); and George
Vernadsky, The Origins of Russia (Oxford: The Clarendon Press, 1959).
For a brief but useful discussion of the whole question see Nicholas V.
Riasanovsky, A History of Russia, (New York: Oxford University Press,
1963), pp. 25-30.

the Novgorodian Slavyane [Slovene], the Krivichi, the Ves and the Chud
exhausted" by internecine warfare sent to "Varangian (Norman) princes for
governance and the establishment of order in the land," and to the fact
that "three brothers from a Scandinavian tribe the Rus' (hence Russia)
responded to their call and settled with a small company in Russia."[71]
However the basic facts about Russia's origins are not so important from
the political point of view as the special complexion which Samarin put on
them. This was an "event", he said, which was

> ...unique in world history; from it the whole of our subsequent
> history developed. ...for us the relationship of two tribes -
> natives and Normans - was altogether different than in France
> and England. For us there was not and could not be conquest,
> because of the geographical position of the country and the
> numerical insignificance of the arriving tribe, consequently,
> there could not be either feudalism, or a military aristocracy,
> in the sense of an independent principle, nor the inimical re-
> lationships of conquered to conquerors, consequently, there could
> not be either revolution or constitution.[72]

Having noted that the relationship between the Slavs and the Normans
was peaceful and mutually advantageous, Samarin goes on to assert that the
Norman "influence" was of short duration and "limited" extent. Nevertheless, he attributed several specific contributions to the Normans (1)
they drew (sblizili) the Slavic tribes together; (2) they put them in

---

[71]Ibid., p. 454. V. Thomsen to whom Cross attributes the "best
modern exposition of the Norman Theory" (Cross, Primary Chronicle, p.
121) is unequivocal in stating that the founders of the Russian state were
Normans and that the major points made in the Chronicles are factually
correct. See V. Thomsen, Ancient Russia and Scandinavia, pp. 16 and 130.
V. Klyuchevsky asserts that the appearance of the Varangians (Normans),
who came to Russia as "armed merchants", who settled in large trading
cities like Novgorod and Kiev, and who soon became rulers is explained in
the "legend of the calling." See V.O. Klyuchevsky, Sochineniya, I:
Kurs Russkoy Istorii (Moscow, 1959) pp. 134-141. After reflection on the
available evidence, S. Solov'yov concludes that the account of the
"calling" in the Chronicles is factual. He asserts that it was an event
of "great significance", because it marked the beginning of "Russian
history" and was the first step "in the foundation of a state." See S.M.
Solov'yov, Istoriya Rossii s Drevneishikh Vremyon (Moscow, 1959) I, 130.

contact with Constantinople; and (3) they introduced them to Christianity.[73] This latter event was of such "great significance"
(vazhnoe znachenie) for the subsequent history of Russia that Samarin
begged permission to tell the story as it appears in the Chronicles:

> In 988 St. Valdimir, on concluding peace with the Greeks,
> married Princess Anne, sister of the reigning emperor, and
> accepted baptism. Instantaneously all the people followed
> his example and said in doing so the following memorable words:
> 'if the prince wants it, then it must be good'.

Samarin concludes from this that the Christianization of his country
proceeded "without war, without force, by the unanimous consent of all the
people...."[74]

Samarin then noted that the short Norman stage of Russian history (no
more than a century), was followed by the appanage stage. He says that it

---

[72]Ibid., p. 454. This repudiation of the possibility of conquest
is a very early expression of an important Slavophil idea. K.S. Aksakov,
who is credited by N.V. Riasanovsky with "contributing most to the
Slavophil elaboration of Russian history," (N.V. Riasanovsky, Russia and
the West in the Teaching of the Slavophiles: A Study in Romantic Ideology,
(Cambridge, Massachusetts: Harvard University Press, 1952) p.74. wrote:
"The Calling was voluntary. The state and the Commune-Land did not mix,
but as separate units formed an alliance with each other. The relations
of the Land and the State were already defined by the spontaneous calling:
mutual confidence on both sides. Not war, not enmity because of conquest,
as was the case with other nations, but peace because of voluntary
invitation." See Riasanovsky, pp. 75-6. From the point of view of the
origin and enunciation of Slavophil ideas, it's worth noting that Aksakov
wrote these lines in 1849, some nine years after Samarin's statement of
the idea in his letter to Mauguin. See K.S. Aksakov, Polnoe Sobranie
sochineniy (Moscow, 1861-80) I. 1. A.N. Brianchaninov, one of the last
Slavophils, made the same point in 1915: "They [the words of the calling]
were not the result of conquest. This is historically proved. There was
likewise no invasion, no peaceful surrender of territory which could leave
its trace on the nation's inward existence." See A.N. Briantchaninoff,
Ideological Foundations of Russian Slavonism, Trans. Madame Sophie de
Bellegarde, (London, 1916), p. 1.

[73]Ibid., p. 455.

[74]Ibid., p. 455.

too, was unique because of the absence of "conquest" - for Russia grew by "the peaceful occupation of savage provinces, by the foundation of cities and principalities." But the appanage period was also characterized by a "lack of political unity" for the Grand Principality of Kiev possessed "only a moral, almost fictitious predominance" in the growing state. Civil war erupted as the nation sought "political unity, a visible centre, a capital" but the "national principle (narodnoe nachalo)", destructive as the war was, survived because the people were united in their "faith".[75]

This appanage period was described by Samarin as a period of "centripetal" development, because of the search for a political centre. During it Moscow, favoured by her central "geographical location" and the Tatar "influence", emerged as the nation's "first and only (edinstvennoyu) capital."[76] It was Moscow that became the "nucleus of the state" and "mustered (splotila) the scattered parts of Russia around her." After Moscow had emerged as the political centre a new "centrifugal" period began; from this moment the nation's main concern was to find "a state idea, a vital centre, a Tsar." The sought after political idea proved to be "the principle of autocracy (samoderzhaviya)" which "materialized (voplotilos') in the fifteenth century in the person of Ivan III." However, autocracy had to fight and win three major battles to acquire the resilience and toughness demanded by the nation. First there was the battle against foreign enemies which Ivan II was compelled to wage. Then

---

[75]Ibid., p. 455.

[76]Ibid., p. 456. Samarin makes the following short comment on the Tatar influence: "It was purely external, it touched in no way our religion, it made very little impact on our language and morals, but it helped our political development." Ibid.

there was the battle which Ivan the Terrible had to fight with "the petty

appanage princes, who formed like an aristocracy around the throne,

separating the Tsar from the people." And finaly there was the battle

which the "temporal authority" Tsar Alexis (1648-1676) had to wage against

ambitious priests seeking to establish "a kind of papacy" in Russia. The

"national principle, autocracy" was securely established by the victories

won in these battles.[77]

Samarin concluded his letter to Mauguin with two remarkable passages.

In the first he summarized his perception of the nationality question:

> And so we did not have either conquest, or feudalism or aristocracy
> (in the sense of an independent principle) and there was no agreement
> (social contract) between the Tsar and the people. Unlimited power,
> indivisible (edinaya) and national (narodnaya), acting in the name of
> all, going at the head of our civilization and completing without the
> horrors of revolution, that which in the West was the result of
> internecine war, religious discord and social upheavals--such is the
> form of government which the Russian people created for themselves; it
> is the holy inheritance of our history, and we do not want any other
> form, because any other would be tyranny.[78]

In the second he summarized his view of the future:

> After everything that has been said, you will understand, why we
> believe in the calling of the Slavic tribes to the great task of
> renewal; this task, we know, we will have to complete ourselves
> without the help of anyone; the people of the West will not sympathize
> with us in this task, and for a long time we will have to reconcile
> ourselves to the thought, that in their eyes we are no more than
> objects of contempt and fear.[79]

While composing the Mauguin leter, Samarin was already engaged in

research on his first major exercise in scholarship, the writing of his

magistral dissertation for the University of Moscow. Begun late in the

winter of 1840, this work occupied his full attention until the spring of

1843. His topic of research was on Stefan Yavorsky and Feofan

---

[77]Ibid., p. 456.

[78]Ibid., pp. 456-457.

Prokopovich, hierarchs of the Orthodox Church, and was assigned, it seems, by the University. While the degree of his personal involvement in the choice of this topic is uncertain, it is very clear that he felt compelled to circumscribe severely the range of his philosophical investigations in order to accomplish his task.[80] It is also very clear that his work on Yavorsky and Prokopovich engaged him in the study of Orthodoxy in relation to Catholicism and Protestantism, and had important implications for his political thought.

---

[79]Ibid., p. 457. While the ideas presented here are quite legitimately attributed to Samarin as an expression of his personal convictions it must be emphasised that Samarin wrote this letter as the unofficial spokesman "of very many in Russia." (Ibid.) In terms of the development of Slavophilism it is interesting to note, that he did not refer to a group or movement, or use the term Slavophil, although it had been coined somewhat earlier as a sarcastic slur against the extreme Russian nationalist, Admiral A.S. Shishkov (1753-1841) and his followers. See Riasanovsky, Russia and the West, p. 5, and M.T. Florinsky, Russia: A History and an Interpretation, (New York: The Macmillan Co.) II, 809. Writing on the origins of the term Slavophilism about 1878, Ivan Aksakov said: "this term, which was an uncomplimentary name for the adherents of Shishkov and Prince Shikhmatov at that time [1843-4], was applied [to Khomiakov, Samarin, Aksakov and their followers] in ridicule by Petersburg literary circles, but was gradually consolidated and, has already acquired a respected place in the history of Russian society." "Pism'a A.S. Khomiakova k Yu. F. Samarinu," Russkii Arkhiv (1879), p. 304. Samarin, himself, first used the term in a letter to Khomiakov of February-March 1846, in which he advised him to be "more careful" during the Tsars visit to Moscow, because the Grand Duchess Maria Nikolaeva, who would be accompanying him, had heard of a secret society of Slavophils in Moscow to which Andrey Karamzin and he (Samarin) belonged, and was determined to discover all she could about it. Sochineniya XII, 412. Peripherally, it is interesting to note that Samarin saw Shishkov as an "individual, ...deserving a more conscientious evaluation" and co-edited his works, see Zapiski, mneniya i perepiska Admirala A.S. Shishkova. ed. N. Kiselev, and Yu. Samarin. 2 vols. Berlin, 1870.

[80]Ibid., pp. 130-131, and Sochineniya V, XXXVI.

Through 1840-41 Samarin worked steadily at his dissertation, immersing himself in religious questions. Soon his views of Catholicism and Protestantism began to take shape, and his religious philosophy to solidify.[81] By the end of 1841 he possessed very definite theological opinions and had begun to participate in vigorous theological debates with Khomiakov, Kireyevsky and A.N. Popov, a young friend of his university days.[82]

The debate with Popov was of special importance because it reached a vigorous polemical stage and was preserved in their correspondence. In all, some seven letters were exchanged and these provide a valuable insight into both the development of Samarin's mind, and the theological convictions, which he arrived at as a result of his independent investigations. The debate concerned the role of development in the Church and appears to be an attempt to apply Hegel's category of becoming to this crucial area of interest.[83] It should be cautioned, that this debate was in no way definitive as Samarin's views would later change substantially under the influence of Khomiakov.[84]

Yuri Samarin began his first letter with the Hegelian sounding statement: "the Church develops, i.e. she constantly brings to her consciousness the eternal, inexhaustable truth which she possesses."[85] The rather involved theological argument which he expounds to substantiate

---

[81]Sochineniya, XII, 14.

[82]Sochineniya, V, XLI. Alexander Nikolayevich Popov (1820-1877) was a jurist and historian who joined the Moscow circle of Slavophils. During the winter of 1841-42 he was living with Khomiakov while preparing to defend his master's thesis, "Russian Justice and Criminal Law." Sochineniya, XII, 51fn.

[83]Throughout the debate razvitie, literally "development", is used to render Hegel's concept. W.T. Stace, author of a standard exposition of Hegel's philosophy in English renders it "becoming". See W.T. Stace, The Philosophy of Hegel; A Systematic Exposition, (New York: Dover Publications, 1955) p. 125 et passim. See p. 66 below.

[84]Sochineniya, XII, 82fn. See p. 64 and pp. 79-89 below.

[85]Ibid., p. 82. Samarin "began to approach the question of Church authority from the point of view of the Hegelian category of development." Nol'de, p. 22. D.I. Chizhevsky states that the Samarin-Popov debate "was conducted in the terms of Hegelian philosophy." D.I. Chizhevsky, Gegel' v Rossii (Paris, 1939), p. 177.

this idea can be summarized in the following manner.

Jesus Christ, incarnated as the son of God, represented a "reconciliation between God and man - in the person of - God-man." At his death and
resurrection Christ created a Church in which "the Spirit of God lives
constantly." This Church, as a result, embraced "two elements: the divine
and the human."[86] The character of the "mutual" relationship between
these two elements is of crucial importance for the Church. If the
relationship between the divine and the human is "indifferent" -- "the
Spirit as eternal truth, in its fullness and immovableness, and humanity
under its obligation (pod svoim opredeleniem) of constant development"--
then two "false propositions" must be allowed: either humanity is separated from God, and the Church converted into a "priestly cast" as in the
Old Testament, or, as in Catholicism, a single person, the Pope, is "constantly materialized as the divine, making him the Church and the general
membership "subjects" in the same way that citizens are subjects of the
state--"members live under the Church, and not in the Church." If, on the
other hand, the relationship is a "close and indissoluble union of the two
elements" of individual persons as the Church and of the Spirit--develop-
ing the consciousness (soznanie) of the Church", a true relationship
consistent with the idea that the "Church develops" is achieved.[87]

This process of development plays a vital role in the elaboration of
Church dogma. "Each dogma contains a living principle" or "embryo", which
"can develop only in the soil of the Church, i.e. become a part of the

---

[86]Ibid., p. 83.

[87]Ibid.

consciousness of the people." Attempts to elaborate this principle, or to bring it to full consciousness by the faithful, produce clashes of opinion, which the Church seeks to allay by convening ecumenical councils. At these councils differences are resolved and dogma established in the light of the spirit which the Church possesses. Through this process the faithful are raised to a level of religious consciousness, which is "as much higher, as rational conviction is higher than opinion."[88]

Samarin concludes this part of his argument as follows:

And so, the Church develops, but its development stands infinitely higher than any human development, because each one of its moments has been imprinted by the Spirit, every result, every word of the Church is necessarily true. Therefore the Church must acknowledge, must bless development, the very path by which she has reached truth. Triumph over evil, victory over death lies in the foundation of the Church. This means, that she has been given the possibility of infallible development, of the attainment of every truth, of the exposure of every lie.[89]

This particular letter ends with a rather long paragraph dealing with a number of specific points that Popov had apparently raised in a recent conversation. In his answers Samarin tried to expand and strengthen his argument that the true Church develops. The "completion" of the sacraments is seen as a "vital" part of the Church's existence, which "can be the object of her rational development." A parallel is seen between the Church's relation to the sacraments, and man's relation to "immediate

---

[88]Ibid., pp. 83-84.

[89]Ibid., p. 84. B. Nol'de makes the following comment on the ideas expressed above: "Whatever the internal worth of these thoughts - Vl. Solv'ev acknowledged that they had great significance in the history of Russian theological doctrine - they weren't much use for the foundation of a refutation of Catholicism from the Orthodox point of view. The latter not only never denied development of the church, but with sufficient foundation pointed out that precisely the Orthodox church was guilty of such a denial." Nol'de, pp. 23-24. "Moment" is a characteristic Hegelian term. See p. 66 below.

life" with the possibility of development in the "sphere of thought." The crucial question is seen to be: "not why is the Church a Church, but can and must the Church develop." The "superiority, the truth" of the Orthodox Church, as well as the "reconciliation of two extreme principles [man and Spirit], are seen to grow from "the recognition and realization of this development." Conversely, the errors of Catholicism and Protestantism are seen to lie in their failure to perceive the importance and substance of development. Catholicism erred by establishing an "immovable Church", that is, a Church which does not develop; whereas Protestantism erred by "recognizing the principle of development, but at the same time "denying the Church", thus committing itself to "abstract fruitless movement."[90]

Popov's reply to this letter is quite relevant because it helps to elucidate Samarin's thought as summarized above. In fact, Samarin began his second letter by stating that his first contained a "gap" and that Popov had filled it by very effectively defining "the relationship of the Church to incarnation."[91] What, then, did Popov say on this important relationship? He said:

> In order to decide what the relationship between the divine and the human principle in the Church is, we must first decide what the relationship is between the Church herself and incarnation, which triumphantly joined these two principles in the person of God-man. The apostle called the Christian a new man. And so this relationship is creation. In the first creation man, and in his person all of mankind, was created, therefore in his fall the fall of all was included; in the second—man was redeemed, therefore Christ is named the second Adam, and man was recreated. From this creation the new world (mir) begins. The Church is this humanity recreated. Incarnation, which was completed in God-man, is not completed anew in the Church, but lives in her as an already accomplished fact, clothing the

---

[90]Ibid., pp. 84-85.

[91]Ibid., p. 85.

Church, as it were; therefore the Church is called the body of Christ. Christ, as the head, and private individuals, as the members, these are the component principles of the body of the Church. The Holy Spirit joins them reciprocally. The constant communion of these principles is the life, the development of the Church. In this development we note two sides: victory over evil and creation.[92]

Because Samarin's support for this statement of belief was "unconditional",[93] it can be said that he believed that the Church was humanity recreated through the incarnation of Christ as God-man, or to state it in a negative way, that without the incarnation of Christ and the recreation of mankind accomplished by it, there would be no Church, no redemption and no possibility of development, that is, growth in the knowledge of the Holy Spirit.

But more important than Samarin's perception of the Church's relationship to incarnation was his perception of "the Church as humanity recreated" (the statement is taken from Popov's letter quoted above). On this point, Samarin believed, that the renewal of mankind accomplished through incarnation found its source in "victory over sin." A victory made possible because man became aware, for the first time, of his sinfulness and could proceed from this new basis of awareness, using reason and will, to the realization of his true potential for development as defined by God. Thus incarnation freed "the new man to realize the divine in real life" by thought; that is, freed him to formulate and express his understanding of the divine in dogma. But incarnation had also given him the possibility of communing with Christ by partaking of his body and blood in the sacrament of Holy Communion, "thus immediate communion with God through the sacrament and communion in understanding

---

[92]Ibid., pp. 459-460.

[93]Ibid., p. 85.

through dogma, was given to the new man by Christianity." In the "church
militant" (the new testament Church),[94] the identity of these two
modes of awareness had been achieved - "the knowledge of God, i.e. dogma
is realized in life, i.e. in the sacraments, and life is raised to dogma:"
-- thus constant growth in her level of consciousness was an ever present
reality for the new testament Church.[95]

Samarin summarized the conclusions to be drawn from the above
arguments as follows. The Church "did not develop into a Church, but
appeared as a full, living organism" having two clearly recognizable but
interdependent sides - "life and consciousness." The "life" of the Church
is complete and unchanging, and is the same for each and every one of her
members. It repeats itself in time, being encompassed by "the full,
closed sphere of the Church year," including the sacraments which "embrace
the whole life of man." On this side, the Church does not develop, but
"is an organ of blessing." On the other side, the side of "consciousness", there is development because the Church constantly tries to comprehend and to justify her "life" by expressing it in dogma. This side of
the church "appeared later in time," but is more "significant" than the
first. To the point:

> The sacraments existed in the Church from the first; but the
> recognition of them as sacraments, the recognition of them as
> seven in number, the justification of them by elevating them to
> dogma--is the result of the development of the Church being com-
> pleted in time, in historical memory, parallel with the develop-
> ment of the thought of man and agreed upon by a whole row of councils.

---

[94]Popov defines the Church militant as the New Testament Church.
Ibid., p. 462.

[95]Ibid., pp. 85-86.

Samarin touched especially on this latter point concerning the role of

ecumenical councils, for they marked "the highest step" in the development

of the Church's consciousness "corresponding in this relationship with

what the sacrament is in life." Therefore the ecumenical council is "the

highest manifestation of the Church in general." Further, Samarin

emphasized, the Church finds her answers by introspection, by becoming

aware of "herself," for she is "the truth" and "the eternal source of

revelation."[96]

Having noted that the Church has two sides, Samarin stressed that they

must be in "constant agreement" if one (life), or the other (consciousness

as expressed in dogma), or both, are not to be "perverted." On the basis

of this argument, he arrived at the far-reaching conclusion, that Ortho-

doxy is superior to Catholicism, for he claimed that the "perversion" and

"falseness" of Catholicism stems precisely from its failure to grasp the

true relationship between these two sides of the Church. Beginning about

the tenth century the Catholic Church manifested its error when it began

"to raise" the fixed unchanging side, the life of the Church, to "rational

consciousness." Since this was attempted "under the influence of the

pagan traditions of ancient Rome, its fruit was Catholic doctrine--a

reflex of Christianity in Latin presentation."[97] On the other hand,

Orthodox doctrine was free of perversion because it understood the

relationship between life and consciousness correctly--"immediate life,

---

[96]Ibid., pp. 86-87.

[97]Ibid., p. 87. In passing, Samarin makes the point that he
explains "the whole Catholic system from the juridical, tight conception
of freedom." It's unfortunate that he did not elaborate on this point.

as final and always real, and consciousness, constantly developing."[98]

By way of illustration, Samarin compared Orthodox and Catholic teachings on the sacraments, establishing that Catholic doctrine was perverted because it does not recognize the validity of the sacraments unless the communicant is as moral and as understanding as the Pope; whereas, Orthodox doctrine was correct because it recognises the validity of the sacraments regardless of the morality and understanding of the communicant. He affirmed that this correct Orthodox understanding is possible, only, because it rests squarely on the idea of development as he had outlined it.[99]

That is the substance of Samarin's thought on development as expounded in his second letter to Popov. However, a small, but perhaps significant, elucidation of it is contained in a small fragment preserved in his notes where he said under the heading "Dogma on Tradition":

> Tradition (we have in mind everything that the Church professes and is not in the scriptures) is the fruit of the developing consciousness of the Church about those things, which are in the open (otkrovennom) teaching, which she bears in herself; consequently, tradition is not a supplement to the scriptures, not something else, which is not in the scriptures and therefore cannot be concluded from it. In order to understand tradition, the organic development of the Church must be recognized.[100]

This debate carried over into a third letter, which was written to refute a number of specific objections which Popov had raised to Samarin's conception of the developing Orthodox Church.[101] Some of the points made are important, because they contribute to a fuller understanding of Samarin's theology, and are summarized below.

---

[98]Ibid., p. 89.

[99]Ibid., pp. 88-89.

[100]Sochineniya, V, XLIV. Italics in the original.

[101]Popov's letter is available in Sochineniya, XII, 462-471.

Firstly, Samarin saw the Church developing through three "moments" or "phases":[102] the Old Testament Church, the New Testament Church, and the Church Triumphant, that is, the Church when her consciousness had risen to the point where it "fused" with, or became identical with God's ideal conception of her i.e., "promise" for her. On this latter point, God's "promise" was seen to exist in the Church's consciousness as a "premonition"; and striving, born out of a sense of incompleteness, was seen as a persistent spur for the development of the Church to her next higher phase, terminating finally in her ultimate phase as the Church Triumphant.[103]

Secondly, he argued that "victory over sin and creation (tvorchestvo)" cannot be separated (Popov saw them as "two sides in the essence of the Church"), because the Church defined sin "as an insufficiency, as the absence of freedom or the living principle at the heart of any creation", and victory over sin "as the return of lost freedom." Therefore, "victory over sin" is "creation" and vice versa. From this Samarin concluded that "the combination of two principles--the law and the promise--" in the Old Testament Church can only be understood "as the striving of the Church, conditioned by the consciousness of her present moment and future."[104]

Thirdly, he stated in the process of stressing that his views on sin were consistent with "the teachings of the Apostle Paul", that "sin was defined by the law", and that "the law" was revealed so that man, who was

---

[102]See Ibid., p. 86, where Samarin uses the term phase as moment is used here.

[103]Ibid., pp. 90-91, and p. 462.

[104]Ibid., p. 91.

inherently sinful, could "know", as opposed "to recognize", the nature of
sin, for mere recognition could not lead to victory over it.[105]

Fourthly, he averred in a well-documented passage that the development
of dogma was not finished. Surveying the record he stated that no
ecumenical council had ever prohibited further elaboration and refinement
of the creed as formulated at the Second Council of Constantinople (381
A.D.). Acknowledging that "prohibitions" had been passed by the Third,
Fourth, Fifth and Sixth Councils, he convincingly demonstrated that these
were "prohibitions" against the "arbitrary" formulation of dogma by
"separate individuals" and affirmed that "development was and will be
constant; there is no reason for it to end."[106]

Fifthly, Samarin stated that it is "impossible" for the Church to
create a "system" or "theological science". Although no conclusive
arguments were presented in support of this contention, for Samarin
emphasized that he was simply seeking clarification of a "contradiction"
in Popov's position, a number of points relevant to an understanding of
his final theological stance were made. One was that the Church "recog-
nising active thought among her members" logically required herself "to
recognize theological science" as an integral "sanctified" part of her,
just as the Catholic Church had done at the Council of Trent (1545- 1563).
Another was that two elements are found in the "writings of the Holy
Fathers"--"reflections" about peripheral or "superfluous questions", which
the Church does not try to answer, and "proofs" or "rational justifica-
tions of dogma". The latter are "most important" for the creation of any

---

[105]Ibid.

[106]Ibid., pp. 91-93.

system, and in fact "condition" it. In another, a system is defined as "a rendering into one logical whole of all dogmas, so that everyone of them appears not as an aphorism, but rationally proven, linked with the foregoing and the following". In still another, he stated, that "systematization is not the creation of new dogmas, but the logical justification of old ones: consequently a system, in agreement with dogmas, will be one in which dogmas have been proven so strictly that from each proof flows not less and not more, than is contained in the dogma itself." In yet another, he said, that the Church in acceding to "the demands of science" was seeking a solution for difficult questions in "philosophy."[107]

From the argumentation and tone of this passage, as much as from specific points, one senses that Samarin feared that the Church by allowing rational proofs true to scripture and dogma would become entrapped in a system which would pervert her real character and restrict her infinite capacity for development.

Sixthly, Samarin explained miracles, prophecy and monasticism as phenomena occurring outside the normal sphere of life, which were comprehensible only if it was understood that the Church is simultaneously "a moment" and "a finished whole", because they were examples of "revelation" growing out of "contemplation" of the Church as life (as a moment), and as promise (as a finished whole).[108] He also maintained that Catholic theology tried "to explain the possibility of miracles" as the result of "independent spontaneous revelations to separate individuals", and that

---

[107]Ibid., pp. 93-94.

[108]Samarin's position is summarized by inference, on the basis of the fact that he expressed "full satisfaction" with Popov's explanation of miracles, etc. Ibid., p. 95. For Popov's explanation see Ibid., p. 467.

this explanation failed, as Protestant theology recognized, because "it presupposed the possibility of numberless separate revelations and suppressed the conception of a general and single revelaton." Further, he agreed that Orthodox theology, in addition to accepting the Protestant grounds for rejecting this Catholic explanation based on "independent personal revelation", rejected it, because it (Orthodox theology) maintained that man had no "independent personality outside of the Church."[109] Samarin did not accept, however, the idea that monasticism had become under Catholicism a "state institution" fulfilling assigned tasks in the realm of "education, propaganada, etc.", because the doctrine de operibus supererogationis provided sufficient "justification" for its existence and its specialized work in education, etc.[110] On this point the theological debate between Popov and Samarin ended.

During the spring and summer of 1842, Samarin worked almost without interruption over the first part of his dissertation--rewriting, revising, expanding--as he reported in a letter of that period. Inevitably, however, his concern over the questions raised in his debate with Popov continued; and by the fall, as evidenced by the following comment, he had definitely reached a conclusion about the possibility of creating a "Church system":

> I have developed...the idea that a Church system, theology as a science, and evidently, by its indifference to the two attempts to create a system (I have in mind the works of Stefan Yavorsky and Feofan Prokopovich) recognized the precise idea of a system as false, foreign to itself, outside of its sphere.[111]

---

[109]Ibid., p. 467.

[110]Ibid., p. 95.

[111]Ibid., p. 96.

However, the range of issues on which he was prepared and able to comment was steadily expanding. Already in September 1842, he observed that it was time for Russia to have its say in the field of science, and dedicated himself to speaking out for her. By December, he was ennunciating an integrated position, revealing some independence and originality, on the relationship between the Slavs, Russia, Orthodoxy and science. His position was set out in a letter to Popov (December 5, 1842) which seems to have been provoked by a fear that he (Popov) might stray from that small group of "Muscovites...working in a single cause, filled by identical hopes..." to which Samarin had already dedicated himself.[112] Unlike "many", and Khomiakov was clearly implied here, who believed that "the future triumph of Slavism" would be a "triumph of life over science", Samarin emphatically believed, that Slavic "life" could and had to be "justified by science." While readily acknowledging that Slavic "life" was "free" and "splendid", he insisted that it must have scientific verification before it could become the sole "inalienable property" of all Slavs. By science he meant philosophy, and by philosophy Hegel, which he saw as a product of German science "expressing a demand for life" which that country and Western Europe as a whole was incapable of realizing. He believed, however, that Russia after absorbing Hegelianism, could achieve that "demand"--that is, the complete "reconciliation of life and consciousness"--and so "triumph over the West." On the other hand, if Russia did not accept Hegelianism, he believed, she would always remain at a lower level of development.

---

[112]Ibid., p. 97.

He made a revealing point about his perception of Russia's role in the Slavic world when he said that studying the history of other Slavic tribes would not serve the interests of Slavic "development" so well as singling out Russia as a model for the other Slavic tribes, because unlike the others she had passed through every stage of development and had achieved an exemplary "wholeness" of "selfconsciousness, conditioned by self-negation." Hence, "liberation" for the other Slavic tribes "from their tribal onesidedness and the realization (osushchestvlenie) in themselves of the common Slavic principle was only possible if they were conscious of themselves in Russia." This was the firm conviction to which he had come after three years of studying Church history. "I will tell you one thing," he said in summarizing his position, "the study of Orthodoxy, limited certainly to a single moment--the appearance in it of two extremes: Catholicism and Protestantism--has brought me to the conclusion, that Orthodoxy will achieve fruition and will only triumph when science justifies it, that the question of the Church depends on the question of philosophy, and that the fate of the Church is tightly, inseparably bound to the fate of Hegel. This is completely clear to me, and therefore in full consciousness I am putting aside my theological occupations and setting to the study of philosophy."[113]

True to his word, Samarin, having finished the work on his dissertation two or three months after this letter was written, threw himself into the study of Hegelian philosophy.[114] This, it seems, was quite a natural, even an inevitable development, for it is reliably reported

---

[113]Ibid., pp. 98-100.

[114]Sochineniya, V, LIV-LV.

that "Hegel embodied European philosophy" for Samarin's generation.
Indeed, Mikail Katkov, publisher, journalist and classmate of Samarin's,
described Moscow of those days as a city in which one "heard only Gogol
and Hegel."[115] But, more significantly, it was still "widely
believed" that philosophy could provide "a rational justification for
belief", and Hegel had produced the most recent and compelling attempt to
establish conclusive rational proof of the existence of a priori ideas
including religious truths.[116] For these reasons it was logical and
appropriate that Samarin should try to justify "slavism" and "orthodoxy"
through Hegel.

The record clearly reveals that this attempt to provide a rational
basis for "slavism" and "orthodoxy" through Hegel was a tormenting and
exhausting experience for Samarin. In a letter to Konstantin Aksakov
(December 31, 1843), he states that he was passing through a period of
"cleavage" and that he had spent many sleepless nights in "bitter tears...
without prayers" as he struggled to resolve questions with which "he had
been long acquainted", but for which he now had to have "definite yes or
no" answers.[117] However, as the following survey will demonstrate,
the record lacks precision, providing only glimpses of this intellectual
and spiritual journey which culminated in the repudiation of Hegel and

---

[115]Nol'de, p. 29.

[116]A.R.M. Murray, An Introduction to Political Philosophy
(London, 1959) pp. 5, 9-12 and 147-159. "Hegel...claimed to show how
thinking can be at once rational and fruitful by defining truth in terms
of the logical relationship of propositions to one another and by
portraying thinking as a process, not of linear inference, but of
dialectical evolution." Ibid., p. 151. cf. W.T. Stace, The Philosophy
of Hegel (New York: Dover Publications, 1955), p. 54.

[117]Sochineniya, XII, 45-46.

rationalism, and a forthright rallying to "slavism" and "Orthodoxy" on the basis of faith.

But first, who were the men who influenced Samarin most during this critical period of development? Certainly one was Peter Chaadayev (1794-1856), an early Westerner and admirer of Catholicism. There were many exchanges between these two, and at least once in 1843, Samarin called Aksakov to his aid with the statement that, "I have already endured his [Chaadayev] attacks, insinuations, etc. for a long time. It is time for a change."[118]   Another was Alexander Herzen (1812-1870), the outstanding Westerner, whom Samarin met for the first time in December of 1842 or January of 1843. Herzen's diary reveals that he and Samarin had frequent discussions, although Samarin's letters record only a brief comment made in 1844: "Yesterday I drank strongly of Herzen and now I am in a muddle."[119] Another was Timofey Granovsky (1813-1855) the moderate Westerner and friend of Herzen and Belinsky about whom Samarin said to Aksakov in 1844: "Let us fall on him together, by surprise: this man is obviously wavering."[120] Still another was Konstantin Aksakov, who had already done so much to solidify Samarin's love for Russia's origins and traditions, including her faith;[121] but whose influence was steadily losing sway as Samarin matured. Concrete evidence of this is contained in a letter of 1844 in which Samarin defends himself from some recent Aksakov reproaches for disloyalty:

---

[118]Ibid., pp. 43-44.

[119]Ibid., p. 47.

[120]Ibid.

[121]Ibid., p. 3.

I love you as much as formerly, although I disagree with many
things [you say] and will dispute them to my last breath. I am
offended more by your unusual exclusiveness and exactingness
than by your opinions. ...if there was something essential in
our difference of opinion I would, reluctantly, submit to
necessity and part with you; but it is painful and disturbing
for me to see that there is no essential difference of opinion
[between us] and that in this situation your exclusiveness,
your impatience, your somewhat insensitiveness to the reality
in which we live, almost always force you to be unjust in your
judgements of people, and among them of me.[122]

But certainly the man who exerted the most powerful and lasting influence

on Samarin at this stage of his career was Alexey Khomiakov, a fact

attested to by Samarin himself many years after in a comment possessing

obvious personal relevance: "For people who preserved in themselves the

sensitiveness of an undamaged, religious sense, but who had become

entangled in contradictions and divided in spirit, Khomiakov was an

original emancipator; he led them to the spaciousness, to the light of

God, and restored to them wholeness of religous consciousness."[123]

What we know about Samarin's investigation of Hegel comes from two

sources: his correspondence with K. Aksakov, and notes and fragments from

his archive. From these sources, we know that he studied Hegel's

Esthetics in preparation for an M.A. exam in 1840, and studied them again

while writing the third part of his dissertation in the spring of

1843.[124] From them we know that he began a study of Hegel's Logic

together with Aksakov in 1841, a study which he soon gave up in order to

---

[122]Ibid., p. 49.

[123]"Predislovie k bogoslovskim sochineniyam A.S. Khomiakova,"
Sochineniya, VI, 347.

[124]Sochineniya, XII, 9, and V, LVI. "The third part contains an
introduction, which is devoted to the theory of preaching and is based on
Hegel's esthetics." D. Chizhevsky, Gegel v Rossii (Paris, 1939), p. 179.

concentrate exclusively on his dissertation.[125] We know that in the

salons of Moscow he was present during, and participated in, many

arguments touching on Hegelian philosophy.[126] We also know that he

wrote extensive summaries of three of Hegel's works: The Phenomenology of

Mind, The Encyclopaedia of the Philosophical Sciences, and the Philosophy

of History: and we know, finally, that some of this work, like the

chapter on perception in The Phenomenology, went with great difficulty (in

fact Samarin told Aksakov he "could not cope" and gave it up); while some,

like The Encyclopaedia, went with ease.[127]

No one can doubt that these investigations made a significant

impact on the development of Samarin's thought and work from the very

beginning. One notable authority who makes the point is D. Chizhevsky.

He states: that "Samarin's Master's dissertation reveals that he studied

Hegel very carefully;"[128] that "the third part [of the dissertation]

contains an introduction, which is devoted to the theory of preaching and

is based on Hegel's esthetics. ...The characteristics of Catholic and

Protestant preaching are established on the basis of this introduction

...";[129] that "Samarin's Hegelianism became an object of derision at his

defence;"[130] and that "the polemical dispute between Popov and Samarin

---

[125]Sochineniya, XII, 25.

[126]Ibid., p. 21, et passim.

[127]Sochineniya, V, LVI.

[128]Chizhevsky, p. 176.

[129]Ibid., p. 179.

[130]Ibid., p. 178.

was conducted in the terms of Hegelian philosophy."[131] Samarin's

biographer, B. Nol'de, makes the same point stating that "his first

acquaintance with the philosophical works of Hegel...was reflected in his

setting of the question of Church authority: he began to approach it from

the point of view of the Hegelian category of development."[132]

An examination of the preceding pages, in the light of Hegel's

philosophy, in an effort to find points of comparison, provides strong

support for these statements of authority. For instance Samarin

frequently uses the term "moment" in the Hegelian sense of designating a

distinctive stage of development inextricably linked with its past and

future.[133] Also Samarin was obviously impressed by Hegel's concept of

"development" applying it to Church history. For Hegel "development" "was

conceived as the coming to light of what was latent and hidden" in a

continuous process culminating in the "actualization of reason, the idea,

in the world":[134] for Samarin "development" was seen as the Church

"bringing to her consciousness the eternal inexhaustible truth which she

possesses."[135] Lastly, Hegel created a philosophical system in which

the principles of logic were rigorously applied to prove that everything

---

[131]Ibid., p. 177.

[132]Nol'de, p. 22.

[133]In Hegel's philosophy of history "every stage, or 'moment'...is
viewed both as a necessary consequence of its predecessor and as radically
different from it." Henry D. Aiken, The Age of Ideology: The 19th
Century Philosophers (New York: Mentor Books, 1956), p. 73. In Hegel's
theory of the dialectic "the first and second terms of a triad are the
'moments' of the third, i.e. the factors which go to compose it." Stace,
The Philosophy of Hegel, p. 109.

[134]Stace, pp. 25 and 214.

[135]See above pp. 48, 52, 53 et passim.

in the universe was rationally deducible or to prove, in his own words,

that "reason is the substance of the universe; ...the design of the world

is absolutely rational."[136] Samarin demonstrated a similar commitment

to reason and rigorous logic in commenting on the characteristics of a

"theological system" or "science", when he claimed:

> ...a system renders into one logical whole all dogmas, so that
> everyone of them appears not as an aphorism, but rationally proven,
> linked with the foregoing and the following. ...systematization is
> not the creation of new dogmas, but a logical justification of old
> ones: consequently a system, in agreement with dogmas will be one in
> which dogmas have been proven so strictly that from each proof flows
> not less and not more than is contained in the dogma itself.[137]

A further example of Samarin's Hegelian commitment to logical proof is

found in his repudiation of Khomiakov's belief that "the future triumph of

slavism" would be a "triumph of life over science", by the contrary belief

that Slavic life had to be "justified by science."[138]

Now what do the documents, comprising a few letters, several

fragments, and a number of diary entries by Herzen, tell us about the

impact of Hegel on Samarin's thought during the period (December 1842 -

June 1844) of preoccupation with the implications of Hegelian philosophy

for Orthodoxy?

---

[136]G.W.Hegel, Philosophy of History, Bohn ed., pp. 9 and 13, as
quoted in W. Durant, The Story of Philosophy (Toronto: Doubleday, Doran
& Gundy, Ltd., 1926), p. 323. Cf. "Thus a philosophy which would
genuinely explain the world will take as its first principle not a cause
but a reason. From this reason it will proceed to deduce the world not as
an effect but as a logical consequent. We shall then see not merely that
things are as they are, but we shall see why they are as they are. This
is the fundamental Hegelian idea of explanation. This is what Hegel's
philosophy attempts to do." Stace, p. 54. See also Ibid., pp. 64, 71,
83, 99 and 113.

[137]Above, p. 57-58.

[138]Above, p. 60.

In the first document, an unfinished letter to Khomiakov of September 1843,[139] Samarin stated that the crucial question on which he and Khomiakov must agree if they were to achieve harmony and consistency of thought between themselves was "the question of the relationship of religion to philosophy."[140] Eschewing any immediate attempt to resolve the question by "scholarly means", because he had just perceived the importance of the question, he proceeded to outline how he became aware of it and "how closely ... it was tied to the fate of the [Orthodox] Church." As he described it even though the work on his assigned dissertation topic necessitated "setting aside many very important questions",it enabled him to grasp the relationship between Catholicism, Protestantism and Orthodoxy. This relationship he defined as follows:

> the essential difference between Catholicism, Protestantism, and our Church is that Catholicism, expressing a pretension to exclusiveness, is together a science and a state; Protestantism, recognizing the full freedom of science and the state and rejecting the exclusivenss of the Church, rejects at the same time the Church and religion in general; our Church is not a science and not a state: it is conscious of itself only as a Church (I do not say, as a moment, because you do not allow this word, and you, it seems, agree with what has been said up to this time). But science and the state must exist: consequently, if the Church does not recognize them in her sphere, it signifies they exist outside her, as separate spheres, and the power of the Church must not extend to them. Therefore, if science and the state really have in themselves this power, and they exist independently, as separate spheres, then the Orthodox Church is right, and her abstention from expressing a pretension to that which is not accessible to her, vouches for her truth. If not--the conclusion would be the reverse. Having set aside the question of the state, about which there is no argument between us, I propose the following question (and you will accept it in this

---

[139]Sochineniya, XII, 130-131: also in Sochineniya, V, LVI-LVIII. The contents of this letter are known from a rough draft which survived among Samarin's papers. Khomiakov's reply is available in I. Aksakov, "Pisma A.S. Khomiakova k Yu. F. Samarinu, "Russkiy Arkhiv (1879), pp. 305-307: also in Sochineniya, V, LXVIII-LXXI.

[140]Sochineniya, XII, 130.

form): does philosophy exist, as a separate sphere from the Church, subjected to her, or on the contrary, does it subject the Church to itself? I think, that if science exists, as a separate sphere of the spirit from art and religion, then it must be a higher sphere, the final stage of the development of the idea...[141]

In a fragment penned at approximately the same time as this letter to Khomiakov, Samarin clearly tried to answer the specific question posed above: "does philosophy exist as a separate sphere from the Church, subjected to her", or vice versa? His answer began somewhat apologetically, for he still lacked proof for what he proposed to say, with a statement of the idea upon which his conviction was based--the idea that "the state, art, religion and philosophy", exist "as separate spheres", which "will never be in conflict, if each of them is conscious of itself only in its own sphere and does not overstep its boundaries." This was so, because "each of them had its own foundation, in harmony with "forces" and "capacities" "deeply rooted in man's nature", and was the logical and natural outcome of a process of self-conscious development. For this reason "the content of each" was "exclusive" and "irreplaceable." When applied to religion and philosophy, "the principal concern of the moment", this theory led to the conviction that there could be "no conflict between them, until one of them expressed a pretension to be the other, to constrain the other and to replace it, until religion accepts a philosophical, and philsophy--a dogmatic character." But since "such a pretension" contradicts the "substance" of both, "the content of religion ... cannot become the content of philosophy" and vice versa, just as "the ability to believe cannot become the ability to understand." And since, "that, in which we believe has been created by faith and can only be assimilated by faith ", the function of "thought is not to comprehend

---

[141]Ibid., p.131.   The letter breaks off at this point abruptly.

the incomprehensible, because then it would not exist, and it must exist, but to comprehend its necessity, as such." Thus "thought" in its most recent "phase" of development, has recognized "religion as a separate sphere with all its peculiarities, with its sacraments and miracles." Hand in glove with this discovery came the realization that religion could only exist as a separate sphere if philosophy exists as a "higher sphere ...which strengthens for its use reason, and, reconciling itself with religion" does not infringe its boundaries. Thus the reconciliation of philosophy and religion can only be maintained when these "limits" are recognized and adhered to--"when each of these spheres is conscious of itself as one sphere, as a moment." As for the Church, it cannot express this relationship in a positive way without "overstepping its limits", without acknowledging "reason", without introducing "the philosophical element" into itself, and so contradicting its essence. Thus the conclusion is reached that the Church has nothing to fear from "an outside force" unless she allows it to act inside her sphere. Finally, the argument is concluded in this statement:

> the Orthodox Church has not expressed pretensions to be either a state, or a science; consequently, if the state and science exist as independent spheres, the Orthodox Church is right; she can and must be justified by contemporary philosophy. Philosophy defines a place for her, as an eternally-present moment in the development of the spirit, and decides in her favour the argument between her and the Western religious denominations. Therefore the fate of Orthodoxy is tightly bound with the fate of Hegel and the question of our Church depends on the question of this philosophy. Outside of this philosophy the Orthodox Church cannot exist, and those, who, not recognizing philosophy, take it on themselves to defend our faith against Catholics and Protestants, are not right and must be overcome.[142]

In another closely related fragment, Samarin tried to clarify the relationship between religion and philosophy by comparing "the parallel

---

[142]Sochineniya, V, LVIII-LX.

relationship of art, another absolute sphere, to the absolute sphere of religion." Pointing out that art and religion co-exist as separate but unequal spheres (religion standing higher), he emphasized: that "each exists in its own way" and has a "normal relationship" with the other; and that this relationship causes neither "doubt" nor "confusion" in the modern age. However, he continued, this was not the case in the early centuries of Christianity when "defenders of religion" were locked in "battle" with art and "persecuted" it remorselessly. As an example in point, St. Augustine is cited as a "great Christian zealot" who denounced "love of the exquisite", "persecuted poets", and "wept" over his own youthful indulgence in art studies. Samarin avers that Augustine was correct in this "because the ancient world never rose above art." "Beauty", which "reconciled all contradictions", and "was for it the divine", was "its ideal"; therefore, the ancient world could not accommodate Christianity, and religion and art had to do "battle"--"the triumph of religion was revealed by the development of a new world." Giving focus to this comparison, Samarin went on to argue that contemporary humanity was living through a similar crisis of development, as "the new sphere" of philosophy was striving to establish its relationship to the sphere of religion. This momentous and stirring "struggle", pregnant with prospects for "spiritual renewal", "must" see the relationship between religon and philosophy "defined" and culminate in "harmony" just as the "battle" between art and religion had centuries before. However, philosophy could "never be reconciled with Catholicism and Protestantism", therefore, Orthodoxy "the only religion that recognized philosophy" had a crucial role to play in this process of definition and harmonization. Finally, commenting on the validity of his

comparison, Samarin began a refutation of the arguments of those who

accepted it for art and religion, but rejected it for religion and

philosophy on the grounds that the "questions" and "interests" of religion

and philosophy were "identical." "Religion", he began, "had its sphere,

its particularity, just as philosophy had, and that sphere was the sphere

of faith --the communication of what is being hoped for, the exposure of

things unseen. Usually they think [the refutors of his comparison] that

the object of faith and knowledge is one and that it is only two means of

the attainment...." On this note the fragment ended, midway in the

explication of an idea.[143]

In another fragment Samarin wrote:

> Our real position...is this: the Catholics and Protestants have
> carried the religious question to the final limit. It is already
> impossible for us to retreat. Two alternatives remain: to recog-
> nize the latest philosophical principle, defining religion as a
> moment; then we will have a chance to completely destroy Catholicism,
> which only seems strong to us, because we have not been clearly
> conscious of our faith, and then a splendid future will open before
> us, -- or we must repudiate Orthodoxy and at the same time all of our
> past and become foster children to one of the Western peoples. But
> this will not happen; we are all convinced of this; and although at
> the present minute we are not agreed about the direction from which
> salvation will come; many of us, if not all, look ahead with hope and
> excitement. In this sense of expectation and high hopes we are all
> reconciled.[144]

Having concluded that Russian Orthodox Christians must recognize

religion as a "moment" in the development of man's consciousness, Samarin

went on to argue that this view must be accepted or everything that he had

said "in praise" of the Orthodox church would have to be said in "censure"

of her. Further, he said, her history would have to be interpreted in an

---

[143]Ibid., LXI-LXII.

[144]Ibid., LXIII.

entirely different way, as follows. After the schism[145] "the Orthodox church maintained its uniqueness" in relation to the Catholic church by allowing the "Protestant element" to develop within its framework -- refused "to recognize the Pope, rejected purgatory etc." The reformation came and the Protestants took possession of that very element which had distinguished Orthodoxy from Catholicism, leaving the former no special ground to occupy. As a result Western influence became very strong, and "two schools emerged" within the Orthodox Church, both professing to be Orthodox, although one, "propogated Catholic teachings" in an incomplete form, and "the other Protestant teachings." Since the Orthodox Church reacted passively, "neither accepting nor rejecting" either of these tendencies, it "must be concluded" that the Church divided into Catholic and Protestant parts, and that "her" separate "existence, from the beginning illusory, was now ended." This conclusion was supported, he said, "...by the sorry position of the clergy in Russia, its enslavement to secular power and the terrible arbitrary opinions of its representatives."[146]

---

[145]Samarin is referring to the schism of 1054, when leaders of the Orthodox and Catholic Churches excommunicated each other. See N. Zernov, Eastern Christendom: A Study of the Origin and Development of the Eastern Orthodox church (London: Weidenfeld and Nicolson, 1961), pp. 99-103. Zernov's comment on the issues separating the two Churches is as follows: "Both sides firmly believed in the unity of Christendom, but their vision of what the Catholic Church ought to be was no longer the same. Not only were their worship, discipline, customs and outlook different, but there was a serious divergence in regard to the structure of the Christian community. The West saw the Church as a sacred monarchy, and the Pope as the source of all authority in teaching and administration. The Greeks had no place for that type of papacy in their system. They were ready to treat the Bishop of Rome as the senior hierarch, but the idea that the Pope was an ecclesiastical monarch to be obeyed by the rest of Christendom was alien to the Byzantine tradition and neither side was prepared to make any concessions." Ibid., p. 102.

[146]Sochineniya, V, LXIII-LXIV.

The line of argument summarized in the above pages reaches its

culmination in a remarkable fragment beginning:

> Let the man who has studied Orthodoxy, and who has read the begin-
> ning of the second part of Mohler's Symbolism[147] in which the idea
> of the Catholic Church is developed, place his hand on his heart and
> say, whether there is anything in the Orthodox Church, as a Church,
> leaving aside that particular definition of it, arising from its
> relationship to philosophy, that could not be in the Catholic Church.
> And could an Orthodox Christian, standing on an exclusively religious
> point of view, not recognize in that Church, the one to which he
> considers himself to be a member. I am convinced that he could
> not.[148]

Pursuing the implications of these words in the remaining lines of the

fragment, Samarin first noted, that they were "a condemnation" of his

dissertation, indeed, "destroying it"; and properly so, for his

dissertation was based on the proposition that Orthodoxy embodied a true

understanding of the Church idea, while Catholicism and Protestantism

embodied two rival extremes of the idea.[149] He then noted that a

"solution" to the continuing debate between Orthodoxy and Catholicism

about "the idea of the Church" could not be found along "the path", which

he had followed in writing his dissertation, because Orthodoxy "would

always lose" until it "transferred" the argument to the "higher sphere of

---

[147]Johann Adam Mohler (1796-1838) was a famous Catholic theologian
at Tubingen University. His field of specialization was Church history,
patristics and Church law. His book Symbolik, oder, Darstellung der
dogmatischen Gegensatze der Katholiken und Protestanten, nach ihern
offentlichen Bekenntniss-schriften [Symbolism: or, Exposition of the
doctrinal differences between Catholics and Protestants as evidenced by
their symbolical writings], (Mainz, 1832), sparked a heated polemical
debate in Western Europe. Samarin offered this evaluation of Mohler's
work: "I have definitely found nothing new in it: but the exposition is
splendid. There are several very unjust accusations against Protestants;
but in general the book is intelligently conceived. From it, it
immediately follows that Protestantism does not exist as a single,
integral teaching; for this reason it so perplexed the Germans."
Sochineniya, XII, 96.

[148]Sochineniya, V, LXIV-LXV.

philosophy." He concluded:

> It falls to me to accept this heavy task; I call it heavy
> because there is no guide for it. To Hegel the fact of the
> Church was almost completely foreign; his philosophy of religion
> is in many ways unsatisfactory; therefore it is necessary to add,
> to say what he did not say, to discover and introduce to the
> content of his philosophy the side, which was hidden from him -
> by Hegel himself to add to Hegel.[150]

And Samarin did try "to add to Hegel", writing a composition (unfortunate-

ly lost to us) in which he claimed "to demonstrate, that Hegel ...divined

the Orthodox Church and a priori placed her, having called religion one of

the moments (middle, but not the last) in the logical development of the

absolute spirit, which is striving towards the fullness of selfconscious-

ness."[151]

As the preceding pages indicate, Samarin was very concerned to define

the relationship between philosophy and religion and to develop therefrom

a rational justification for his commitment, hitherto based on family

tradition, to the Orthodox faith.[152] The idea which he applied in his

analysis was Hegel's idea that the "absolute spirit" manifests itself in

---

[149]"The spirit of God lives in the unity of Christian humanity,
consequently not in one chosen individual of any sort, and not in each
individual, taken separately in disassociation from the whole. Having
defined these two extremes, we have identified Catholicism and
Protestantism." "Rech' proiznesennaya pred zashchishcheniem dissertatsii
na stepen' magistra v publichnom sobranii Imperatorskago Mosk.
Universiteta, 3 iyunya 1844 goda," Ibid., pp. 452-453. See also pp.
77-78 below.

[150]Ibid., p. LXV.

[151]Samarin, as quoted in Chizhevsky, p. 177.

[152]Konstantin Aksakov and Yuri Samarin "both passionately loved
Russia, for both Orthodoxy was a family tradition and possession,...." I.
Aksakov "Predislovie, Pis'ma A.S. Khomiakova k Yu. F. Samarinu," (Russkiy
Arkhiv, 1879), p. 301.

three ascending stages "art", "religion" and "philosophy."[153] Art in
which experience and the Idea are synthesized in art forms indicating the
nature of absolute spirit: "beauty is the sensuous body, so to speak, of
the Spirit, in which the nature of the spirit is indicated."[154]
Religion in which experience and the Idea are synthesized at a higher
level, although the imagination continues to play a crucial role - finite
spirits (men) are seen to be creations of the Absolute Spirit, and the
movement of life and the spheres a manifestation of its purpose. And
philosophy, the highest stage of all, which synthesizes the perceptions of
art and religion to produce a clear rational statement of the relationship
between finite spirit and the absolute - finite spirit becomes fully
conscious of itself in the absolute.[155]

This general conception of Hegel's was applied in a creative way, as
Samarin developed original arguments consistent with the concept of self-
conscious development, to prove that the "state, art, religion and
philosophy" were "separate spheres."[156] However, in a Hegelian sense,
the argument is strained when he maintains that the content of each is
"exclusive" and "irreplaceable", especially where religion and philosophy

---

[153]See p. 69 above. "Philosophy" can generally be substituted for
"science" in these passages, consistent with Samarin's equating of the
terms, see p. 60, above. Aksakov and Samarin, "avid admirers of German
philosophical speculation and literature. ...attempted to construct, on
Hegel's principles, a complete world view, a complete original system of
the "phenomenology' of the Russian national spirit with its history,
existential appearances and even Orthodoxy." Ibid.

[154]B.A.G. Fuller, History of Philosophy (New York: Henry Holt and
Company, 1947), p. 311.

[155]Ibid., pp. 310-311; and A.K. Rogers, A Student's History of
Philosophy (New York: The Macmillan Company, 1912) pp. 463-465.

[156]See p. 69, above.

are concerned, because there is no place for exclusiveness in Hegel's
system, for movement through boundaries, forward and back, is a foundation principle established in the first triad "being, not-being, becoming."[157] Samarin is in conflict, too, with his mentor when he argues
that "the incomprehensible must exist",[158] for in Hegel's system
"...all mystery is at last dispelled in the clear light of reason, and the
whole course of creation may be watched, as it moves with logical
necessity from one step to the next."[159] Nevertheless, Samarin argued
that religion and philosophy had set "limits", philosophy being "higher",
and that the Orthodox Church was "a separate sphere" that could and must
be "justified" by Hegel's philosophy.[160]

Another creative application of Hegel's concept appears in the
historical argument that art and religion were "separate absolute
spheres", which were once locked in battle in much the same way that
religion and philosophy were in the 1840's. However, the argument becomes
strained and tendentious when Samarin begins to plead a special position
for Orthodoxy as the "only religion that recognized philosophy."[161]

Samarin was clearly aware of the unsubstantial character of some of
his arguments. At least his repeated assertions that "the latest philosophical principle" must "be recognized"; the rather cataclysmic fate,
which he foresaw for Orthodoxy if it was not; his response to Mohler's

---

[157]Stace, p. 92.

[158]See p. 70, above.

[159]Rogers, p. 465.

[160]See p. 69-70, above.

[161]See pp. 70-72, above.

Symbolism; and his assertion, that Hegel knew little about "the fact of

the Church" and had produced "a philosophy of religion that was in many

ways unsatisfactory", suggests a high level of doubt and uncertainty.[162]

This perception of Samarin's state of mind as a result of his attempt to

reconcile Orthodoxy and Hegelianism is given credence by several comments

in Alexander Herzen's Diary, comments which are doubly meaningful because

Samarin himself, on reading them in 1875, confirmed that they were

accurate.[163] In October 1843, Herzen wrote:

> Kireyevsky is more consistent than Aksakov and Samarin: they
> want on the basis of contemporary science to build a Slaviano-
> Byzantine structure. They, through Hegel arrive at Orthodoxy and
> through Western science at the rejection of Western history; they
> accept progress, they look through our eyes on the future of man-
> kind, and for this they have lost necessary consequentiality.[164]

On November 10, he wrote:

> A long very interesting conversation with Samarin. He is agreed,
> that it is clearly impossible to develop logically his idea of the
> immanent coexistence of religion and science, that das Aufheben by
> science leaves the Church in all her reality. They are agreed, that
> the rastorzhyonost' (dissolubility?) of man, which destroys by
> thought that which is accepted by fancy and the heart, and, on the
> other side, which lulls thought, and again gives a place to idea, is
> irreconcilable.[165]

---

[162]See pp. 74-75, above. Cf. Stace's comment: "It must not be
supposed that Hegel has actually succeeded in rigorously applying his
principles throughout his system. ...For example, in the philosophy of
spirit Hegel puts forward as one of his triads the notions of art,
religion and philosophy. Here art is supposed to be the thesis, religion
the antithesis, philosophy the synthesis. It is very difficult to see in
what sense religion is the opposite of art; and it is quite impossible to
see that art and philosophy are related as genus and species, or that
religion can be regarded as the differentia." Stace, p. 97.

[163]Sochineniya, V, LXVI.

[164]A.. Herzen, Sobranie Sochineniy v Tridtsati Tomakh: Stat'i
Fel'etony 1841-1846, Dnevnik 1842-1845 (Moscow, 1954) II, 311.

[165]Ibid., p. 314. Hegel used the term aufheben (to abolish, to
preserve), sometimes translated "to sublate", to signify the two-fold
activity of the synthesis of a triad in abolishing and preserving the
thesis and antithesis. See Stace, p. 106.

and on January 18, 1844 he wrote:

> Samarin has returned; he has begun with horror to view the impossi-
> bility of holding to [his] Orthodox-philosophical point. The fine
> structure of his mind does not allow him to rest on formal external
> coexistence or better on a juxtaposition. In Kazan a priest, assured,
> peaceful in his Orthodoxy, impressed him. But he is sad, the process
> is being completed suddenly, and I know by my own experience, how
> difficult it is to part with some dreams even though I was not so
> committed to them as he is. [166]

Alexey Khomiakov was a deciding influence in freeing Samarin from this

doubt and uncertainty. When Samarin met him in 1840, Khomiakov already

held a mature ideological position, impregnable to Hegelian attack, for

when Hegel's philosophy began to become a force in Moscow, it is recorded,

"Khomiakov locked himself away with the Logic for several days, after

which, emerging from his seclusion, he declared, that he had gnawed four

holes."[167] Being "a passionate and skilful debater" he became a

principal opponent of Hegelianism in the salons of Moscow. Speaking in

the larger context of Russian thought, Chizhevsky claims, that "the

strength of Khomiakov's inner conviction and the energy of his presenta-

tion" was more remarkable, "than the subtlety of his distinctions, and the

logical consistency of his thought."[168] Whatever the merit of this

assertion, Samarin, as an enthusiastic young Hegelian, clashed with

Khomiakov in their first fateful meetings. However, frequent clashes were

soon followed by fast friendship, and in late 1843, when Samarin was

acutely aware of the inadequacies of Hegel's philosophy and the inconclu-

siveness of his own efforts to produce a satisfying synthesis therefrom,

---

[166]Ibid., p. 327. Samarin had just returned from a long journey
which had taken him to Yaraslavl, Simbirsk and Kazan. See Sochineniya, V,
LXXVII.

[167]Chizhevsky, p. 185.

[168]Ibid.

a long and decisive series of discussions on the relationship of philo-

sophy to religion and Orthodoxy took place between them. I. Aksakov

left posterity valuable evidence on this development:

> The young people [Samarin and Konstantin Aksakov] bravely entered
> into battle with this athlete of the dialectic (as Herzen called
> him in his memoirs, it seems). The debates extended over more
> than two years, always more intimately and strongly, gradually
> bringing the opponents together. In any case the debate was not
> about the significance of nationality in general and of Russian
> nationality in particular, nor about spiritual essence and the
> differences of the Russian people from West Europeans, etc.,
> etc., but for the most part about the relationship of philosophy
> to religion, and about Orthodoxy, being justified or deduced by
> the young people from the principles of Hegel.[169]

A good indication, at least of the nature of this relationship, and

more importantly of the burden of Khomiakov's thought as set out in these

discussions, is contained in a long letter which he wrote to Samarin on

October 15, 1843:

> Dear Yuri Fyederovich! Your letter of September 26 made me very
> happy, in spite of the fact that it was written with a heavy heart.
> Thank you for remembering and fulfilling your promise to write; I
> am glad, that your free time has not been spent in vain. The
> content of your letter was not unexpected by me. You, perhaps,
> remember the conversation with you and Aksakov, when I promised you
> both an internal struggle and even predicted, that it would begin
> with you first. In his nature there is more dreaminess, and not in
> anger against him it can be said, femininity or artisticness, which
> willingly avoids the demands of logic. You have set to the matter
> manfully, conscious of your inner split. I expected this, but I
> must confess, not so quickly. God knows how a conscious split will
> end, but it is good that it is conscious. An unconscious split
> could continue for a century without producing a reconciliation.

> A man does not have the right to retreat from the demands of
> science. He can close his eyes from exhaustion, forcefully impose
> oblivion on himself; but following on this peace is a whitened
> grave from which neither life nor anything living will ever come.
> If he was once conscious of the dichotomy between science
> (analysis) and life (synthesis), he would have only one exit - in
> analysis, because synthesis cannot trust itself.

> Is the position of science reliable? That is the question. That
> is, can science rely strictly on itself? On this test depends the

---

[169]I. Aksakov, pp. 303-304.

possibility of reconciliation. With your frankness to yourself and
your preciseness of thought, I believe completely in a final
conclusion. Science has not been true to itself up to now,
confusing what is recognized with what is conscious and (don't
laugh) suffering constantly from that ailment, in which it
reproaches mystics. This is strikingly reminiscent of Schelling, to
whose defense you will not rise; this seems clear to me in Hegel in
the opposition of conscious Being to immediate Being, from which
the first emerges with the character of a negation in the form of
not-Being, and which is impermissible, because the conscious is
legitimately contrasted only with what is conscious. In other
words the relationship (no matter what it is) bears again only the
character of what is recognized and must not have a place in the
science of consciousness. In any case this is only by the way.
You will find a great deal that will not leave you and return to
you freedom of life, having exposed in a lie the excessive
pretensions of science - the anatomy of the spirit.
...In passing you speak about Hegel's view on one of the basic
facts of Christianity. You do not agree with him, or it would be
better to say, recognize that his view is not in agreement with the
teaching of the church. You are completely correct. But Hegel is
guilty not of a bad interpretation, but of the child-like faith
with which he set to interpreting the text, because this text has
long been interpreted according to the philosophical schools, i.e.
in a truncated form. Frenchmen, Englishmen and Germans have
already discussed the tree of knowledge a great deal and constantly
left aside the addition: of good and evil. Our long-standing
argument with you is linked with this. Forgive me, if I repeat
what I have already said; but, it seems to me, it was said not in
your presence but in the presence of Aksakov and Bobarykin. Of two
men one knows about light only that it shines, while the other
narrates all the laws of the refraction, diffusion and reflection
of rays, etc. Of two men speaking about love one knows only the
word to love, and the other explains all the actions of love so
clearly, that it is possible to conclude correctly how one who
loves will act in a given situation. You will say, that the second
two know light and love much better than the first. Just so. But
the great specialist in light is a congenitally blind professor,
and the specialist in love is the devil. Do they know? Evidently
less than the first. Their knowledge is external, while the
knowledge of the first is internal, much fuller, in spite of the
absence of logical definition. The tree of knowledge is in any
case a myth about the knowledge of good and evil by means of whatever law. Spontaneous, instinctive life, was not defined for
rational being. The law reveals freedom. Free violation of the
law opened the door of knowledge, just as free fulfillment; but in
the one circumstance man received positive knowledge of evil and
recognized good as its negation; and in the other the opposite. You
see what follows. Knowledge, as logical knowledge, has nothing in
common with the knowledge of good and evil. Truly we know only
that in which we live and by which we live. Hegel's mistake
(leaving aside the truncation of the text) stems from the one-sided

and scholastically haughty concept of knowledge in general. And in truth, it is funny to think how scholars on one side and praisers of ignorance on the other, for various reasons, have tried to accustom and have partly accustomed people to understand the story of Moses about the law in the sense of a more or less just satire on knowledge.

When will we see each other? At what point on your path will I find you? God grant, that you will quickly receive a presentiment of inner reconciliation, if still not full reconciliation. But allow me to give you some advice. Don't leave yourself without work, except the work, which you are now undertaking for the clarification of your own thought. Outside work will be a relaxation for you and ease your main intellectual task. ...

P.S. No matter what your present or future conclusion from the full study of science, do not regret the achievements of thinkers, as if they had been in vain. True, all this could or could not have been, just as history could or could not have been; but seeds, which have been sown a long time ago must give fruit, and the work of one who brings their time of ripeness closer is not lost in vain.[170]

Comments scattered throughout Khomiakov's works indicate that he had

the highest regard for Hegel's philosophical achievement. German idealism

"alone of all the philosophical schools fully completed its course strict

to the final conclusion." "All future attempts by means of pure philo-

sophy are impossible after Hegel."[171] German idealism, initiated by

Immanuel Kant, achieved its consummation in Hegel.[172] Nevertheless,

Khomiakov had a fundamental objection to Hegel and it is voiced in the

above letter to Samarin. Logical and strictly rational though he was,

Hegel made the same error as science "confusing what is recognized with

what is conscious...suffering constantly from that ailment in which it

---

[170]Pis'ma A.S. Khomyakova k Yu. F. Samrina, pp. 305-307. Also in Sochineniya, V. LXVIII - LXXI. Dmitry Samarin claims that this letter "contains, in embryo, the whole view of Khomiakov, as revealed by him subsequently in his theological writings." Ibid., p. LXXI.

[171]Khomiakov as quoted in Chizhevsky, pp. 185-186.

[172]P.K. Christoff, An Introduction to Nineteenth Century Russian Slavophilism. A Study in Ideas. Volume I: A.S. Xomjakov (The Hague: Mouton & Co., 1961), p. 129.

reproaches mystics."[173] Or as Chizhevsky says in explicating this
passage, "Hegel gives us only knowledge, but at the same time, knowledge
which was only addressed to our consciousness, knowledge incapable of
standing as an object of recognition. Because recognition is a function
not only of the intellectual sphere, to which German idealism addressed
itself, but also in no small measure of feeling and will."[174] In
other words Khomiakov asserted that Hegel's claims to having created an
"all encompassing universal system" was negated, because "the sphere of
intellectual knowledge is linked in the closest manner with feeling and
will, defining them but also being defined by them."[175] This is the
point made so eloquently in the allegory of the blind professor and the
devil and articulated in the passage "logical knowledge has nothing in
common with the knowledge of good and evil. Truly we know only that in
which we live and by which we live. Hegel's mistake...stems from the
one-sided and scholastically haughty concept of knowledge in
general."[176]

Herzen's Diary provides another valuable source of information about
Khomiakov's critique of Hegel. Therein Herzen wrote an apparently
verbatim summary of Khomiakov's critique as developed in a long debate
on December 22, 1842. Samarin must have been very familiar with these
oral arguments, considering that he spent so much time in privte discussion with Khomiakov, who "talked very much, talked more than he wrote or

---

[173]Above, p. 81.

[174]Chizhevsky, pp. 186-187. Italics in the original.

[175]Ibid., p. 187.

[176]Above, pp. 81-82.

acted."[177] According to Herzen, Khomiakov argued that "it was impossible to derive either the personality or the transcendentality of God" from Hegel's first principles--that these could lead only to the idea of the "immanence" of God, and the idea of life as an "inner fermentation."[17] Khomiakov attacked what he saw as the fundamental weakness in Hegel's philosophy--the development of the "logical idea", that is, the failure to recognize the impossibility of making a "transition" from an idea to the fact, because of the unpredictable impact of "chance." "Chance" was a necessary element in every fact; therefore, any logical understanding of that fact was unavoidably an "abstraction": "Man in the fetal state must develop into a mature adult, the necessity lies in the understanding of the embryo; but chance cuts the thread of life, and the fact is no more. Therefore chance is essential to the fact, but is taken by the idea to be unessential."[179] Thus Hegelianism was logically consistent, and represented the final highest stage in the development of philosophy, but it was self-annihilating because it could only create an "ideal construction" of the universe, "parallelling the real...leading in the final analysis to immanence and disintegrating chaotic atomism. Consequently, to an absurdity."[180] Thus Hegel proved, by remaining in the sphere of abstract reason (razsudok), that it was impossible to know the truth by logic alone, negating in the process the whole scientific movement, and leaving religion as the sole source of knowledge

---

[177]N. Berdyaev, Aleksey Stepanovich Khomyakov (Moscow, 1912), p. 63.

[178]Herzen, p. 250.

[179]Ibid., pp. 250-251.

[180]Ibid., p. 251.

understanding.[181] Khomiakov was convinced that his criticism of Hegel took him beyond the limitations of German idealism. As will be seen, it provided Samarin with a rationale for remaining loyal to his religious roots.

When Khomiakov finally undertook to systematize Slavophil philosophy in the last year of his life (1859), using letters to Samarin as a vehicle, he reaffirmed much of what has been said above. For example he wrote: "Hegel is the most complete, and I would boldly say, the only rationalist in the world"; "Hegel could, and did, bring rationalism to its ultimate limit..."; "Kant's great school" found its culmination in Hegel; "Its highest development as also its extreme one-sidedness were expressed by Hegel. This one-sidedness consisted in accepting the laws of under-standing for the law of the all-embracing spirit..."; "The common error of the whole school, not clearly prominent in its founder Kant, and sharply characterizing its consummator Hegel, consists in this, that it constantly accepts the movement of concepts in personal understanding as identical with the movement of actuality itself (of all reality)...."[182] There is no doubt that these inadequacies served to strengthen Khomiakov's religious commitment.

But what were the religious ideas that Khomiakov espoused? They were a counter-weight to his critique of Hegel, and were of critical importance because they contributed decisively to the resolution of Samarin's philosophical and religious dilemma.[183] First of all Khomiakov was an

---

[181]Ibid., p. 252. Cf. Chizhevsky, pp. 187-188.

[182]Christoff, p. 130.

[183]"Only the spiritual influence of Khomiakov freed Yu. Samarin from philosophical rationalism and brought him to the Church." Berdyaev, p. 63.

Orthodox theologian who believed that "divine truth" had been revealed "at the very beginning" and provided "the solution for all problems."[184] Both his theology and his philosohy were rooted in his faith. Faith was primary, as his affirmation of I. Kireyevsky's statement that "philosophy itself is nothing but a transitional movement of human reason from the realm of faith into the realm of multiform application to indigenous thought", and his concluding observation that "in this deduction are determined at once both the rational independent freedom of philosophy, and its lawful though unconscious (lawful, precisely because it is unconscious) subordination to faith..." attests.[185] Khomiakov's basic idea, and the cornerstone of Slavophil philosophy, was the idea that "the source of all theology and philosophy must be the whole life of the spirit (tselostnaya zhizn'dukha)...."[186] Central to "the wholeness of the spirit idea" was the conviction that faith and reason were not in "struggle and conflict" with one another, but in "agreement and Harmony." Faith was first in importance. Reason was second, having the special

---

[184]Chizhevsky, p. 188.

[185]As quoted in Christoff, p. 135. Berdyaev identifies Kireyevsky and Khomiakov as the joint founders of Slavophil philosophy (Berdyaev, p. 114). Zenkovsky, however, states that Khomiakov had "unquestionable priority" even though his "fundamental philosophical articles were written more or less as a continuation and development of those of I.V. Kireyevsky...." (V.V. Zenkovsky, A History of Russian Philosophy (New York: Columbia University Press, 1953) I, 180.). Slavophil philosophy suffered an unfortunate fate. Soon after Kireyevsky began a systematiza- ton of it, he died of cholera (June 10, 1856). Tragically, the same fate overtook Khomiakov soon after he took up Kireyevsky's philosophical work (September 23, 1860). (Berdyaev, p. 114).

[186]Berdyaev, p. 108.

function of attaining to "the level of sympathetic agreement with faith."[187] Reason itself could not discover eternal truth without assistance from the whole battery of man's cognitive faculties including "sentiment" and "aesthetic sense" acting in concert and "inspired and illuminated by faith."[188] "The whole life of the spirit" was an "organic" phenomenon accessible only to those who lived a vigorous religious life focussed on the Orthodox Church. The Orthodox Church was "love" and "freedom" and the source of Russia's uniqueness and messianic promise for the future.[189]

Khomiakov became the leader of the Slavophil movement because of the force and steadfastness with which he propounded these religio-philosophical ideas. But perhaps Samarin, who was converted through his discussions with Khomiakov into "a loyal student"[190] should be allowed the final word:

> We want...to refresh in the memory of those readers, who personal-
> ly knew Khomiakov, the main themes and characteristics of his
> polemical conversations. Their effect, it seems, can be express-
> ed in this way: lively minds and receptive spirits, carried from

---

[187]Christoff, p. 135. Christoff credits Kireyevsky with going farthest in elaborating "the wholeness of the spirit" idea. The phrase "the level of sympathetic agreement with faith" is a direct quotation from Kireyevsky.

[188]Ibid., Cf. Khomiakov's statement: "Truly we know only that in which we live and by which we live." Above, p. 81.

[189]Berdyaev, pp. 109, and 114. Speaking about the roots of Slavophil philosophy, Berdyaev comments: "Kireyevsky and Khomiakov... converted the influence of Hegel and Schelling into an original philosophy, which laid the foundation of the Russian philosophical tradition. That was the concrete philosophy of the wholeness of the spirit and not the philosophy of truncated reason. The Slavophils revealed in the highest degree a creative relationship to that Western thought, by which they were nourished . They were not passive adapters of Western influences." Ibid., p. 19.

[190]Ibid., p. 64.

friendship with Khomiakov the conviction, or, let us propose, even feeling, that the living vitalizing truth is never revealed to simple curiosity, but is always given in accordance with the demand of the conscience, which is seeking understanding (vrazumlenie), and that in this circumstance the act of intellectual comprehension demands an achievement of the will; that there is no kind of scientific truth, which would not agree or would not definitely coincide with revealed truth; that there is no such sense or aspiration, in the moral sense irreproachable, no such rational demand of no matter what kind, from which we must refrain, in spite of our consciousness and our conscience, in order to buy peace in the bosom of the church; in a word: that it is possible to believe honestly, conscientiously, and freely, that it is even impossible to believe otherwise than honestly, conscientiously and freely. This is what Khomiakov explained, developed, proved with his powerful, irrefutable words, and to his word, he himself, with all his substance served as a living confirmation and witness. This is the sense in which we have named him an emancipator of people, inclined to believe, but frightened and confused by meeting with seemingly irresolvable contradictions. Having come to know him, they began to breathe freely, feeling as if their religious consciousness had been liberated and as if they had been justified in their inner protest against all dual and illegitimate, even though sometimes attractive agreements with the mixture of lies, untruths and conventions, by which the image of the Church is covered in our conceptions. For many, friendship with Khomiakov was the beginning of a turn for the better, and therefore will remain forever in their conscious memory as a significant event in their personal inner life.[191]

Thus Samarin, unsuccessful in his attempt to build a convincing rational foundation for his Orthodox faith on the basis of Hegel's abstract reason found comfortable ground for it in the religious philosophy of Khomiakov. Having examined Samarin's intellectual and spiritual journey one has the impression that Hegel was not so much refuted as transcended. In any case, whatever the process, Samarin had completed a dramatic reversal of the position expressed in his letter to Popov of December 1842. Then he emphasized the importance of Hegelian

---

[191]"Predislovie k bogoslovskim sochineniyam A.S. Khomiakova," Sochineniya, VI, 349-351. Also in Sochineniya, V, LXXV-LXXVI. Even though these lines were written in 1867, their relevance for the arguments advanced above is obvious. They are the closest thing to a personal comment on the impact of Khomiakov that Samarin ever wrote.

science and repudiated Khomiakov's view that "the future triumph of slavism" would be a "triumph of life over science."[192] Now, having repudiated Hegelian science, he affirmed Khomiakov's view, a position which has interesting links with that of the anti-rationalists, who emphasize the crucial importance of imbibed tradition and experience - essentially non-rational elements - in man's knowledge of life, religion and politics.[193]

As near as can be judged Samarin adopted Khomiakov's position in the spring of 1844. From this time forth he was a reliable student and co-worker of Khomiakov's. This was unquestionably a major event in the development of Samarin's religious and political philosophy. On the testimony of close observers, it was also a major event in the consolidation of Moscow Slavophilism. I. Aksakov, whose brother Konstantin adopted Khomiakovism a short time before Samarin, claimed, that the "spiritual, moral and intellectual union" between these three "laid the foundation of Slavophilism."[194] According to Samarin's brother Dmitry, who also commented on this matter:

> The mutual relationships of the members of the Slavophil circle changed from this time. The division into two parties: Khomiakov's and Kireyevsky's on one side, and Aksakov's and Samarin's on the other, disappeared completely; more and more the ideological unanimity of Khomiakov, Samarin and Aksakov was consolidated; finally pushing them forward as the leading representatives of the Slavophil movement.[195]

---

[192] See p. 60 above.
[193]Cf. Michael Oakeshott, Rationalism in Politics and Other Essays (New York: Basic Books Publishing Co., 1962), pp. 1-36.

[194]I. Aksakov, p. 304. By way of interest, Ivan Aksakov says that his brother was less logical and consistent than Samarin was, and found the transition to Khomiakovism much easier as a result. Ibid.

[195]Sochineniya, V, LXXVI-LXXVII.

CHAPTER III

Church and State

Samarin's master's thesis, "Stefan Yavorsky and Feofan Prokopovich",
was finished in the spring of 1843 and presented to the University of
Moscow soon thereafter--a full year before it was defended in public on
June 3, 1844. This was before Samarin tried to justify Orthodoxy
through Hegel and before he was converted to Khomiakovism; thus, his
thesis cannot reflect the conclusions which he reached during the year
which was so fateful for his final philosophical, religious and
political stance.[196] Yet the dissertation cannot be ignored for it
presents important Samarin ideas on the relationship between Orthodoxy,
Catholicism and Protestantism in the areas of both doctrine and
politics. Further, it has special instrinsic value. Chizhevsky, the
authority on Hegel's influence in Russia, is most emphatic in praising
the scientific value of the dissertation. Writing in 1929, he said:

> It retains its value even now--after 95 years!--and not
> only in separate points, like the work of Aksakov,
> but as a whole. Samarin shows that the systematic
> theologians of Peter's time, Stefan Yavorsky and Feofan
> Prokopovich, who determined the direction of Russian
> theology for many decades, were dependent, the first
> on Catholic and the second on Protestant theology.
> The latest work on this theme simply repeats Samarin.[197]

Although the thesis was divided into three parts, the defense was
restricted to Part Three "Stefan Yavorsky and Feofan Prokopovich as
Preachers." This was because the controversial character of Parts One
and Two, dealing with Stefan Yavorsky and Feofan Prokopovich as
theologians and officials respectively, led the University to delay

---

[196]Sochineniya, V, pp. LV and LXXXIX. This volume of the
Sochineniya, "Stefan Yavorsky i Feofan Prokopovich," pub. D. Samarin,
Moscow 1880, was the first and only full edition of Samarin's
dissertation.

[197]Chizhevsky, p. 178.

publication of them until they had been approved by the Committee for
the Censorship of Religious Books.[198] For this reason Samarin
prepared a summary of the conclusions, advanced and proved in Parts One
and Two, and then applied in the analysis of Part Three, the least
important part of his work. This summary served as the basis for a
speech to the assembly and was later published as a kind of appendix to
the dissertation.[199] However, before examining it a few points must
be made.

The Orthodox churchmen, Yavorsky and Prokopovich, had outstanding
careers as hierarchs, theologians, politicians, scholars, preachers and
poets - a level and range of accomplishment that created serious
problems of scale and organization for any investigator. Samarin
resolved these problems by concentrating his attention on discovering
the essential general principles "upon which the work of these men was
based and on showing their significance for the development of Russian
life."[200]

The general ideological framework of his investigation was set out
quite succinctly in a few prefatory remarks, and merits particular
attention. It can be summarized in the following manner. Christianity
was "in essence a single whole", which had fragmented over time to
produce "three main faiths" organized in three main churches. Of these,

---

[198]Sochineniya, V, pp. VII and LXXVIII.

[199]Ibid., pp. LXXIX and 451-463.

[200]Ibid., p. 4.

the Orthodox Church, which still preserved "undamaged revelation" in its
bosom, was the only true church, while the Catholic and Protestant
Churches were nothing more than West European aberrations of it.
Writing as an Orthodox Christian for Orthodox Christians, Samarin felt
under no compulsion to prove this point.[201]

The Catholic aberration, "a reflection of christianity in Latin
form", did not result from a calculated repudiation of "the conception
of the church, its dogmas and its rites", but grew naturally under the
impact of principles and exigencies dominant in Western Europe. It was
an aberration, nevertheless, because the church assumed "the form of a
state" and all the features of the church assumed a different form:

> the idea of unity conditioned (uslovila) monarchical
> government, the character of ecumenicity was per-
> verted into the conception of universal possession,
> and propaganda assumed the character of a longing for
> conquest.[202]

This transformation of the church into a state occurred inevitably,
because the idea became entrenched among Westerners that unity in faith
must be accompanied by political unity. This led logically to the idea
that state power was "the property (prinadlezhnost')" of the church, and
in due course to the conception of a Pope, who concentrates this power
in his person, who symbolizes the church idea, who has full infallible
knowledge of revelation and who passes that knowledge on to his
successors.[203]

---

[201] Ibid., pp. 4-5.

[202] Ibid., p. 5.

[203] Ibid., pp. 5-6.

The effect of singling out an individual to represent the church in this way was destructive, for it cut that individual off from "the general law of development", giving the Western Church a false appearance of stability and isolating it from the rest of humanity. More importantly, however, it created a gulf between the church and her individual members by converting them from actively involved members into passive "subjects." Thus the real life of the church was snuffed out, and those two alien principles, the state and science, which the Catholic Church had adopted, developed within her structure.[204]

This is what Samarin called "the Romano-church idea." In relating it to the appearance of Protestantism he noted that the German peoples were natural individualists, a fact which had manifested itself in the political sphere by "feudalism" and in the religious sphere by the rejection of "church-state power." As individualists they had felt constrained and oppressed by "the Romano-church idea" and had advanced the Protestant idea, which rejects "the visible church", which repudiates "the principle of submission" and which recognizes the free "striving of the isolated individual to God." The effect of this idea was also negative, for while it "freed science and the state" and ended the subject status of church members, it made "agreement and unity" impossible leading to "the fragmentation of Protestantism into a multitude of sects and teachings", or in short, to a rejection of "the church in general."[205]

---

[204]Ibid., p. 6.

[205]Ibid., pp. 6-7.

Bringing the threads of his argument together, Samarin maintained
that:

Catholicism presents the idea of unity to us; but this idea,
understood abstractly and confined in a symbol, does not
penetrate Christian humanity. By contrast, in Protestantism
separate, private individuals appear with vital religious
strivings, but they are incapable of rising to the general and
are therefore divided among themselves.

In neither one nor the other do we see the church, as a vital
manifestation: but we do recognize her two abstract sides.

The church perfectly expresses her consciousness of herself,
calling herself the spiritual body, of which the members are
in essence all the believing, and the head is Christ himself.
Consequently, the idea of the church is not incarnated in a
single person, as her representative, but in the whole
collectivity of Christian humanity.

The spirit of God lives constantly in the Church, i.e. in the
vital collectivity of her members, and not in one of them in
particular."[206]

Thus Church unity and the individual worth of each one of its

members is preserved. This reconciliation of two apparently contradic-

tory principles had occurred only in the Orthodox Church, giving it a

completeness which neither its Catholic or Protestant rivals had

managed to achieve. Those faiths, in fact, occupied "two abstract

sides of the Church ", and were incomplete in spite of their individual

claims to a monopoly of "truth and exclusiveness." It was precisely in

this "one-sided exclusivenss" that "their falseness" and inability to

find "an artificial reconciliation" lay.[207] This explained why the

Catholic and Protestant Churches had not rejected Orthodoxy in total.

Each one of them was attracted by that facet of the Orthodox church

---

[206]Ibid., p. 7.

[207]Ibid., pp. 7-8.

which it shared and understood, hoping to bring about a union with it

on that basis. Their efforts were successful in penetrating the

Orthodox Church, because individuals with Catholic and Protestant

tendencies appeared among its members; however, their two-sided

challenge, made possible only because "the Orthodox principle" was "so

complete," that it contained both extremes within it, had failed,

serving only to prove the superiority of Orthodoxy.[208]

Thus Samarin was able to argue: firstly, that the appearance of

Catholic and Protestant tendencies in the Orthodox Church and their

struggle within her bosom "as two deviations represented the strongest

possible refutation of Catholicism and Protestantism"; and, secondly,

that the importance of Stefan Yavorsky and Feofan Prokopovich, the most

important Russian exponents of the Catholic and Protestant deviations

respectively, resided in the fact that their theological systems and

political roles "expressed this moment of diversion and

conflict."[209]

In the speech presented as a part of his defence Samarin set out the

ideas which had grown from his investigation of the theological works of

Stefan Yavorsky and Feofan Prokopovich. It is a synopsis of the first

part of his dissertation "Stefan Yavorsky and Feofan Prokopovich as

Theologians," and expands and clarifies the ideas summarized above.

Therefore a paraphrase of the speech will serve a useful purpose.

During the times of Stefan Yavorsky and Feofan Prokopovich Russia

came under vigorous proselytizing attacks from both the Catholic and

---

[208]Ibid., p. 8.

[209]Ibid., p. 9.

Protestant Churches. This experience had important lessons for "the substance of the Orthodox Church and its relationship to the Western faiths."[210]

The Church expresses her substance in a neat formula: she is a "spiritual body" animated by "the holy spirit", - Christ is her 'head' ", and "all believers are her members." Thus disparate members of the Christian community become "a living organic whole", "a unity", united not by compulsion, but by common voluntary self-sacrificing participation in "the blessed life."[211]

Through this formula the Church eliminates two false conceptions of herself: "the spirit of God lives in the unity of Christian humanity,... not in one chosen individual of any sort, and not in each individual, taken separately in dissociation from the whole."[212] Catholicism occupied one of these extremes and Protestantism the other. Neither managed a full definition of the Church idea. Neither managed to reconcile "the unity of life with the multiplicity of phenomena." This "wholly organic living condition" could not be understood by either of the Western faiths because they tended to view each part as separate and antagonistic one to the other.

The Catholic Church focused on the aspect of unity and through the process of abstraction came to express it by means of a living symbol - the Pope. The Pope came to symbolize the Church and was given possession of the Spirit of God. Inevitably this created a chasm between the

---

[210]Ibid., p. 452.

[211]Ibid.

[212]Ibid., pp. 452-453.

Pope, representing the Church, and the "totality of separate

individuals" constituting her membership. The members of the Church

became, in effect, her subjects. Thus the institution created by this

failure to reconcile unity in diversity resulted in a parody of the real

Church:

> In the sphere of theory the relationship of the individual to
> the Church became like the relationship of knowing to being known;
> in the practical sphere like the relationship of subjects to state
> power. Instead of the kingdom of faith and love, appeared the
> kingdom of knowledge and rights.[213]

Protestantism resulted from a natural rebellion against this

Catholic failure to recognize the legitimate demands of "individuality"

(lichnost'). A fixation on "the onesidedly held idea of unity" provoked

an equally contrary fixation on "the onesidedly understood idea of

multiplicity" (mnozhestvo). This was the origin of the Reformation -

the Protestants, asserting the right of every individual to consummate

his own personal reconciliation with God, separated individuals and lost

sight of the idea of "a united, objective Church." However, rejecting

and destroying the Roman Catholic Church, the Protestants left in its

place a great many sects incapable of unity. [214]

From this Samarin's definition of Catholicism and Protestantism and

their relationship to the Church emerged: Catholicism and Protestantism

develop opposite sides of the Church idea in an exclusive and abstract

way; therefore, neither one of them has realized the Church idea "as a

complete and living organism."[215]

---

[213]Ibid., p. 453.

[214]Ibid., p. 454.

This perception made it easy to explain why the Western faiths
looked upon Orthodoxy with some optimism, never rejecting it in its
entirety. Catholics and Protestants saw in Orthodoxy the side which
they shared and understood. The rest they saw as contradiction which
could be extirpated "moving Orthodoxy a step forward."[216]

The campaign which Catholics and Protestants launched against the
Russian Orthodox Church at the beginning of the eighteenth century grew
out of this perception. It was a test imposed by Providence. Its
"universal-historical significance" was that the Orthodox Church
preserved its integrity while demonstrating the "onesidedness" of
Catholicism and Protestantism.[217]

---

[215]Ibid. At this point Samarin departed from the main line of
his argument to advance an idea of special interest to this project. It
follows in its entirety. "We have defined the western faiths, as
divergencies from the Orthodox Church; but we only defined them, and did
not deduce them from the historical conditions of all of western
development. Such a study would present much of interest. If time
would allow, I would try to develop the idea that all western
development was conditioned by the meeting and the eternal conflict of
two one-sided principles: the idea of generality and the idea of
individuality, of Roman substance and of German substance; that all
living organisms, falling under the corrupting action of these two
inimical forces, were broken into two parts, one of which suffered the
fate of the Roman world, and the other of the German. This phenomenon
was repeated in all spheres. In the sphere of religion it was expressed
in the antagonism of the two faiths. In the Roman manifestation
christianity is reflected in Catholicism, in the German by
Protestantism. A little insight is necessary, in order to join these
two phenomena with other similar ones. The idea of world government is
clearly resurrected in the idea of Catholicism; the juridical
relationship of the person to power is in the relationship of the member
of the Church to the Pope, and in the process of external justification.
It is also clearly understandable that Protestantism is religious
feudalism; that knight and protestant are one man in two different
spheres." pp. 454-455.

[216]Ibid. p. 455.

[217]Ibid.

In this time of testing the real champions of Russia's Orthodox Church were Stefan Yavorsky and Feofan Prokopovich. Both men were devout Orthodox churchmen. They best understood the issues and arguments. Yavorsky understood and articulated the anti-Protestant principle in Orthodoxy and Prokopovich the anti-Catholic one - defending the Orthodox Church from both sides they assured her triumph and were the real heroes of the contest.[218] For Samarin, the fact that Yavorsky and Prokopovich could defend their Church from two different sides like this was sufficient proof that both the Catholic and Protestant principles were successfully reconciled in her - that she was in other words "a complete living organism."[219]

Working in concentric circles of increasing specificity Samarin proceeded to flesh out his argument about the roles of Yavorsky and Prokopovich by examining their significance as theologians. Once again he stated that Catholicism, by adhering to the principle of unity in the abstract, had destroyed the organic relationship between the Church and its members and had isolated itself from mankind. Thus it was inevitable that the Catholic Church should feel compelled to prove herself through science, which seemed the only logical way to heal the split between individuals and the Church. This in turn produced fertile ground for the growth of scholasticism for there was an urgent need to reunite the two sources of religious understanding which were being interpreted in isolation from one another - the dogmas of the Church and

---

[218]Ibid., p. 456.
[219]Ibid., p. 457.

the ideas of mankind, that is to prove by finite reason the eternal truths already revealed by God.[220] However, the agency of scholasticism and science was of no avail for there is no "artificial way" to recreate "the organic union of life." In fact, science itself contained irreconcilable contradictions. It could not, therefore, reunite "authority" and "reason" for the Church. The only union it could offer was a syllogistic system which had the appearance, but not the substance of logical consistency -- "the general idea, evident truth (lumine ratione nata) occupies the position of the first premise; a text from the scriptures occupies the position of the second; and the conclusion provides a proven proposition, a logically justified dogma."[221]

Thus, a deficiency in Catholicism produced a drive to prove dogma, to create a "church system." Scholasticism which resulted from this drive was an "exclusively Western phenomenon." The Orthodox Church had never experienced it. Science had an entirely different significance for her, because she had a profound sense that she did not need external proof. She knew that she could only be comprehended by those who lived within her in full harmony with her life. She knew that truth was revealed by "religious force" and that everyone possessed the capacity to absorb it. "In a word -- faith is called the object, the content, and the subjective capacity, the form. In the unity of the blessed life (blagodatnaya zhizn')the break between being known and knowing disappears."[222]

However, even though the Orthodox Church had not relied on "reason,

---

[220]Ibid.

[221]Ibid., p. 458.

cogitation" to prove dogma, she had used it. Firstly, she had used it
for the related tasks of understanding and clarifying dogma. This was
an important function, going beyond the assignment of scholasticism,
which was only to prove dogma. Secondly, she had employed it in a
polemical fashion to protect both the Church and dogma, neither of which
needed proving, from "false teachings." This was certainly a different
and important function.[223]

Convinced that he had established the importance of the Catholic
Church system, Samarin chose to examine two questions of special
importance for the Orthodox Church, because the argument between
Catholics and Protestants turned on them -- the question of the Church
and the question of justification.

Dealing first with the Catholic side of the matter, he claimed that
Catholic doctrine was "an answer to the illegitimate demand for an
external sign, by which it would be possible to know Church revelation."
Accordingly the doctrine of justification grew from the attempt to
arrive at a "clear formula" by which man could justify himself before
God, thereby making it possible to be saved by the relatively simple
expedient of mechanically fulfilling a formula.[224]

---

[222]Ibid., p. 57. These paragraphs contain the positive arguments which Samarin used to justify his claim that it is "impossible"
for the Church to create a "system" or "theological science." See p.
57 above. Although the arguments advanced in the third letter to Popov
(summarized on pp. 56-59 above) indicate that Samarin had some trouble
reconciling this position with observed Orthodox Church practice and his
own predilecton for rational proofs and science, he held fast to it.
See also p. 59 above.

[223]Ibid., p. 459.

[224]Ibid., p. 459.

When scholasticism made its way into Russia in the sixteenth century, the Orthodox clergy of the south were attracted by the logic and clarity which it gave to Catholic propaganda. As a result courses in theology taught by western scholars were introduced in the Academy of Kiev and Orthodox dogma was recast in the western scientific pattern. In the meantime Protestant influences had appeared in northern Russia posing a serious threat so that Orthodox clergymen found themselves occupying common ground with Catholic scholars and adopted their method of doing battle with Protestantism.

Stefan Yavorsky emerged as the most powerful Orthodox opponent of Protestantism in Russia. In his "colossal book" The Stone of Faith he, on the one hand, conclusively refuted Protestant doctrine, and on the other "affirmed the proofs of Orthodox church dogma."[225] The latter affirmative side of Yavorsky's work, which very naturally revealed the influence of Catholic writers like the Jesuit scholar Bellarmine, was not as important as the negative side, which revealed that "he understood and expressed only the anti-Protestant principle in the Orthodox Church."[226]

Samarin began his discussion of the Protestant case with the Newtonian sounding observation that "every one-sided development provokes an opposite one-sided one." On this analogy Protestantism was an inevitable reaction to Catholicism's failure to achieve a genuine reconciliation between reason and authority. Protestant reformers did not begin by disputing the possibility of a system, or by repudiating the need to prove

---

[225]Ibid., p. 460.

[226]Ibid., p. 461.

dogmas, but by attempting to verify these basic principles of the
Catholic system. By careful examination of scripture they discovered,
first errors of interpretation, and then evidence to demonstrate that
Catholic dogmas were not proven as claimed. Correct to this point, the
Protestants now went astray, concluding that having disproved the
proofs of dogmas they had disproved the dogmas--a patent logical error,
for to disprove the proof of a position is not to disprove the
position, or as Samarin put it:

> From the fact that a position has not been proven, it follows
> that he, who accepts it as proven does not possess the gift of
> infallibility, but it does not at all follow, that the position
> itself is false.

The Protestants judged the Catholics correctly, but not the Church for
its view was not "similarily limited."[227]

Having fulfilled its negative task, Protestantism entered a new
phase, when it moved to create a positive doctrine. In this phase,
building "on the ruins of Catholicism", it retained the idea of a system,
but gave foundation-stone importance to "scripture and personal reason."
However, because of its "purely negative character" it was not able to
produce "a unified Protestant doctrine." Many teachings emerged but none
of them had anything "common or essential" except their negativeness, as
exampled in "the rejection of tradition, and the rejection of the
possibility of justification by good works", the two doctrines around
which the first disputes between Catholics and Protestants turned.[228]

---

[227]Ibid.

[228]Ibid., p. 462.

The counterpart to West European Protestantism in the Orthodox
Church was the school founded by Feofan Prokopovich, who came under the
influence of Catholic teaching while studying for the priesthood in
Kiev. The heavy emphasis placed on the work of scholastic and Jesuit
theologians there repelled Prokopovich, turning him against "their
artificial, protracted explanations and fruitless subdivisons." As a
reformer his answer was to adopt the Holy Scriptures as the norm and to
subject contemporary religious doctrine to a thoroughgoing revision.
His "great unforgettable merit" was that he became a "brilliant Catholic
antagonist smashing their doctrines on tradition, on the origins of the
holy spirit, and on justification by good works!", which were so
widespread in Russia during his day. That Prokopovich became "one-
sided" and developed a Protestant school within the Orthodox Church was
manifest in his view of the Holy Scriptures and of revelation, and in
the fact that he lost sight of the idea of the Church as an "organic
spiritual whole" seeing it as "only a collection of individuals united
for the sake of advantage."[229]

That is how Samarin characterised the relationship between Stefan
Yavorsky and Feofan Prokopovich. Obviously their differences were so
fundamental that it was impossible for them to act together, yet, as he
saw it, the impact of their theological work was of vital importance to
the Orthodox Church because it revealed the "onesidedness" of both
Catholicism and Protestantism, and in the process of elaboration struck
"a blow at Catholicism, erected a barrier against the influence of

---

[229]Ibid., pp. 462-463.

Protestantism, and enabled the Church to triumph in her two-front battle."[230]

The theological part of the dissertation does not provide a single religious idea going beyond those summarized above. What it does provide, however, is the evidence which Samarin used to support his major theses. That evidence comprises a number of elements. There is a short, rather romantic history of the development of Christianity in Russia from its beginnings in the ninth and tenth centuries. In it Samarin emphasized that the Russian conversion to Orthodoxy, when once it was decided upon by Vladimir, was almost unprecedented for its unanimous character and spontaneity.[231] But this was not his only romantic-patriotic perception, for he also emphasized that the Russian people joined the Church "trustfully, cooperatively, uncontradictingly," and were unusually Church-centred in their understanding of Christianity.[232] Further he emphasized that there was a special affinity between Russianness and Orthodoxy which made "continuous relations" between heterodox Christians and Russians impossible.[233] Striking a more realistic note, he also pointed out that the heavy weight of formalism in the early Russian Church was natural and inevitable considering that the theoretical aspects of Church life were still beyond the comprehension of the majority.[234]

---

[230]Ibid., p. 463.

[231]Ibid., p. 11.

[232]Ibid., pp. 11-12.

[233]Ibid., p. 18.

[234]Ibid., p. 12.

Finally he praised the inherently progressive character of the Russian
Orthodox Church as exemplified in the way it undertook to correct
scriptures in the seventeenth century.[235] There is also much hard
analytical evidence. It includes a detailed statement of Catholic
doctrine as enunciated in the decrees and catechism of the Council of
Trent and a close analysis of its influence on Russian Orthodox Church
doctrine especially as manifested in the theology of Stefan Yavorsky.
It also includes an examination of Protestant doctrine as set out in
"the Augsburg Confession", and a crude analysis of the content and
significance of the Protestant-leaning theology of Feofan Prokopovich.
Remarkable features of Samarin's work in the first part of his
dissertation include the thoroughness of his scholarship, the romantic
idealism which permeates so many of his perceptions of the Orthodox
Church and Russian nationhood, and the tendency to examine problems from
an historical point of view.

Although religious ideas going beyond those summarized above are not
to be found in the body of Samarin's dissertation - the ideas are even
expressed in the same idiom, as for instance in the following striking
example:

> The Catholic system as a whole and in each of its
> dogmas taken separately presents itself as a correct
> syllogism. General ideas, so-called evident truth,
> appear in the position of the first premise; and texts
> from scripture or tradition appear in the place of the
> second, which are harmonized with the first premise like
> facts acquiring sense and significance from the general
> idea. The conclusion appears as a proven proposition, a
> logically justified dogma.[236]

---

[235]Ibid., p. 16.

[236]Ibid., pp. 22-23.

- his position on the feasibility of creating a "church system" is more

extensively and clearly articulated. Because Samarin was so positive in

rejecting the possibility of creating a church system in his letter to

Popov of December, 1841 and did so without providing any reasons

whatsoever, this is a matter of some importance. Briefly stated, he

argued that the doctrine, liturgy, norms and traditions of the Church,

what he called at one point "the positive content of religion, founded

on the authority of the Church",[237] are revealed by God and,

therefore, are beyond comprehension and systematization by man's finite

reason. In his opinion this proposition was proven by the experience of

all three major Churches. By applying the "philosophical principle", by

attempting to rationalize "a priori content and historical evidence", by

trying to create a "system", in short by attempting "to prove herself",

the Catholic Church had lost the sense of true community and had reduced

doctrine to a body of tenuous unconvincing syllogisms.[238] As for

Protestantism it fell into the same rationalist trap by setting out to

prove dogma. Further, it compounded its error by rejecting church

authority in preference for the authority of "private individuals" and

by accepting holy scripture alone as the "norm". On this basis Protes-

tantism was successful in its attempt to prove the falseness of Catholic

dogma, but unsuccessful in its attempt to create a system, achieving

nothing more in this regard than an "aggregate of opinions."[239] In

contrast, the Orthodox Church had never lost sight of the fact that

---

[237]Ibid., p. 22.
[238]Ibid., pp. 22-24.

revelation and life in the Church community were of decisive importance when it came to assimilating "the positive content of religion" or, as he put it, "In the life of the Church lies her rational justification, and reason (rassudok) with its questions, doubts and proofs cannot have a place in it."[240] On the basis of these arguments Samarin affirmed his faith in Orthodoxy and reached his final conclusion that the Orthodox Church "could not have and must not have a system."[241]

Samarin essayed the tasks of political investigation and speculation for the first time in writing the second part of his dissertation "Stefan Yavorsky and Feofan Prokopovich as Officials of the Church." The point has already been made that Samarin liked to examine problems in their historical context. Certainly, the main political conclusions of this study grew out of his analysis of the historical development of the Catholic, Protestant and Orthodox Churches.

As it was characteristic of Samarin to examine problems from an historical perspective, so also was it characteristic of him to root his

---

[239]Ibid., pp. 60-63.

[240]Ibid., p. 24.

[241]Ibid., p. 163. Nol'de comments on this conclusion as follows: "In all justice, such a conclusion for a Russian religious thinker may be called both negative, and suicidal. No matter what the religious truth being professed by it, the rejection of the possibility of its systematic development is to deprive the Church of a powerful means of influence and preaching." Nol'de, p. 26. In making this comment Nol'de seems to have lost sight of the fact that Samarin in concert with Orthodox Church practice assigned reason the analytical function of understanding dogma and the polemical one of defending it. See Sochineniya, p. 459, and above, p. 102.

analyses in theological propositions. In this case he began by stating that the divine and the human were reconciled in Christ and that the Church was a constant, immortal testimony to that fact, being an "incarnation of the divine in the human."[242] From this proposition it was an easy step to his conclusion that the Church had to enter the stage of history and develop as an integral part in an universal process subject to diverse influences and cross-currents. Thus Samarin investigated the history of the Church with the aim of determining how Catholicism and Protestanism had influenced the relationship between Church and State in Orthodox Russia. Although the conclusions which he reached can be simply expressed, the analysis which brought him to them is not at all simple, and merits close examination. Samarin began his analysis by reiterating that the Catholic Church was not a true Church but a "pretension".[243] Because of this it was compelled to seize "temporal power...manifesting itself as a state."[244] The main argument advanced by early Catholic writers in defence of this act was the "divine right" argument that "the spiritual and temporal

---

[242]Samarin's footnotes indicate that he used as sources: Bellarmine, De Summo Pontifice, Carrarius, De potestate romani pontificis adversus impios politicos; Pouvoir du Pape sur les souverains au moyen age; Bossuet, Defensio declarationis; Fleury, Histoire ecclesiastique, and Institutions au droit canonique; Ranke, Histoire de la Papaute pendant les seizieme et dix-septieme siecles; Lamenais, de la religion consideree dans ses rapports avec l'ordre politique; the works of de Maistre; and others.

[243]See above and especially p. 94 where Samarin's reasons for claiming that the Catholic Church could be no more than a "pretension" are summarized.

[244]Ibid., 166.

power of the Pope came directly from God."[245] Therefore the Church had to be a state and because there could only be one church, there could only be one Church state.

This doctrine coupled with the elaboration of it in administrative structures made the Catholic Church the dominant organization of religious and political control until the Middle Ages. Known as the ultramontane doctrine from the Middle Ages on, it was, in Samarin's opinion, "the preferred Catholic principle, and the sole logically possible justification of the Western Church."[246]

Parallelling the rise of national consciousness, a new doctrine known as the Gallican doctrine emerged. It claimed that spiritual and temporal power came from God, but that spiritual power belonged to the Popes and temporal power to the kings. This doctrine made it possible for the kings to repudiate Papal claims to temporal authority as "an illegitimate infringement" on their power as national rulers. About the same time another doctrine originating with the French theologian Fenelon was propagated in Catholic circles. It, like the Gallican doctrine, repudiated Papal claims to temporal authority on the basis of divine right, but unlike Gallican doctrine it did not accuse the Popes of illegal powers. Rather the Fenelonists took the position in line with the "general convictions" of the Middle Ages that temporal authority had been "voluntarily"entrusted to the Popes.[247]

---

[245]Ibid.,

[246]Ibid., p. 167.

[247]Ibid., pp. 167-8.

Expressing mild incomprehension of the fact that large numbers of
Catholics could accept the latter two doctrines, Samarin emphasized that
the Catholic Church as an institution accepted the ultramontane doctrine
that temporal power was an "essential property" of the Church.[248]

According to Samarin's analysis the ultramontane doctrine evolved
naturally out of the western historical experience. An important part
of that experience having special relevance for the Church was the
collapse of the Roman Empire, because the idea of "universal monarchy"
which it represented, survived in the Church. Thus the Church inherited
the state idea from Rome and perpetuated it in western political
history. Thus the Church gave birth to the states of Western Europe and
legitimatized political power as power sanctioned by God. In joining
the Church the people of the West met the idea that spiritual and
temporal power were one, that is, began to regard the Pope as both first
priest and sovereign, and became "constituent parts of a single
Christian monarchy."[249]

However, in Samarin's opinion the identity of spiritual and temporal
power, while being rational and legitimate under the conditions of the
ancient world, became under Christianity anachronistic and even more
culpably "a contradiction to Christianity itself."[250] This, Samarin
explained, was a result of the evolution of "religious consciousness".

---

[248]Ibid., p. 169. Samarin cites without specific reference the
Papal Bulls of "Gregory VII, Innocent III and many others" as evidence
confirming this assertion.

[249]Ibid., p. 170.

[250]Ibid., p. 171.

In the ancient world religious consciousness had still not grown beyond the real world of "finite manifestations", so it was inevitable that religious consciousness would coincide with national consciousness and spiritual power with temporal power. In the new Christian era, however, religious consciousness had transcended the finite world, penetrating to the world of the idea, thereby making possible a clear distinction between spiritual power and temporal power as expressed in the biblical pronouncement: "my kingdom is not of this world, give to Caesar what is Caesars, and to God what is God's."[251] Hence the Catholic Church's policy of consciously perpetuating the identity of these two antithetical powers contradicted "God's word", and was therefore, "a crime."[252]

The fact that Samarin described Catholic policy as criminal should not be allowed to obscure the central point of his analysis, which was that the Catholic Church claimed to be the source of temporal power and gradually organized an enormous monolithic state in Western Europe. In the process she subjected local secular rulers to her authority and simultaneously legitimatized their political power.

This monolithic church-based system reached its apogee during the Papacy of Innocent III (1198-1216). But this remarkable organizational success facilitated by the honest, high-minded endeavor of generations of Popes, could neither mask nor reconcile the basic contradiction between temporal and spiritual power.[253] What Samarin meant, it becomes

---

[251]Ibid.,

[252]Ibid.,

[253]Ibid., pp. 172-3.

clear, was the contradiction between ends and means manifested in the work of the Popes who "preached the general principle of love and peace, but put them into effect by compulsion, dressing them in the form of laws...."[254] Lacking faith in moral suasion's power to transform the character of man in line with Christian norms, the Popes employed naked state power to compel outward obedience to those norms. Thus the people of the West submitted to the Church as citizens submit to the state, and the Church, becoming entrapped by a contradiction, lost its moral force.[255]

The decline of the Catholic Church, which began paradoxically, at the very moment when she reached her highest point of development under Innocent III, was hastened by the growth of national consciousness among the peoples of Western Europe. "The illegitimate identity of Church and State" was brought into sharp focus by the rise of this new phenomenon. By the fourteenth century certain people were beginning to distinguish between the Pope's spiritual power as head of the Church and his temporal power as ruler of separate provinces, and to challenge the latter in the name of independent national statehood. As a result a conflict developed for Catholics between loyalty to the Pope as behooves a member of the Church and loyalty to the sovereign as behooves a member of the State. This conflict was especially difficult for clergymen, who eventually rallied to their temporal rulers, thus facilitating the break-up of "the single Church into separate national churches, and her future enslavement."[256]

---

[254]Ibid., p. 173.

[255]Ibid.

[256]Ibid., pp. 174-175.

Thus the rejection of Papal claims to temporal authority was a development of epic importance for the religious and political history of the West. In all of North Western Europe where Protestantism triumphed the conflict between Church and State was resolved by the "rejection of Papism" and "the reduction of religion to the level of national interest."[257] In those lands which remained Catholic the Church's claim to temporal power was also rejected in the name of national interest. In every case the impact on Church-State relations was profound, because in proclaiming their independence from the Church, temporal rulers sacrificed their legitimacy and were propelled into a search for a new principle on which to base their power. The Gallican Church adopted the idea that temporal power derived its legitimacy directly from God. This variation was accepted in France and ratified by Louis XIV. Thus the Gallican Church by recognizing a new doctrine separated from Rome and became a servant of the State. However, the new doctrine, because it was introduced over Rome's opposition, was itself illegitimate and therefore proved to be a shaky base on which to establish supreme power:

> It could not have been otherwise. Becoming independent of the Pope, the King lost the significance of a holy person, annointed by God. The vital focus of political life was destroyed, and the conception of an organic state fell in the national consciousness to the conception of an accidental union of separate individuals, who have entrusted conditional power to a single selected individual by mutual agreement. The contract theory arose and out of it the idea of an artificial, mechanical union of parts into one external whole by means of the maintenance of equilibrium between them.[258]

---

[257]Ibid., 175.

Accordingly, Samarin took the position that one of two things could happen in the West: either, "the domination of the Church and the negation of the state", or, "the domination of the state and the negation of the Church." The extreme of the latter "false relationship" occurred in France where the state came "to recognize no Church and profess no faith." On the other hand, even in the former situation the Church suffered a serious setback for "reduced to the level of a private separate state and deprived of external material power she had never enjoyed full independence."[259]

Samarin's final conclusion on the relationship of spiritual power to temporal power in the Catholic and Protestant West can be summarized as follows. The Western Church had become a "state" because it had contested state power. As a state the Church was weak for the reasons given above and declined as is the case with weak states. This decline undermined her stature as a church. In other words, the Church by

---

[258]Ibid., pp. 175-6. In a footnote dealing with this question, the legitimacy of separating Church and State, Samarin makes a comment of considerable importance for this study. "De Maistre", he said, "develops the idea in many of his works of the necessary fall of a supreme power, which repudiates its dependence on the Pope. From this point of view he justifies the French Revolution, as a just retribution. Therefore, he does not at all recognize the legality of the emancipation of the state from the Church and sees a possibility of salvation for it only in the restoration of the life of the middle ages. The onesidedness of this view is obvious. The state must be freed from its submission to Church power. Unconditional independence is its essential, necessary right, which it can never give up. On the other hand the Church can never repudiate pretensions once expressed by her. Therefore, in the sphere of Catholicism, there cannot be a reconciliation between Church and State. Except for mutual rejection and constant enmity, there can be no other relationship between them." Ibid., p. 176(My italics).

[259]Ibid., p. 176.

"illegitimately" placing her faith in temporal power had condemned
herself "to ruin."[260] However, this rather terse summary has to be
supplemented by a direct quotation, before Samarin's perception of how
total and precious the difference between temporal and spiritual power
really is, can be appreciated.

> A Church, founded on an unshakeable stronghold, cannot be
> conquered by any external force. 'The Gates of Hell will
> not overcome her!'
>
> Private individuals, her representatives, can be oppressed
> and hounded, but the Church herself, filling a sphere, be-
> longing to her exclusively, cannot lose it and no power can
> ever eject her or replace her. In vain they talk as if
> temporal power could deprive the Church of her freedom, her
> independence; temporal power has force only over the external
> side of the Church. The state cannot rise to her level, but
> the Church herself can lower herself to the level of the state,
> and then betraying herself, she voluntarily gives up her
> independence.
>
> She does not perish, when external power marshals against her,
> but when, having begun to doubt herself, having lost faith in
> the invincible power of the spirit, she extends her boundaries
> and takes into herself a principle foreign to her.[261]

Thus "the Western Church had to perish" because her "fear of the world
prompted her to seek salvation in the assimilation of...temporal
power." However, unfortunately, in achieving her aim she was punished,
for "her triumph over the world was by enslavement to the
world."[262]

Turning to an examination of the relationship between Church and
State in the Orthodox world, Samarin stressed that the situation was
entirely different. The critical element making for this difference

---

[260]Ibid., p. 177.

[261]Ibid., p. 177.

[262]Ibid., p. 178.

was the understanding which the Orthodox Church had of her charcter and role. "The Orthodox Church, conscious of herself as a living manifestation, concrete in herself, never ever sought to exist as a state. She lived in her pure-spiritual sphere, as a complete whole, as incarnated spirit." Thus the Orthodox Church distinguished herself from the State and at the same time recognized it as "a separate, independent sphere, possessing its own legality, its own justification." This perception she expressed clearly in the following dogma: "The power of the Tsar (in general supreme temporal power) takes its principle directly from God; the people invest what is selected from their environment in it [temporal power]; but the power itself comes from God and not from them."[263]

According to Samarin, then, the Orthodox Church saw the State as a distinct autonomous province. But if the Church recognized the State, could it be assumed that the State must recognize the Church? Or put more broadly, how should the State relate to the Church? For Samarin, the answer to this question seemed to reside in the fact that the Church only possessed spiritual power, and the closely related fact that this power was manifested through her clerical representatives.

Starting from these facts Samarin elaborated the following system of relationships. The State recognizes the "spiritual power" of the Church, and as a natural consequence, her clerical representatives. To the latter it assigns a definite place and status as a separate class. And so the clergy has dual status. On the one hand, as representatives

---

[263]Ibid.

of the Church it exercises spiritual power and is completely free of

State authority ("The State does not give spiritual power, therefore it

cannot take it away, and cannot legitimately participate in the

activities [of the Church]"). On the other hand the clergy lives in

the State and is subject to the supreme State power in the same way and

to the same degree that other classes are ("The State gives rights

[i.e., of property and of civil law], consequently it can take them

away."). Obviously, it was imperative for the clergy to keep its dual

status in mind, because it symbolized the essential relationship between

Church and State.[264]

Therefore, contrasting powers and commitments, along with over-

lapping functions, required that Church and State take cognizance of one

another. Samarin describes the proper relationship between Church and

State in the Orthodox World very clearly, as follows:

> The normal relationship of Church and State in the
> Orthodox World is one of mutual recognition and full
> reconciliation. The Church gives supreme, state power
> religious significance.... The State, in its turn,
> defends the Church from external attacks, helps her in
> the eradication of abuses, protects the interests of ...
> her representatives. Only in this sense are the represen-
> tatives of temporal power called defenders, protectors of
> the Church.
>
> But the materialization of this relationship in reality,
> as a fact conditioned by the free agreement of the State,
> is beyond the power of the Church. The Church always re-
> cognizes the State, but the State need not recognize her,
> and therefore the Church does not assume that this latter
> recognition is a necessary condition for herself. No matter
> how the State relates to her, even if it does not recognize
> her, even if persecution befalls her representatives, full

---

[264]Ibid., p. 179.

of the promise which has been given to her from above, she
does not appeal to external means of support, and does not
repulse force by force. In this possibility of repudiating
the State lies the freedom which no earthly power can take
away from her."[265]

According to Samarin's analysis the Catholic Church, convinced that

she was accountable for the strict adherence of her members to

Christian moral principles, sought and exercised temporal power to that

end: "Her influence on life was purely external, and was expressed by

laws...which established limits to the external manifestation of

personal will."[266] The Orthodox Church, on the other hand, very

correctly had no such perception of accountability. Her task, as she

understood it, was "to cultivate in man a sense of spiritual love, to

compel him to understand and to hate evil, so that the law itself could

lose for him the character of an outside obstacle and penetrate his

whole life, as a freely accepted fruitful principle."[267] In other

words, the Orthodox Church understood that only spiritual power, "the

word", was efficacious in the struggle against evil, and therefore she

never once sought temporal power or had recourse to external methods of

compulsion in order to fulfill her mission.

On the basis of these premises Samarin launched into an historical

examination of the relationship between Church and State in Russia,

which produced some very interesting results. Such prominent scholars

as Klyuchevsky, Riasanovsky and Pipes have claimed that Peter the Great

---

[265]Ibid., 180.

[266]Ibid., pp. 180-1.

[267]Ibid., p. 181.

was anathema to the Slavophils;[268] however, Samarin saw Peter as a positive hero whose reforms were necessary and proper, although definitely one-sided. But this is only one of the interesting assessments to be found in this part of Samarin's dissertation.

Samarin began his analysis with an examination of the political situation in ancient tribal Russia. He concluded that the demise of tribalism, with its characteristic local loyalties and fragmentation, was facilitated by the adoption of Christianity, because it introduced "unity of faith" to Russia. By drawing separate tribes together and uniting them in a single spiritual body, the Church created "the possibility for the formation of political unity, based on the recognition of a single supreme power." From the very beginning the Church claimed spiritual power and assumed the existence of a separate, independent temporal power, so "calling it into being."[269]

---

[268]Klyuchevsky claimed that "the Slavophiles, and especially Khomiakov, revived Karamzin's criticism that Peter had interrupted Russia's natural development by alienating educated people from their customs and traditions. Khomiakov compared these people to a colony of Europeans thrown among savages." V. Klyuchevsky, Peter the Great, trans. L. Archibald (New York, 1958) p. 251. Riasanovsky is bluntest of all: "Those who hated the reformer and his work included...such quixotic romantic intellectuals as the Slavophiles...who regarded the emperor as a supreme perverter and destroyer." N. Riasanovsky, A History of Russia, p. 265. Pipes states that "according to the Slavophiles, it was the Russian tradition to draw a sharp line of demarcation between the state or authority (vlast') and the 'land' (zemlia). ...This tradition was violated by Peter the Great, and ever since his reign Russia had been following a path entirely alien to her nature." R. Pipes, Russia Under the Old Regime (London, 1974), p. 267.

[269]Sochineniya, V., 181. In commenting on the tribes of Russia, Samarin observed that "consciousness of national unity, which in its final manifestation is the state, had not yet awakened in them." In other words Samarin believed that the State came into existence when national consciousness peaked. Ibid.

Thus, the Orthodox Church, by introducing the State idea to Russia,
helped her political development; however in doing so, and this was a
point of critical importance to Samarin, the Church left the State with
full scope for autonomous development.[270] Conversely, a point of
equal importance, during the centuries-long development of the Russian
State, the Church acting through her Metropolitans as heads, even
although they were dependent on the patriarchs in Constantinople,
cooperated on a basis of full equality and independence with the
princes as temporal authorities.[271]

The Russian State finally emerged at the end of the fifteenth
century during the reign of Ivan III. Significantly, its emergence was
in harmony with "the aspirations of the Princes and the Metropolitans."
For the Princes, Moscow became "the Capital of Russia": for the
Metropolitans, "the idea of the union in one organic whole, under one
supreme power, of all parts of Russia, the idea, which the Church had
so long preserved for a better time, and preserved in a holy way, like
somebody else's property, was finally realized." In concert with this
idea the Church recognized the new State and "voluntarily submitted to
it."[272]

Samarin observed that at this point the Church entered into a new
phase of her historical development in which she lived and grew within
the State. Naturally, she possessed certain rights. Some of these

---

[270]Ibid., p. 182.

[271]Ibid., pp. 182-191.

[272]Ibid., pp. 192-3.

were "essential inalienable rights" which belonged to clergymen as
representatives of the Church, and some were "civil rights" which had
been granted to clergymen by the temporal authorities.[273] The first
included the right to judgement by an "ecclesiastical court" operating in
accordance with "apostolic laws."[274] The latter included such rights
as the "free possession and administration of estates" and a "court" to
judge "Church people living on these estates."[275]

As one might expect these rights had become confused by the
fifteenth century, so that the clergy itself lost the ability to
distinguish between those rights which were intrinsic (belonged to it
from the Church) and those which were extrinsic (belonged to it from
the State). Furthermore, the clergy, by dint of being drawn into the
administration of large estates and handling legal disputes
(non-spiritual affairs), had been corrupted.[276] So when the Church
became an integral part of the "organically formed" Russian State the task
of reconciling the acquired traditional rights of the Church with the new
political realities was a formidable one, and required diligent
application over "many reigns" to accomplish.[277]

---

[273]Ibid., p. 193.

[274]Ibid. Samarin uses the term dukhovnyi sud po Nomokanonu. V.
Dal' defines Nomokanon as a "Collection of Church regulations": Slovar'
sovremennogo russkogo literaturnogo yazyka defines it as a "collection of
Church regulations, containing statutes, touching various sides of life
(byta) and family relationships (semeynoy zhizni).

[275]Ibid.

[276]Ibid., pp. 195-6.

[277]Ibid., p. 197.

Of these many reigns Ivan IV's (1533-1584) was of special importance,
because Ivan as the supreme temporal authority asserted "his right in
accordance with the general demands of the state   to limit and to
abolish the civil rights of the clergy, to correct abuses, and to
undertake measures for the maintenance of propriety."[278] Ivan's
legislation affected three areas:" (1) Church estates, (2) administration and Church jurisprudence, and (3) the conduct of clergymen and
religious ceremonies."[279] And it revealed "one constant objective:
to establish an unified administration" consistent with the demands of
an autocratic power.[280]

As noted above, Samarin was concerned to emphasize that the Russian
state was "organically formed." In keeping with this perception of
organic growth Samarin stressed that Ivan did not strive to create "an
artificial, formal uniformity", but created a new unity synthesized
from traditional customs and current needs, and so "did not destroy the
ancient multiform life, but raised all customs and rights, which had
existed for a long time in the various provinces of Russia, to a single
supreme principle, acknowledged them, and in so doing gave them legal
status in the state."[281]

Ivan's attempts to redefine the relationship between Church and
State focused on the Stoglav Council of 1551[282] and were motivated
by a determination to harmonize Church-State laws in an unified codifi-

---

[278]Ibid., p. 201.

[279]Ibid.

[280]Ibid., pp. 204-5.

cation.[283] As this very necessary undertaking exemplifying "the

best side of Ivan's reign, his work, as a lawmaker and ruler"[284]

was not completed during his lifetime, it remained as a major task for

the new Romanov regime, which came to power after the devastating chaos

of the Time of Troubles. However, Michael (1613-1645), the first

Romanov, beset by foreign wars and domestic disorders, was unable to

tackle the question of Church-State relations, and it was not until the

reign of Alexis (1645-1676), his son and heir, that progress was made

on this critical question.

Alexis carried Ivan's work forward in the Ulozhenia (statute) of

1649. From Samarin's analysis of those parts of the Ulozhenia bearing

on the Church, one conclusion seems particularly relevant. It is the

conclusion that in harmony with Orthodox perceptions, the Ulozhenia

defined the juridical relationship between Church and State and

regulated only civil matters, leaving spiritual affairs entirely to the

---

[281]Ibid., p. 205. Although the following quotation could be omitted without harming the present exposition, the political orientation of this study along with the fact that Samarin later wrote a vigorous polemical attack on the Jesuits ("Otvet Iezuitu otsu Martynovu (1865)", Sochineniya: Iezuity i stat'i bogoslovsko-filosofkogo soderzhaniya, pub. D. Samarin, (Moscow, 1887), VI, 23-262) requires that it be included: "Let us remember," Samarin said, "that at that time the Jesuits in the West were propagating the democratic, revolutionary principle, the domination of the people, which was first proclaimed by them, were inciting citizens to revolt against sovereigns, who were not submissive to the Church, and were justifying regicide as a godly affair." Ibid., p. 210.

[282]Ibid., p. 204.

[283]Ibid., pp. 217-8.

[284]Ibid., p. 205.

prelates.[285] In elaborating this conclusion Samarin maintained

without equivocation that it was a prerogative of the soveriegn

temporal authority to limit clerical rights when they infringed upon

the interests of good responsible State governance.[286] No less

relevant is the concurrent observation that the ecclesiastical courts

did not at any time meddle in the "sphere of temporal state

jurisprudence." "It is remarkable", Samarin concluded, "how strictly

this distinction was observed in ancient Russia before Peter, not as a

result of juridical laws, but by itself, by the force of custom."[287]

The correspondence between this conclusion and Samarin's exposition of

the Orthodox view of the proper relationship between Church and State

is obvious.

However, in terms of the relations between Church and State the

challenge which Patriarch Nikon put to Alexis, and in his person to the

State, was of far greater importance than any of the Church-related

measures of the Ulozhenia. Nikon's challenge to the authority of

Alexis was rooted in his perception of the proper relationship between

spiritual and temporal power. Samarin's research convinced him that

Nikon believed that any interference whatsoever in Church jurisprudence

was illegitimate, and that all Church lands and properties should be

administered by the Church without any kind of control or interference

from the State; in other words, that "the civil rights of the clergy,

as a class, should be raised to the level of essential rights of the

---

285Ibid., p. 219.

286Ibid., p. 221.

287Ibid., p. 219.

Church herself."[288] Nikon also believed that the Church should be ruled by the Patriarch in accordance with the monarchical principle. These two beliefs taken together were the essence of Nikon's determination "to raise the Church to the level of an independent state within the state."[289]

Obviously Samarin's opinion about the correctness of Nikon's challenge is of major concern. That opinion was unequivocal. Nikon's idea - "an independent state within the state" and "unlimited autocratic power" for the Patriarch - amounted to establishing, Samarin said, "a separate national Papism" in Russia, and was therefore "contrary to the spirit of the Orthodox Church."[290] Expressed in political terms "the spirit of the Orthodox Church" meant a Church-State relationship in which the Church existed in a recognized nation-state and voluntarily accepted the supreme power of the duly established temporal authority in all matters except those relating to the exercise of spiritual power.[291] Therefore Nikon's challenge was "a logical, necessary impossibility" in Russia, and was doomed to failure.[292] As an inevitable result the confrontation between Nikon and Alexis, Patriarch and Tsar, Church and State, ended with the fall of Nikon and the preservation of that relationshp between Church and State, which the Orthodox Church and Samarin so favoured.

---

[288]Ibid., p. 226.

[289]Ibid.

[290]Ibid., 231.

[291]Ibid., p. 232, and pp. 121-125 above.

In Samarin's opinion a far more serious threat to the proper
relationship between Church and State emerged in Russia at the end of
the seventeenth century when Catholic influence reached its peak. From
this eminence Catholic theory was able to make a direct impact on the
nation's political life.[293] As always Samarin advanced specific
arguments to support his claims. Firstly, he argued that the influence
of Catholic theory was manifested in the idea of the Patriarchate
advanced by "several" Russian writers of the period. These writers
were clearly influenced by the Papal idea (remember that Nikon is
described as a Papist) for they "raised the Patriarchate to the level
of a divine institution." For this reason, Samarin concluded, the
Patriarchy had to be destroyed.[294] Secondly, he argued that the
influence of Catholic theory was manifested in the predilection for
persecuting heretics and schismatics which the Orthodox Church and her
divines demonstrated during these years. This use of persecution for
religious dissent was contrary to "the spirit of Orthodoxy" and had
"never been justified" by the Church. On the contrary, however,
persecution was an integral part of Catholic practice being justified
on two counts. Firstly, by the argument that the Church "conscious of
herself as a state founded on unity of faith, had to look on any
calculated contradiction to dogma, on any heresy, as a revolt against
legitimate state power, as on a political fact." Thus, "a heretic

---

[292]Ibid., p. 231.

[293]Ibid., p. 236.

[294]Ibid., p. 237.

necessarily acquired the significance of a revolutionary and was subjected to civic execution." Secondly, by the argument that persecution
was "a means of turning the errant to the path of truth."[295] The
corollary of the first argument - the Orthodox Church was not conscious
of herself as a State - validated Samarin's argument that persecution
was not characteristic of the Orthodox Church. To clinch his argument
about Catholic influence Samarin quoted a long passage from Stefan
Yavorsky's Kamen' very (Stone of Faith) ending with the evocative
phrase "...where the spiritual sword fails, the real sword succeeds."
Samarin's pungent comment speaks volumes: "Bellarmine himself could
not have said it better. This whole page is an unexpungable stain on
the memory of Stefan Yavorsky."[296] In the light of these arguments, Nol'de's comment that "Samarin's political ideal was freedom of
the Church and freedom of conscience"[297] seems most appropriate.

According to Samarin, the intrusion of Catholicism split the
Orthodox Church into warring camps, demoralized the clergy, and most
characteristicaly led the Church into open rebellion against State
power. By 1696 the first year of Peter the Great's reign, "religious
interest had become a political weapon and fanaticism a main mover of
parties."[298] As a result Peter, who felt the brunt of this

295Ibid.

296Ibid., p. 241.

297Nol'de, p. 28.

298Ibid., pp. 242-3.

religiously-based lawlessness, learned to look upon the Church as a
force inimical to the State and inevitably and very properly took
extreme measures against her.[299] Samarin summarized the situation
in these words:

> And so, the Catholic interest in Russia at the end of the
> seventeenth and the beginning of the eighteenth centuries
> acquired a political character having raised up in the
> clergy a party hostile to the state; counteraction was
> necessary. The influence was political, directed against
> the state, therefore the counteraction had to be completed
> from the offended principle, from the state. Further, the
> influence originated in a one-sided principle - in Catholicism,
> therefore the counteraction could incline to the opposite
> one-sidedness. This possibility became a reality because of
> the personality of Peter.[300]

Thus Samarin was convinced that Peter's personality was a key factor in
the reform of Church-State relations at this critical juncture in
Russian history. However, what was the personality trait of decisive
importance? It was Peter's "one-sided" preoccupation with statecraft,
for Samarin saw Peter as a "practical genius", a master politician who
understood religion, art and science solely in political terms.[301]
Thus Peter saw religion as "a necessary condition of the power and
well-being of the state, the foundation of popular morality, without
which there could not be a durable true relationship between subjects
and sovereign." However, and this was critical for Samarin's charge of
"one-sidedness", Peter was "fairly indifferent to the content of faith"
concerned only that it be "simple" and work towards the improvement of

---

[299]Ibid., pp. 244-5.

[300]Ibid., p. 245.

[301]Ibid., pp. 245-6.

"popular morality".[302] It was this practical attitude to religion

that made Peter tolerant of all faiths and even somewhat preferential

towards Protestantism, which had a superior record for raising the moral

tone of nations.[303] Also, it was this practical attitude which led

him to expect the clergy to provide "didactic instruction" on moral

living, supplemented by "good example." Without question Samarin felt

that Peter's expectations of the clergy accorded well with Russia's

needs at that time and were to be welcomed.[304]

However, this perception of the Church as a tool of State was also

Peter's weakness and the reason for his "exclusiveness", his "Protestant

one-sidedness." Peter "did not understand what the Church was, he

simply did not see her."[305] Because he did not understand the

higher spiritual side of the Church - what Samarin described elsewhere

as "...the vital connection and combination in the total organism of the

Church of her abstract side, of dogmas, with rituals and the moral

development of separate individuals",[306] "he acted, as if it did not

exist."[307]

Samarin's assessment of the implication of Peter's "Protestant one-

sidedness" provides as explicit a statement about the special construc-

tive role which the Church must play in the State as it is possible to

[302]Ibid., p. 246.

[303]Ibid., pp. 247-8.

[304]Ibid., p. 251.

[305]Ibid., p. 252.

[306]Ibid., p. 254.

find in the whole corpus of his dissertation:

> Therefore [Peter] did not understand that it is only in the
> Church that a strong, true, lasting, premeditated penetration
> of the national life by Christian morality is possible;
> that man devoted to himself alone, torn away from the Church,
> is necessarily separated from God and from his neighbours,
> that the absence of a positive faith and authority leads
> to arbitrariness in opinions and from there to arbitrariness
> in affairs, and that if in Protestantism, and in general in
> societies, that do recognize the objective Church, morality
> sometimes flourishes, then it is only a fading lustre, thrown
> on it by the fading Church, or the fruit of fleeting efforts,
> of artificial tension, originating from the consciousness of
> what has been lost and from a desire to replace it.[308]

Therefore, Samarin was convinced that any state - past, present or future

- is dependent on the objective Church for the establishment of that

minimum standard of behaviour based on ethical principles which is so

necessary for the development and maintenance of a reliable, just, social

and political order.

But, to return to Samarin's assessment of Peter's understanding of

the Church, one point remains to be made. Peter, because he was unable

to comprehend the Church as an integrated whole, saw it as a number of

separate parts comprising: "doctrine, to which he was fairly indifferent;

rites, at which he laughed, like they were food for fruitless supersti-

---

[307]Ibid., p. 252. Alexander V. Muller seems to approve of
Samarin's assessment of Peter's perception of the Church's role and
position: "...Peter's efforts may be seen as having been directed toward
importing into the Muscovite state the basic tenets of the Protestant
territorial system in keeping with which the visible church on earth was
envisaged as 'a religious projection of the state itself.' As for the
indigenous Orthodox church, it is perhaps not far from the mark to say, as
Iurii Samarin did, that Peter simply did not see it. Accordingly it
becomes clear why Florovsky calls the Spiritual Regulation 'a program for
a Russian Reformation.'" The Spiritual Regulation of Peter the Great,
trans. and ed. by Alexander V. Muller (Seattle & London: University of
Washington Press, 1972), p. XXXVII.

[308]Ibid., p. 253.

tion; and clergy, which he saw as a special class of civil servants to whom the state had entrusted the moral education of the people." As regards this latter part, the clergy, Peter believed the State had the right to arrange its "structure, administration and duties" just as it did for any other group or organization in the State.[309]

Accordingly Samarin concluded that the need for Church reform and the one-sidedness of Peter, the reformer, were the critical factors determining the shape and the course of Church-State relations at the beginning of the eighteenth century. However, in ranking these factors Samarin was careful to stress that the two Church officials Stefan Yavorsky and Feofan Prokopovich made contributions of such significance that "a detailed study of their work, in the sphere of Church adminis-tration, presents a fairly full picture of the external fate of the Church during Peter's reign."[310]

In Samarin's opinion Peter probably decided for political reasons to destroy the Patriarchate during the lifetime of the last Patriarch Adrian who opposed his reforms. But he was afraid of the opposition which this would create and therefore approached the task with caution, weakening the Patriarchate itself by postponing the appointment of a new Patriarch to replace Adrian when he died in 1700, and gradually undermining popular support for the instituton. His practice of ridi-culing Church ceremonies as in 1702, when he organized a funny wedding of his jester Shansky which featured Nikita Zotov dressed in a costume

---

[309]Ibid., p. 254.
[310]Ibid., p. 257.

like the Patriarch's, was a part of his strategy.[311]

Entering onto the path of Church reform, Peter aimed to change Church administration in those areas where church activities overlapped those of the State and fell logically under the State's jurisdiction.[312] This aim was wholly justified in Samarin's opinion because it was in full accord with Orthodox theory and Russian practice. It was also justified because the Patriarchate had adopted Papal practices and attitudes to the point where the clergy looked upon it as "a necessary institution, the only possible form of administration for the Church", and the people looked upon the Patriarchs as autocrats with power at least equal to that of the Tsars. Therefore, the Patriarchate under Catholic influence had become "a false" institution requiring "in the general consciousness of all Russia...abolishment."[313]

The Orthodox Church had developed different forms of administration from Metropolitanate to Patriarchate, depending on the requirements of time and place, including the general will of the populace, which it was the prerogative of temporal power to satisfy.[314] Without question, Samarin believed that Peter could and should abolish the Patriarchate in line "with the demands of the people."[315] However,

---

[311]Ibid., pp. 281-2.

[312]Ibid., p. 268.

[313]Ibid., p. 281.

[314]Ibid., p. 283.

[315]Ibid.

acknowledging this fact, he observed that the question of what kind of organization should replace the Patriarchate, or more specifically, the question whether the collegiate organization created by Peter was a suitable replacement still remained. Characteristically, Samarin sought an answer to this question in both the ideology and the historical experience of the Russian Orthodox Church.

Nol'de complains at one point that Samarin, by denying "the possibility of the systematic development" of the truths which the Church professed, was denying the Orthodox Church a weapon that she could hardly afford to be without in the struggle against heresy and unbelief.[316] However, Samarin's reason for denying that a Church system could be developed did not mean a repudiation of the usefulness of a systematic elaboration of doctrine on the basis of experience and close rational analysis, but an affirmation of his basic conviction that the essence of the Church, "the eternal unconditional substance of the Church [had to] be manifested ", and could not be developed, explained or proven by any rational Hegelian type system. For this reason, he argued, the Church was constant through time and place and "was not subject to the laws of historical development."[317] In the final analysis it was, for this reason, that Peter's Spiritual College was an unsuitable replacement for the Patriarchate.

The proof of this latter statement is found in Samarin's analysis of the implications of the fact that "the eternal unconditional substance

---

[316]Nol'de p. 26. See also above, pp. 102 and 109. Fn. 241.

[317]Sochineniya, V, 283.

of the Church had to be manifested", or "could not exist in the

abstract."[318]   Because of this, he maintained there is a side of

the administration of the Church which "grows from inside the Church

herself and exists in all times and among all peoples without

change."[319] Because of this the administrators of the Church enjoy

certain rights and powers entrusted to them by the whole Church. Thus

each separate and equal bishop and each separate and equal bishopric is

a part of the whole. Each bishopric comprises a part of the Ecumenical

Church, and each bishop, representing in his person a bishopric,

belongs to a Council (Sobor), comprising representatives of all of the

bishoprics.

> And so, the Church, being a vital union of all believers,
> a loose council, not accidentally, but because of its very
> substance, is administered by a Council (Sobor) - in other
> words, she administers herself. The Council (Sobor) is
> organic, free, fixed from inside the Church and is therefore
> her only-possible manifestation."[320]

Thus the Church, an organization necessarily manifesting constant

truths, was a democratic union administered by officials responsible to

a general Council.

This general principle of responsible Church government by Council

was very flexible allowing for the creation of a changing administra-

tion including bishops, archbishops, metropolitans and patriarchs, and

for different methods of governance from direct rule by Council to

direct rule by a patriarch. What was constant under this principle was

---

[318]Ibid.

[319]Ibid.

[320]Ibid., p. 284.

the concentration of power in the Council and the Council's character as a "free administration constituted from within the Church itself."[321]

According to Samarin this principle of Church government had prevailed in Russia down to the time of Peter the Great. During that period all officials had been selected by the Council, all important decisions had been made in accordance with its regulations, and even the Patriarchs had recognized their dependence on it. Thus, Samarin stated:

> Peter the Great could, with the agreement of the Ecumenical Church, abolish the Patriarchate and establish another form of administration; but at the same time freedom of administration, which was fixed by freedom of selection, had to remain untouched.[322]

Samarin's final word on Peter was determined by a major event of 1718. In that year Peter decided to push his long-projected reform of the Patriarchate forward. In that year he instructed Feofan Prokopovich to compose a new Spiritual Regulation. Completed in 1719, Prokopovich's document was amended and suplemented by Peter himself, and then dispatched to the Senate and clergy for critical examination. Later it was read twice before their assemblies, amended in some places, and then signed by the hierarchs, the Senators and the Tsar, following which it was sent to Moscow and other cities for signature by those churchmen who had not been present for the earlier readings. Finally at the opening of the Synod on September 16, 1721 it was published under the title A Regulation or Statute of the Spiritual College.[323]

As indicated above, when it came to assessing the suitability of

---

[321]Ibid.,

[322]Ibid., p. 285.

the Spiritual College or Holy Synod which Peter created to replace the
Patriarchate, the critical question for Samarin was "freedom of
administration" guaranteed by "freedom of selection" maintained in the
new institution of Church government? His answer was negative for two
reasons: firstly, the Holy Synod was a permanent council, whereas the
Sobor was a temporary council which met on an occasional basis for
specific purposes; and secondly, the Holy Synod had not developed
naturally from the Church herself but had been created by the state on
the collegiate model. Thus Peter's "one-sidedness", as revealed in his
inability to understand "the eternal unconditional substance of the
Church" as well as the inherently free character of the Church Council
(Sobor), lead to the creation of a College of Spiritual Affairs with a
mandate to administer the church like any other department of the state
administration.[324]

Samarin concluded from his analysis that Peter's main reform objective was to eradicate ambiguities, contradictions and superstitions from
Church teachings, that is to render Christian doctrine clear, simple and
concrete. Furthermore, he concluded, that Peter was more concerned

---

[323]Alexander Muller states that this statute was the most
important piece of legislation affecting the Orthodox Church to come
from Peter's reign and the following comment certainly supports the
burden of Samarin's argument: "It established within the framework of
public law, i.e., the division of law relating to the state in its
sovereign capacity, as opposed to canon law, the law of the Church, the
basis for a new relationship between the spiritual and secular powers of
Russia. It marked for the Russian Church the suspension of the system
of patriarchal administration and the beginning of the synodal period,
which was to last for nearly two hundred years, coterminous with the era
of the Russian Empire, 1721-1917." Muller, The Spiritual Regulation of
Peter the Great, p. ix.

[324]Ibid., p. 190.

to protect the faith from "superstition" than he was to protect it from "un-belief"; and that it was precisely for these reasons that the College and its Regulations reflected the Protestant variety of "one-sidedness" which was so misguided. Intriguingly, Samarin observed that Peter's aim was justified by the degree to which "superstition" outweighed "unbelief" in Russia at that time.[325] In this judgement he revealed much more sympathy for Peter than was characteristic of the Slavophils if their criticism "that Peter had interrupted Russia's natural development by alienating educated people from their own customs and traditions" can be taken as a guide.[326]

The Spiritual Regulation revealed the one-sided character of the reform which it codified, and Peter as a very capable politican was well aware of it. Thus it was that he pressed the reform forward as a project of the whole Church and prevailed upon the Catholic-leaning Stefan Yavorsky to support it and to accept a position of first importance in the new Holy Synod. In this way Samarin maintained, Peter, either "consciously" or "unconsciously", set a limit to the Protestant tendency of his reform.[327]

The premises and analysis summarized above, supplemented by a wealth of data, led Samarin to the following concluding statement about the relationship between Church and State in Orthodox Russia:

> The normal relationship of Church and State in the
> Orthodox world is defined as one of mutual recognition.
> The influence of Catholicism destroyed the harmony, in

---

[325]Ibid., p. 291.

[326]Klyuchevsky, Peter the Great, p. 251.

[327]Sochineniya, V, 300-1.

which Church and State existed in Russia. It threw on
the Patriarchate the reflection of Papism and raised up
in the clergy a hostile political party to the State.
The Catholic influence provoked a counteraction from the
State, which was necessary in itself, but which was inclined to Protestant one-sidedness. This counteraction
was the work of Peter the Great and Feofan Prokopovich.
We have called it one-sided, consequently, we will not
dwell on it. Having given it its due, we have freed ourselves from its one-sidedness and acknowledge it only, as
a moment, - and this conclusion is already the beginning
of an exit.[328]

At least three distinguished Russian writers were present at

Samarin's defense of his dissertation on June 3, 1844. The first of

these was Sergei Aksakov, the famous author and father of Konstantin

Aksakov, Samarin's closest friend, and he was thrilled by the event:

I have never seen anyone on the stand so free, noble and
moderate, but the last epithet does not express my thought;
I wanted to say, that everything about him was in measure;
fervour, virtue, peacefulness, humility, evasivenss and bold-
ness. Everyone was enraptured by him, especially those who
objected to him....[329]

The second was Peter Chaadayev, the outstanding philosopher and

Westerner. He stated in a letter to a friend that:

...not having the chance to defend the whole position of
his discourse, Samarin in brief terms laid bare its content and with rare bravery expressed before everyone his
position on Christianity - the fruit of long study of the
holy fathers and of the history of the church - inspired
by deep conviction and especially striking for its new-
ness. Never, of this I am sure, from the time of the
existence of universities on the earth, has a young man,
who has scarcely left the benches of the university,
decided so successfully such big questions, pronounced
with such power, so autocratically, so unselfishly a
sentence on everything that had created that science, that
educatedness, which had been cherished, which he had
breathed, the language of which he spoke. I was touched

---

[328]Ibid., p. 331.

[329]Ibid.,, LXXX.

to tears by this splendid triumph of a contemporary
direction in our fatherland, in our godloving humble
Moscow. Our young theologian did not feel the least
bit of confusion, the least bit of restraint, deciding
in a completely new and unexpected way the highest problem in the province of reason and the spirit.[330]

The third was the brilliant philosopher-polemicist Alexander Herzen,

whose impression contrasts sharply with Chaadayev's as quoted above.

Herzen wrote in his Diary as follows:

Yesterday Samarin defended his dissertation. The con-
junction of high dialectical capacity with pitiable
orthodox theories and exaggerated slavism in this man
is incomprehensible; in him this contradiction is most
striking, because his logic definitely prevails over
everything. He, it is true, sees the shakiness of his
fantastic foundation, but he does not retreat from it.
Perhaps youth, always ready to give itself up to abstract
theory, an insufficiency of factual information and an
inability to submit to the historical element, is the fault
of this trend. In general the dissertation and its defence
produced a sad feeling. In all of this there is something
retrograde, inhuman, narrow, as in the whole national party.
A terrible gulf remains, which divides and is uncrossable, as
there is no agreement with them on several questions.[331]

Khomiakov was not present at the defense but he did offer an inter-

esting comment on Samarin's work, which at least places in question

Berdyaev's opinion that Samarin had written his dissertation under

Khomiakov's influence and guidance.

It is very difficult for me to answer you, dear Yuri
Fedorovich, because I am almost in agreement with you
in everything. Several places, in which I am not in
agreement have been seized on by others. If time allowed
I think I would attack you for reproaching Stefan for not
having sympathy for contemporary questions while at the
same time you praise Feofan for having it. Stefan could
not speak out against the reform because it was done in
the name of reason, but Feofan could speak out against the
Old Believers, because they acted in the name of the
church; consequently the church was obliged to repudiate

---

[330]Ibid., p. LXXXII.

[331]Herzen, VII, 356.

them. In the same way Feofan said in praise of Peter
that he wanted simple-hearted bishops. Erudition does
not come from this, but the spiritual fullness necessary to the christian, because christianity is not a
science and cannot be scientific, consequently he was
wholly orthodox. In the same way his theology has been
called a "Polemic"; from this it is just as evident
that he did not adopt positive, but only negative
theology. Therefore there is no proper protestantism
in him.[332]

---

[332]Sochineniya, V, LXXXIX. Berdyaev said: "Samarin reworked his
dissertation...under the influence of Khomiakov and developed in application to a concrete situation Khomiakov's idea about the relationship of
Orthodoxy to Catholicism and Protestantism." Berdyaev, Khomiakov, p. 63.

CHAPTER IV

The Civil Service

On August 7, 1844, not long after the successful defence of his

master's thesis, Samarin left Moscow to join the government service in

St. Petersburg. In taking this step he suppressed his own inclination

which was to pursue a career in scholarship and submitted to the will of

his father[333] who, like so many Russian aristocrats of the period,

was driven by a family commitment to state service. Samarin began his

service career in the Ministry of Jusice, and terminated it in February

1853 some eight and one-half years later, by resigning from the Ministry

of the Interior. During these years he acquired varied and valuable

experience as he acknowledged in a letter to Konstantin Aksakov of

December 11, 1850.

> You will not believe how many institutions, bureaus, res-
> ponsibilities, and classes, the existence of which I did not
> suspect, have been revealed to me. I have devoted myself
> to the study of everything: it is necessary that one of us
> possesses a knowledge of our official reality. Perhaps some-
> time this knowledge will be useful.[334]

Samarin's in-service "school", as he called it on another

occasion,[335] saw him fulfill secretarial duties in the Senate from

February 1845 to February 1846, and serve as research historian,

committee-man and official in the Ministry of the Interior from February

1846 to February 1853.[336] Without doubt his most important

experience during these years was gained in the Livonian city of Riga

---

[333]Sochineniya, VII, 1.

[334]Sochineniya, XII, 211

[335]Ibid., 308.

[336]Ibid., 135.

where he served on committees dealing with the problems of peasant land
reform, and of administrative and economic reform for the city of Riga
itself. This work provided him with his first knowledge of the peasant
and Baltic questions - the two questions which he laboured to solve
during the 23 years of active life and work left to him after his
resignation from the Ministry of the Interior in 1853.[337]

However, Samarin's life and training in state service was not as
positive an experience as the above facts suggest. In general he found
his duties repetitious and burdensome during the whole of the period,
especially as they left him little time for independent research and
writing. Furthermore, his months in St. Petersburg were oppressive and
very unsettling, because his spiritual orientation and the ideas which
he had adopted through interaction with Khomiakov and his other friends
in Moscow had not yet been consolidated and were constantly under
challenge in his new environment. Just how frustrating and unsettling his
life in government service was is revealed in a letter which he wrote to
Khomiakov in the fall or early winter of 1845:

> It is already a year since I came to Petersburg, and not
> only have I not done anyone a service in all this time,
> but I have myself experienced much spiritual harm.
> In the circle of my acquaintances I am seen as a repre-
> sentative of a form of thought which is feared and disliked
> here, or better, which is not understood....I am not re-
> conciled to this society but feel that it acts on me, like
> the damp air here, like a sedentary life. Everything is
> stirred up in my head; that which provoked indignation
> and contempt in me, is clothed by my eyes in pleasant forms
> and cunningly creeps into my soul. The rest, in which I
> believed and which I loved, seems to lose value for me and
> becomes suspect.... It is unbearably difficult. I am dying
> to leave here, but I don't know where to go, because I have

---

[337]Ibid., pp. 136-7.

lost the consciousness of my calling....I have decided
to leave here forever; the end of my stay in Petersburg
will be the spring. After that what am I to do?
Leave the service or go to serve in the province? I
am thinking of Little Russia or the Pre-Volga region....
This is what distresses me: there is no possibility
to join my service pursuits with my scholarly pursuits--
I cannot live without them, but to leave the service
would not only go against the oldest and favorite thought
of my father, but raise up persecution again, which would
not fall on me alone.[338]

This letter accurately transmits Samarin's mood and frustrations

only for the date of writing, it is true, but from his comments in other

letters of the period coupled with his eventual resignation from the

Ministry of the Interior, it is fair to conclude that it expresses his

real and abiding attitude to state service. Certainly, one frustration

was constant above all others, causing him a permanent feeling of

dissatisfaction, and that was the frustration of being prevented by his

onerous service responsibilities from undertaking and sustaining

independent scholarly investigations of the many historical and contemp-

orary problems requiring a particular Slavophil answer.

However, even with the burden of service and the inadequate amounts

of leisure time which it allowed for scholarly endeavour, Samarin

managed to produce several articles of value. That his focus was his-

torical and that he was committed to explaining and buttressing the

Slavophil position on crucial questions is clear from a letter which he

wrote to Aksakov in February of 1845:

Our general insufficiency is poverty of factual knowledge.
I am now studying Russian history and I sense a need to refrain for the time being from general conclusions and general
constructions; I want to subject our whole position to investigation: on the absence of conquest, on the absence of an

---

[338]Ibid., XII, 411-13.

aristocracy, on the significance of personal power, etc.
For this all Russian and foreign sources must be examined;
I have much work ahead of me. For this reason, I definitely
do not read anything except books that relate directly to my
object.[339]

From the topic of his first study, "Vyeche i Knyaz'" (Town Assembly and

Prince), it is also clear that his theoretical interest in political

questions was continuing to develop--no doubt this interest was

stimulated by governmental work and life at the political centre of the

Empire, St. Petersburg. At any rate "Vyeche i Knyaz'" was an historical

study of the two principal political institutions of Kievan Novgorod,

apparently undertaken with a view to discovering the relationship

between the people, represented by their town assembly (vyeche) and the

supreme authority, represented by the prince (knyaz').[340]

His next two articles are examples of the "favorite literary genre

of the period--universal, aesthetico-political criticism."[341] Both

reveal the influence of his historical studies and his skill as an

analyst, and both made a notable impact in the sharpening debate between

Slavophils and Westerners. The first, a critical examination of V.A.

Sollogubs Tarantas, was published in Moskovskiy Sbornik (Moscow

---

[339]Ibid., 156. Nol'de provides the useful and interesting
information that "Samarin and his friends got the idea, that conquest
played a huge role in the history of the West from Guizot; it seemed to
them, that in Russia the political structure was raised quite
differently -- by means of the free unity of the people and the supreme
power." Nol'de, p. 35.

[340]See ibid., 143, fn. 4, where it is stated that: "...'vyeche i
Knyaz' was finished at the beginning of 1845 and sent to Khomiakov....
The article was not published. Only the second part 'Knyaz' has been
preserved to this time. It explains the notion of princely power
established in ancient Russia." For an analysis see pp. 160-164 below.

[341]Nol'de, p. 35.

Miscellany) under the initials M..Z..K. in 1846. It made a considerable impact at least on Belinsky, who said that it was " remarkable for its intellectual content and masterly exposition."[342] The second, "O mneniyakh Sovremennika, istoricheskikh i literaturnykh" (On the Opinions of Contemporary--historical and literary), was published in Moskvityanin (Muscovite) in 1847. It made the greater impact and is a better measure of Samarin's evolution as a political thinker.[343]

The three other works to come from this period vary in value. Two of them were official documents, which even though based on extensive historical research and important for Samarin's career as a political thinker, merit little more than passing mention. Published only much later in volume VII of the Sochineniya, they were Zapiski po ostzeyskomu voprosu (Notes on the Baltic Question) and Istoriya Rigi (The History of Riga).[344] Far more important than these documents was his fourth major piece of these years Pis'ma iz Rigi (Letters from Riga) which was written in 1848 after two years of protracted work on the Baltic question. Although Pis'ma iz Rigi was not published either until volume VII appeared in 1889, it was passed around in manuscript form in government circles as well as among his friends, and made a great impact, bringing him instant notoriety. It also brought quick arrest and a brief period of incarceration in the Peter-Paul fortress. Pis'ma iz

---

[342]V.G. Belinsky, "Vzglayad na Russkuyu Literaturu 1846 Goda," Polnoe Sobranie Sochineniy, (Moscow, 1956) X,46.

[343]For an analysis see pp. 164-197, below.

[344]See the bibliography of this dissertation for additional information including the table of contents for these works.

Rigi was not only his first journalistic work, but was one of the first

political tracts in Russian literature.[345] Like the other works

mentioned above it revealed "literary and critical talent" as well as a

level of "scholarly preparation, which made it possible for him to

support his political views with comprehensive and carefully tested

factual information."[346]

There is no question at all, that "Veche i Knyaz'", "O mneniyakh

Sovremennika, istoricheskikh i literaturnykh" and Pis'ma iz Rigi are

important sources for the study of Samarin's political ideas for the

period 1844-1852. However, his correspondence is also an important

source, for during all of these years Samarin lived far from his

emotional and spiritual base, Moscow, where his closest friends and

intellectual confrères lived. While he served in St. Petersburg, Riga

and Kiev, therefore he maintained close and constant contact with his

friends by letter, keeping them fully informed about his work and

thought. Thus the articles mentioned above are more relevant when

examined in the context of his correspondence. In fact his corres-

pondence contains important political clues reflecting on his primary

commitment to scholarship, his distaste for St. Petersburg and the

bureaucracy, his Muscovitism, his political talent and his inchoate

strategy for political action.

---

[345]Nol'de, p. 44.

[346]Sochineniya, XII, 138. Peter Samarin, Yuri's nephew, made
this comment in his preface to the second part of volume XII containing
the correspondence from 1844-1853. Compare it with Nol'de's comment
that "for Samarin in these years Russian history was not simply an
object of pure scientific curiosity, but a way to the proof of political
theses." Nol'de, p. 35.

His primary commitment to scholarship is revealed as early as the first letter to his parents,[347] and emerges as a frequently repeated theme throughout his correspondence. Perhaps the clearest expression of it is found in a letter to his parents of January 9, 1845: "...I know that what wishes, hopes and dreams were in me have long been fused in a single love of scholarship, in a single demand for knowledge and the dissemination of what is known.... Everything else has become silent."[348] Thus, even while he was confronting his first duties as a civil servant he undertook a scholarly investigation of what he called: "...the most ancient period of Russian history" by means of reading The Chronicles.[349] "Vyeche i Knyaz'" grew out of this investigation.

His distaste for St. Petersburg and the bureaucracy is manifested in many negative comments dating from his arrival in the capital. His first impression of the highest levels of St. Petersburg society seems to exemplify his opinion, that is, he saw it as inert as well as disinterested in the problems that concerned Moscow so deeply.[350] He was especially distressed to note that thinking people were at one and the same time, deeply pessimistic because of the government's powerlessness and without "positive convictions" or "hopes" for the future. These people, he said: "expressed a kind of peaceful,

---

[347]Sochineniya, XII, 310

[348]Ibid., p. 314.

[349]Ibid., p. 312.

[350]Ibid., p. 141.

apathetic despair, spiritual death in the most frightening form....

This formless, dumb force is the most terrible enemy, that we can

meet."[351] In another letter he described a full evening and the

flaccid bureaucrats whom he met at Vladimir Dal's:

> ...it was a disappointment! There was not that freedom, that
> gaiety, that warmth; civil servants came, not stupid, but dead-
> ened by service, exhausted by deadening work and physically
> unable to tear themselves away from their stuffy circle of
> petty concerns and activities. They relaxed quietly over a
> cup of tea or told anecdotes, or, finally, talked about the
> opera.[352]

In still another he referred to St. Petersburg as the city in which

"inimical fate had commanded him to live",[353] and scarcely more than

a year after the beginning of his service career he referred to

bureaucratic practice in terms of bitter reproach:

> Most distressing of all time and work pass in vain. In this
> pile of papers, which I have read, I knew in advance, are un-
> conscionable calculated lies; you read and you sense that
> they are deceiving you, but there is nothing you can do.
> Tomorrow quickly, superficially, you will narrate all this,
> but not only will they not listen, but they will not even try
> to adopt the appearance of listening. You cannot imagine with
> what offensive carelessness all this happens.[354]

But perhaps the best piece of evidence supporting the claim that Samarin

disliked St. Petersburg and the bureaucracy are these comments from a

letter which he wrote to his parents in September, 1845: "There is

definitely nothing for me to do in Petersburg; I am leaving it forever

---

[351]Ibid., pp. 322-3.

[352]Ibid., p.145. V.I. Dal' (1801-72) was an outstanding
lexicographer. His monumental Dictionary of the Russian Language
(1861-1868) is still a valuable reference work. He was also a writer of
tales and a collector of proverbs.

[353]Ibid., p. 146.

[354]Ibid., p. 166.

and no enticement whatsoever will bring me back here. I am too deeply
convinced, that to live in it one must serve it, and to serve Petersburg
means to betray Russia," and further on in the same letter commenting
specifically on the government, he likened its work to a "comedy" about
which it was ridiculous to speak either in terms of "duty to the
fatherland" or "duty as a Christian."[355]

Samarin's Muscovitism or commitment to the orientation of thought
and action represented by his Moscow friends, and in particular Khomiakov and Aksakov, cannot be gainsaid. The specifics of this Moscow
orientation were not very clearly defined in 1844-45, but certainly they
contained these elements: a shared love of the past, a deep faith in
Russian Orthodoxy, and a profound respect for the Russian people.[356]
In any case, in this particular instance lack of precision was no
obstacle to Samarin, for the evidence indicates that he gave unequivocal
support to the Muscovite orientation.[357]

Samarin's letters also indicate that he had fine natural political
talents. This fact is illustrated for instance when he wrote to Aksakov
of the need to approach people with "prudence" and "calculation" in
order to win their acceptance and support:

---

[355]Ibid., pp. 322-3.

[356]In a letter to K. Aksakov, Samarin said: "The desire to
argue ebbs; you remain silent and with inner discontent allow offensive,
haughty statements about our past, about our faith, and about the
Russian people in general to pass." Ibid., p. 155.

[357]Ibid., p. 146. On this page Samarin tells Aksakov that he
considers himself "enslaved to Moscow." See also pp. 149, 152, 153 and
164, where similar comments appear.

I became convinced that those who I thought were lost
were capable of being converted. They could be inclined
to another line of thought, but it would be necessary to
act prudently.... If I demanded that they wear a murmolka
[old-style Russian cap], or read them several of your verses,
if I expounded my whole line of thoughtto them suddenly
and at one time, they would turn away in horror. It is
necessary to act on them in different ways: with one to
speak about Moscow and not to mention Orthodoxy until the
right moment, with another--the reverse.... I act with an aim,
prudently, pressing more on that in which we are in agreement....
I am convinced that, speaking with and for another, we are
obliged to speak his language, a language accessible not only
to his understanding, but his heart; all of this presupposes aim,
calculation, prudence. Prudence![358]

Shrewd political calculation was also evidenced in the advice which he
gave to Aksakov about the best way to resist certain petty government
regulations about the wearing of beards and Russian clothes by noblemen.
Aksakov's approach was to confront the government in a manner compelling
a harsh authoritarian response. Samarin's was to assume a misunderstanding and to write a letter to the government affirming respect for
the law and established authority on the one hand, and stating the reasons for wearing Russian clothes and a beard on the other: "Inevitably
prohibition will follow, but you at least will have explained your
action and done what you could. But in any case I insist that this
letter must not have the appearance of a request about the retention of
Russian clothes, but of an explanation, begun with a declaration of a
willingness to take them off."[359] Political calculation also
underlay his frequent and sometimes passionate appeals to his Moscow

---

[358]Ibid., p. 181.

[359]Ibid., pp. 203-4.

friends "to write and to print", for he maintained that Moscow's case had to be stated and defended on the grounds that: "recognition is compelled, a place is taken by storm, it is never given up voluntarily; it counts for little that there are rights, it is necessary to declare them."[360] Finally the possession of uncommon political talent was manifested in his awareness that flamboyant "toasts and exclamations", being no substitute for the sound, clear statement of policy and position, served only to stimulate "fear and hatred" in government circles and "ridicule" on the part of society, thereby ending all hope of realizing some kind of peaceful, just accommodation of conflicting interests.[361]

Important elements of Samarin's developing political strategy have been adumbrated above. They included: firstly, a conviction that work as a government official was dissatisfying and unproductive; secondly, a sense of belonging to a group with a particular orientation; thirdly, a conviction that substantial incontrovertable arguments based on scientific investigtion had to be advanced in support of political positions; and fourthly, a conviction that moderate action in search of viable compromises was a more constructive form of political action than flamboyant confrontationism.

It would be possible to expand on all of these points, but it would be most profitable to expand here on the latter two. Already in a letter to Aksakov of November or December 1844, Samarin wrote:

---

[360]Ibid., p.146.

[361]Ibid., pp. 149-153.

What we now need are conscientious works, even unfinished
ones strengthened by sholarship... It is time for each of us
to concentrate on some object, whether it be grammar, history,
is immaterial, if only the fruits of our work are seen. This
will be the very best answer to every kind of mockery and other
stupid...gossip.362

Writing jointly to Khomiakov and Aksakov a short time later, he asked:

"How should the relationship between Moscow and Petersburg be under-

stood?", pointing out that the Moscow group had not produced a single

positive statement of its position. As a result St. Petersburg was

convinced that Moscow had "unjustified pretensions" and harboured "a

passionate feeling of hatred" towards it, to the extent that it believed

"a political party was being formed in Moscow... which had as its

slogan: 'Hail Moscow, Perish Petersburg'--meaning hail anarchy, and

perish all power."363 Thus he concluded that Moscow's blatant

negativism and failure to state its case had stirred up a political

storm which could only be abated by exercising "restraint",364 and

more importantly, by expounding, proving and justifying its position.

This latter point is at least partly proven by his assertion that:"...

the thought must be proven and justified not only for the sake of

rejections, which it will meet during its circulation, but for its own

sake. We have still proven nothing or very little, everything that we

maintain about our past development, all this is divined not concluded.

... Our general insufficiency is poverty of factual knowledge."365 So

---

362Ibid., p. 147.

363Ibid., pp. 150-1.

364Ibid., p. 153.

365Ibid., p. 156.

it was that scientific investigation of critical questions became a
basic element of Samarin's political strategy.

Even though commitment to the scientific investigation of critical
questions had so much political importance to Samarin, attention to it
should not be allowed to obscure the more important epistemological
basis of his thinking. For no matter how often Samarin affirmed by
exhortation or personal performance the importance of scholarly investigation for the enlargement of knowledge as in the following words from a
letter to Aksakov of 1845: "I am learning so as not to fall behind, in
order to prepare a full arsenal for the use of our convictions";[366]
and no matter how often he urged support for the journal Moskvityanin as
a vehicle of Moscow's message,[367] he never lost sight of the certain
fact, in his view, that the basis of knowledge lay in religion. The
proof of this statement is contained in the following words from a
letter to Aksakov of early 1846:

> I have begun to write an article about the people or, better
> about the religious character of the question of the signifi-
> cance of the people. In it I want to develop the idea that the
> justification of the people, as a people (not the raising of it
> to another level by means of the diffusion of literacy, etc.)
> presumes undoubtedly the recognition of the one-sidedness and
> falsity of logical knowledge, on which is founded all contempor-
> ary enlightenment and the recognition of the supremacy of that
> knowledge which Khomiakov calls living.... In a single word, the
> people, as a people, can be justified only from the religious
> point of view.[368]

---

[366]Ibid., p. 163.

[367]The first number of Moskvityanin was published on January 27,
1845. It was established as the voice of the Moscow group (Slavophils),
under the editorship of I. Kireyevskv. When Kireyevsky resigned as editor in May 1845, M. Pogodin took over. Ibid. pp. 155 and 162. Samarin's article "O mneniyakh Sovremennika" was published under the initials
M.Z.K. in Moskvityanin, No. 2, 1847. Sochineniya, I, 28-108.

[368]Ibid., pp. 175-6.

It was Samarin's rejection of logical knowledge in preference for the

religious point of view, which was at the heart of his differences with

Herzen as the following quotation from Herzen's Diary so elequently

testifies:

> The other day I received a letter from Samarin. It is a surprising
> century, in which a man so intelligent as he, as frightened by the
> terrible irreconcilable contradictions in which we live, closes the
> eyes of reason and rushes toward the assuagement of religion, to
> quietism, talks about the connection with tradition! His letter
> saddened me. Today I wrote him an answer; in it I said to him:
> 'Another star which spins and disappears (Encore une etoile qui file
> et disparait)! Goodbye, go a different road! We will not meet as
> fellow travellers, this is certain.369

Of course this was the "impregnable line", as Samarin called it in

another place, separating the Westerners and the Slavophils;370 it

was also a powerful force in shaping his political strategy.

Expanding on the proposition that Samarin's political strategy

favoured moderate action in search of viable compromises leads naturally

to an examination of a very long letter which he wrote to Aksakov on 19

July, 1846. In a general way its content supports the above proposi-

tion; at the same time however it provides specific additional infor-

mation about his developing political strategy. For instance in

commenting on government service once again, he emphasized his personal

unsuitability for it, stressing that he was wasting his time or making

poor use of it; and then, foreshadowing his role as an independent

expert on the peasant and Baltic questions, he said:

> I am convinced that in general service, under present
> circumstances, under the present ruling conceptions about
> the civil servant and his obligations, under his present

369Quoted in Ibid. p. 159.

370Ibid., p. 160.

mode of life, it is the most ignoble form of work. All the
important questions, which occupy the government, will be
resolved...by private people, acquainted with those spheres
of life, with which they join their free sympathy or interests,
i.e., by scholars, merchants, landlords, etc., functionaries,
by their very ignorance, will only be letter writers and
executors.[371]

In stressing the unprofitability of government service, however, Samarin

was far from taking the uncritical position that no advantage whatsoever

could come from service, and that, consequently, no idea or programme of

the government should be supported, as is clear from the following

quotation:

What does [total rejection of the government service] mean?
Either that the government cannot conceive anything of
general benefit, or that no matter what useful act it decides
to accomplish it must not be supported. The first seems
stupid to me: the second is purely conditional opposition
systematique, which scarcely flows from a vital view of life.
I recognize a whole row of government measures which are
possible at the present time, and which are in themselves
useful; these measures, principally negative, freeing from
a line of obstacles, taking off applied chains, will directly
and positively help the development of the national spirit
and, consequently, serve the land problem.[372]

Having made these points he went on to compile a very interesting list

of government reform measures: allowing a journal to publish in Moscow

free from the threat of censorship; granting the right of peasant land

ownership; beginning the process of emancipation; allowing a free voice

in city government to every citizen regardless of class; destroying the

privileges of the gentry; and allowing the Latvians to convert to

Orthodoxy; all or anyone of which he would enthusiastically support on

the grounds that:

---

[371]Ibid., p. 177.

[372]Ibid., p. 178.

...a measure in any case is good in itself: the national life
flows in an open channel, every privilege, every granted right
of free movement will bring unforeseen blessings, but the cupi-
dious aim of an individual will fall and be forgotten. I am not
saying that rebirth can be accomplished only by negative measures.
That would be absurd. But in general their insufficiency is the
insufficiency of all governmental spheres. The government does
not create life, but it can suppress it consciously or unconsciously, and it can also help its development.[373]

To clinch his argument that reform measures which promised to benefit

the nation should be supported regardless of the motives and ambitions

of either the government or its many functionaries, he advanced the

theory, epitomizing moderation itself, that absolute judgements

embodying black and white distinctions like, for instance, identifying

Petersburg with evil and Moscow with good, drawing "a sharp line between

them, and branding them by external signs [like] dress, place of

residence, and...service occupation" could not be made without falling

into the error of simplyfying a reality made complex by the interaction

of factors like personal accident, the confrontation of contradictory

principles, and the spirit of indifference.[374] Thus Samarin adopted

a moderate reform-oriented political stance which placed a high premium

on principles, expertise and direct personal involvement as a private

individual. What's more, he repudiated confrontationism and revolu-

tionism, taking a political stance which demands comparison with that

implicit in Khomiakov's statement that:

We must show everyone, that [our principles] are just as
far from conservativism in its absurd onesidedness, as
from revolutionism in its immoral and passionate self-
assuredness; that they, finally, constitute the beginning
of rational progress, and not senseless fermentation.[375]

---

[373]Ibid., pp. 178-9.

[374]Ibid., p. 180.

[375]"Pis'ma A.S. Khomiakova k Yu. F. Samariny," Russkiy Arkhiv,
(Moscow, 1879), p. 314.

Finally, his commitment to direct personal participation in reform programmes contrasts dramatically with that of the later generation of political activists at the turn of the twentieth century like Peter Struve and Vladimir Lenin, who laboured successfully, in the latter case at least, to build strong united political parties as vehicles of political action.

The examination of Samarin's articles for this period begins naturally with a look at "Vyeche i Knyaz'" (Town Assembly and Prince), which resulted from his study of the relationship between popular and princely power in Kievan Novgorod. This article was finished in rough form in 1845 and sent to Moscow where it was received by Khomiakov at the end of February. Put into circulation among Samarin's Slavophil friends it provoked a lively debate in which Khomiakov, Aksakov and the Elagin brothers agreed with Samarin, and the other members of the circle split, with Popov, Valuyev, Panov and Pogodin in partial agreement and Kireyevsky in complete disagreement.[376] An offshoot of this debate was a valuable exchange of letters from the point of view of this examination, because the article itself was never published. In fact "Vyeche", the first part, was lost, and "knyaz'", the second, which has survived in manuscript form, is scarcely decipherable.[377]

---

[376]Ibid., p. 316.

[377]Sochineniya, XII, 143, fn. 4. See also Manuscript, pp. 99, and 103. This writer was successful in acquiring "Knyaz'" (38 pp.), plus 136 additional pages of manuscript material consisting mainly of prefaces to the articles destined to appear in Volume XI of Samarin's Sochineniya from the Department of Manuscripts of The State Lenin Library in Moscow. This material has been bound and paginated by the writer. All subsequent references to it will be made as above.

Two letters about "Vyechei Knyaz'" are particularly useful for the
light which they throw on its contents. One of them was written by
Khomiakov and the other by Kireyevsky. Khomiakov was obviously thrilled
by the article for he commented enthusiastically on its soundness,
strict logical consistency and vitality. But these strengths did not
seem to mean as much to him as the fact that "Vyechei Knyaz'" represented a triumph for the Slavophils because it showed how little they were
moved by prejudice, arbitrariness and passion.[378] Still having said
these complimentary things, Khomiakov stressed that the article could
not be published at that time because it was incomplete, and at the same
time open to misinterpretation as a defence of things against which it
"pronounced a strict sentence."[379] Interestingly, Peter Samarin,
who prepared the unpublished eleventh volume of Samarin's Sochineniya,
made the same point, but with much greater specificity, in his preface
to "Knyaz'", saying:

> They would have called him a defender of the existing
> state structure, declared that he justified autocracy
> and autocracy in all its appearances and stepped out against
> all laws and institutions, which could regularize somewhat
> Russian life and even in some degree guard the freedom of
> private social life.[380]

But these comments, which indicate that Samarin was no uncritical
defender of nineteenth century Russian autocracy and no enemy of
personal freedom, acquire still greater relevance as indicators of an
essential liberalism when interpreted in the light of Khomiakov's
further comment, that:

---

[378]"Pis'ma Khomiakova", p. 316.

[379]Ibid.

[380]Manuscript, pp. 117-9.

Since the normal relationship [understood in the idea of
the prince and] existing as a law, as a demand rather than
as an historical fact, presupposes the full independence
of the individual and his full union in a free society, it
is obvious that it can only be realized in a strong whole
society; otherwise the person from being free becomes
arbitrary.[381]

Kireyevsky's letter was filled with negative commentary on Samarin's

article.[382] To begin with, however, he praised Samarin's "unusual

giftedness", observing that it was the source of his "intelligent

exposition, coherence of thought, faithfulnes of language to thought",

and economy of expression. However, he did not linger on these

qualities, but moved directly to the heart of his criticism, which was

that Samarin's thought was not only untrue but a compound of "the most

harmful sophisms", which could only work to the disadvantage of Slavo-

phil ideas.[383] However, in extenuation, Kireyevsky pointed out that

Samarin's position marked a transition point on his "intellectual

journey from Hegel to more vital and profound convictions", and stated

that "Vyeche i Knyaz'" expressed only his first opposition to Western

ideas. Then, identifying the particular Western idea against which

Samarin was reacting, as the mechanistic one that man can be "consti-

tuted in a retort", Kireyevsky stressed that Samarin jumped to the

opposite extreme and adopted the equally one-sided view that "when

society has inner vitality, the external mechanism is completely use-

---

[381]"Pis'ma Khomiakova", pp. 316-7.

[382]This letter was found among Samarin's papers and is quoted at
length in Peter Samarin's preface to "Knyaz'". Apparently it was
written to a member of the Moscow circle and given by him to Samarin.
Manuscript, p. 107.

[383]Ibid.

less ." What's more, Kireyevsky complained, he adopted this idea in an
abstract way, and applied it in his analysis of Russian history in an
unscientific manner, selecting proofs without proper objectivity and
discrimination. Kireyevsky concluded:[384]

> I am surprised only that Samarin does not see that his opinion is
> Western...and still more surprised that w i t h his extraordinary
> mind he does not see that everything evil amongst us...derives only
> from the fact that our conceptions fall into these two conflicting
> opposites of which his is without comparison the most harmful,....
> He sees the inadequacy of formal restrictions and thinks sufficient
> moral restrictions, as if they can exist without the other. ...He
> thinks, that a person, who has developed in the midst of a morally
> and religiously closed circle, will always be faithful to that
> circle, and not being constrained by an kind of external conditions,
> will never separate himself from his circle. As if man is an
> angel.[385]

In short, Kireyevsky accused Samarin of having a one-sided and therefore unrealistic faith in the regulatory power of moral principles, and
hence of having lost sight of the necessary role which the whole gamut
of political and social institutions, including norms, plays in a vital
society.[386]

To conclude this examination of "Vyeche i Knyaz'" it seems important to note that an extended quotation from "Knyaz'" itself, which appears in Peter Samarin's preface, at least places in doubt Kireyevsky's
conclusion that Samarin denied the usefulness of political and social

---

[384]Ibid., p. 110.

[385]Ibid., pp. 110-11.

[386]Kireyevsky finished his letter with an interesting comment
comparing Khomiakov and Samarin: "Khomiakov holds the very same idea
[as Samarin], because reality (sushchestvennost') does not exist for
him; the game of the mind is everything for him; he is too indifferent
to reality. Aksakov holds the very same idea because he is too volatile
and draws his thought from his passion. But for Samarin, I am sure, it
is only a bridge to the furthest development." Ibid., p. 111.

institutions ("the external forms of statehood" as Samarin seems to have called them in his manuscript).[387] In this quotation Samarin clearly maintained that forms of social life were useful and necessary, but that they were "one-sided", and therefore, could not adequately express the full complexity of life. In the real world, he said: "elusive...imponderable moral strengths complement the inadequacy of forms". Carrying the argument a step further he maintained that state and social forms were necessary, but that their rigid operation by formula without regard for these "elusive moral strengths" or "free impulses", as he later called them, could produce nothing of benefit to society:

> Where everything is calculated, subjected to a law, and compelled by necessity, the participation of life is constrained. Gifts are accessible only to the enlightened; but are foreclosed to those who have no need of them or want to receive them by force. Life is jealous of its freedom and aims cruelly at one who encroaches on it.[388]

From the point of view of this study the article "O mneniyakh Sovremennika, istoricheskikh i literaturnykh" (On the opinions of Contemporary - historical and literary) deserves special attention. Written in the spring of 1847 and published in issue no. 2 of Moskvityanin for that very same year under the initials M..Z..K.., "O mneniyakh Sovremennika" contained critiques of three separate articles which had been published in the first issue of Sovremennik, the voice of the Westerner group. These articles were: K. D. Kavelin's, "Vzglayad

---

[387]Manuscript, pp. 113-117.

[388]Ibid., p. 117.

na yuridicheskiy byt drevney Rossii" (An opinion on the juridical life

of Ancient Russia); A. V. Nikitenko's "O sovremennom napravlenii

Russkoy literatury" (On the contemporary direction of Russian litera-

ture); and V. G. Belinsky's, "Vzglyad na Russkuyu literaturu 1846 goda"

(A view of Russian literature for 1846).[389] "O mneniyakh Sovremin-

nika" deserves special attention for at least three reasons. Firstly,

Samarin himself attached considerable importance to it as a refutation

of Kavelin's article which had made "a strong impression" in St. Peters-

burg.[390] Secondly, Samarin valued it as a statement of basic Slavo-

phil theses.[391] Thirdly, it provoked a vigorous polemical argument

with the Westerners.[392]

Samarin was avowedly pleased to see Sovremennikh renewed under the

editorship of N. A. Nekrasov and I. I. Panov in 1847 because he knew

---

[389]"O mneniyakh Sovremennika, istorisheskikh i literaturnykh",
Sochineniya Yu. F. Samarina, I (Moscow, 1877), 28-108. See also
Sochinenija, XII, 192, fn. 1.

[390]Letter to Aksakov, Sochineniya, XII, 192.

[391]Letter to Pogodin, Ibid., p. 252. Khomiakov valued the
article for the very same reason. cf. "It is necessary, without fail to
publish them ["O mneniyakh Sovremennika"]. I say: necessary without
fail, because in them for the first time definite [Slavophil] theses
have been set out, and consequently the beginning to a positive science
has been laid, and we have emerged from that negative tendency, in which
the confusion of our readers reproaches us." "Pis'ma Khomiakova", p. 327.

[392]See the following articles: V. G. Belinsky, "Otvet Moskvityaninu," Polnoe Sobranie Sochinyeniy, vol. 10 (Moscow, 1956), pp.
221-269; A. I. Herzen, "Moskovskiy panslavism i russkiy evropeizm," in
A. I. Herzen, Sobranie sochinenii v tridtsati tomakh, vol. 7 (Moscow,
1956), pp. 244-248; and K. D. Kavelin, "Otvet 'Moskvityaninu'", Sobranie
sochineniy K. D. Kavelina, vol. I (Moscow, 1897), pp. 67-96.

their views and respected their impartiality.[393] Convinced that a
serious literary dispute w i t h St. Petersburg was due, he revelled in
the fact that it was now possible. As he saw it, the St. Petersburg
journals had greeted the new Moscow "party" with "mockery and self-
satisfied scorn," derisively calling its zealots "old believers" or
"slavophils" and consciously or unconsciously refusing to take their
"pattern of thought" seriously.[394] The result of this cavalier
attitude was a total misunderstanding of what the Moscow party stood for
and a misrepresentation of its ideas and aims. "Now, at last," thought
Samarin, "the opinion of our literary opponents will appear in the
worthiest form and our opinion will be understood and valued."[395]
However, he was disappointed by the appearance of the first number,
and for three reasons: firstly, the new journal lacked "unity of
direction and agreement," secondly, it was "one-sided and narrow," and
thirdly, it "perverted the thought of its opponents."[396]. It was in
the course of substantiating these claims against Sovremennikh that
Samarin developed his criticism of Kavelin, Nikitenko and Belinsky.

Opinions on the merit of Samarin's criticism differed dramatically,
even violently between Slavophils and Westerners. To Khomiakov, Sama-

---

[393]Sochineniya, I, 28. Sovremennikh, a literary journal, was
founded by A. S. Pushkin in 1836. Purchased in 1846 by N. A. Nekrasov
it became the major vehicle of liberal Western and radical opinion. V.
G. Belinsky was its principal literary critic in 1847 and A. V.
Nikitenko was its official editor.

[394]Ibid.

[395]Ibid., p. 29.

[396]Ibid., pp. 29-30.

rin's work possessed great power. It was excellent "in exposition, in ideas and in scrupulousness and strictness of analysis," to the point that it simply overwhelmed "the trivality" of his opponents.[397] To Herzen, Samarin's work, by some mystical process, took its conclusions from the Slavonic chronicles, the Greek catechism and Hegelian formalism and was therefore "an immoral verbal fornication, a perverted dialectic."[398] In contrast, he praised Kavelin's work, in particular, for both its thoroughness and its rational scientific objectivity.[399] Such contradictory assessments beg a close look at the substance of Samarin's article.

To begin with, Samarin noted that Kavelin's article "Vzglyad na yuridicheskiy byt drevney Rossii" was a well structured logical whole, in which a single clear idea was advanced and then supported by historical examples. Samarin found this main idea easy to identify and express in the author's own words:

> An opinion, a theory is necessary in order to understand the deep meaning (taynyy smysl) of [Russian] history and in order to revive our historical literature. [This opinion/theory is to be found] in ourselves, in our internal mode of life, and not in impossible abstract thought, or in almost fruitless comparison with the history of other peoples.[400]

Having acknowledged this much, however, Samarin had three caveats to make. Firstly, that it wasn't enough to be aware, as Kavelin was, of

---

[397]"Pis'ma Khomiakova," p. 327.

[398]Herzen, Sobranie, VII, 244-5.

[399]Ibid., p. 244 et passim.

[400]Sochineniya, I, 30.

the danger of applying some "abstract idea of what the history of a
people ought to be" to the study of a people's past, because to a certain extent all thinking is a process of abstraction.[401] Secondly,
that truly, comparing the history of other peoples is "fruitless,"
because it produces only negative knowledge of the laws of development
of the people being studied.[402] And finally, that Kavelin seemed to
be unaware, that studying the inner lives of a people requires an extra
dimension, or an especially close examination in order "to separate the
essential from the accidental, the primary from the secondary, the
direction and aims from the mass of events...a method of study pre-
supposing two conditions: the absence of any prejudices and thorough
observation." [403]

One of the first propositions advanced by Kavelin was as follows:
"the Russo-Slavonic tribe was formed in most ancient times exclusively
by birth.... There was no mixing with other tribes nor was there any
borrowing of foreign national character."[404] Samarin accepted this
proposition as a truth applicable to all tribes whether Russo-Slavonic
or not. However, he had strong criticism for another more important
Kavelin proposition, that "in the most ancient times the Russian Slavs
had an exclusively 'kinship' mode of life based only on blood beginnings

---

[401]Ibid.

[402]Ibid.

[403]Ibid, p. 31.

[404]Ibid., p. 32.

and relationships."[405] Samarin identified this proposition "as the

basic historical datum of the whole article"[406] and went on to argue

that Kavelin's evidence,consisting solely of facts indicating that rela-

tionships with the ancient Russo-Slav community were defined in terms

like father, mother, brother, sister, aunt and uncle taken from family

life, did not prove the proposition. On the contrary, it demonstrated

that there was at least one other larger dimension:

> The point is that his type of terminology, met to a greater or
> lesser degree in all tribes, proves nothing, or better, proves
> something quite different than the author supposes. It ex-
> presses the idea, that besides the fulfillment of necessary
> obligations by law, man wanted to find sympathy, counsel, and
> love in addition; and very aptly expressed those demands by
> borrowing the terminology from family life.[407]

Thus Samarin concluded that "the Russo-Slav tribe carried its demand for

[sympathy, counsel, love] from family life into the social struc-

ture."[408] Further, he emphasized that the Russo-Slav tribe was

mature enough even at that early date to understand "the benefits of

order, based on law and compulsion."[409]

On the basis of his premise that the Russo-Slav mode of life was

rooted exclusively in kinship and was unaffected by outside forces,

Kavelin concluded, that Russia's "ancient domestic history was the gra-

---

[405]Ibid., p. 31. Italics in the original.

[406]Ibid., p. 32

[407]Ibid., pp. 32-33.

[408]Ibid., p. 33.

[409]Ibid.

dual development of an exclusively blood, kinship mode of life."[410]
Samarin countered this argument by reinforcing his general thesis that
early Russian life was shaped by more than considerations of kinship
with evidence taken from the first lines of the Chronicles. This
evidence comprised those lines, which "acknowledged the inadequacy of
the kinship principle and the need for an arbitrating power freely and
consciously summoned."[411] This evidence,taken along with the "al-
ternation of the family and kinship principle without decisive outside
influence",demonstrated that "other principles" influenced Russian life
from the earliest times, thereby proving that it was not an "exclusively
family, kinship mode of life."[412]

The next points which Samarin had to make focused on the role
Kavelin assigned to Christianity as a shaping force in the domestic
history of ancient Russia. To Kavelin the appearance of Christianity
was of profound importance, because it had awakened and nurtured man's
spiritual forces. When once awakened, they came to dominate the material world, and even transferred "holy significance" to man's "personality" (lichnost'). Ultimately, the Christian perception of man's
unlimited capacity for virtue, coupled with the perception that he was
"God's representative on earth," had a profound impact on society: man
began to define his relationships, "to master nature and circumstances,"
and above all to focus on enhancing his "moral and intellectual develop-

---

[410]Ibid. Kavelin's words as quoted by Samarin.

[411]Ibid.

[412]Ibid.

ment."[413] To Samarin, this analysis fell short because it attached too much "historical significance" to the "negative side" of Christianity, or in more precise terms, "to the right of personality to define itself spontaneously from within;" thereby it ignored the "positive side of Christianity, which imposed a real obligation,... a blessed burden on man in the very act of liberating him."[414] Further, Samarin argued, man was "defined" by Christianity as well as being introduced to the idea "of repudiating his personality ... and subjecting himself unconditionally to the whole."[415] Thus, he concluded:

> This self-denial of each to the advantage of all is the beginning of a free, but at the same time unconditionally obligatory union of people between themselves. This union, this commune (obshchina), consecrated by the eternal presence of the Holy Spirit, is the Church.[416]

How did Kavelin come to ignore or miss this well-known positive side of Christianity, and what was the explanation for his "one-sided point of view?" Samarin asked. He found the answer in a long passage in which Kavelin developed the argument that the German tribes and the Russo-Slav tribe developed along contrasting lines. The German tribes, because of the unsettled, warlike character of their ancient history "early developed a deep sense of personality," which became the foundation of their "family and fraternal campaign life (druzhinnyy byt)."[417] Christian-

---

[413]Ibid., p. 34.

[414]Ibid.

[415]Ibid., pp. 34-5.

[416]Ibid., p. 35.

[417]Ibid., pp. 35-37.

ity, adopted from Rome, augmented this "sense of personality." Over a period of time "the personal principle" became so highly developed among the German tribes that it penetrated every facet of the emerging state structures, finally becoming an obstacle to the upbuilding of a single unified state. Consequently the task of the German tribes was "to develop the historical personality which they brought with them into the personality of humanity."[418] The Russo-Slav path of development was quite different, Kavelin argued: "The principle of personality did not exist among them,...their family and domestic life could not develop it," and since the Russo-Slavs, who were destined to play a world role, could not play it without "the principle of personality," their main task "was to create personality."[419]

As mentioned above, Samarin found this analysis to be "one-sided." As well he found it too simplistic: it presented a narrow, limited view of Christianity; it ignored the impact of at least half the nations of Western Europe; and it reduced German history to the development "of a single principle - personality." "Surely," Samarin quipped, "this is contrary to the very simplist, elementary conceptions, drawn from the whole of French and German historical literature."[420]

As concrete evidence in support of this assessment, Samarin cited Guizot, whom he credited with first understanding the development of

---

[418]Ibid., pp. 36-7.

[419]Ibid.

[420]Ibid., p. 37.

Western Europe as "a harmonious whole." According to Samarin's exegesis
of Guizot, three principles met and found "equilibrium" in the West.
They were "the three principles: of personality, being expressed by the
German tribes; of abstract authority, transferred by inheritance from
ancient Rome; and of Christianity." Christianity, although intrinsical-
ly whole, appeared in two forms in the West "under the very categories
of authority and personality" mentioned above - in the Roman world as
Catholicism and in the Germanic world as Protestantism. The German
principle of personality gave birth to a series "of similar manifestations:"

> ...in the realm of politics - to various forms of artificial
> association, the theory of which was expounded in Rousseau's
> Social Contract; in the realm of religion - to Protestantism;
> in the realm of art - to romanticism. In these very same
> realms completely different manifestations developed from the
> Roman principle: the idea of abstract, supreme power formu-
> lated by Machiavelli, Catholicism and classicism.[421]

Samarin concluded that in the face of Guizot's powerful analysis,
Kavelin could not convince anyone that the Germanic principle had
contributed more to the formation of Western Europe than the Roman
principle had, nor could he argue that it was "the embryo of the
future."[422]

Samarin subjected this latter point to particularly close criticism.
Acknowledging the European-wide popularity of the theory, he dubbed it
"an impossible dream," as affirmed by the many doubts and reservations
expressed about it in European quarters. When examined they all "repea-

---

[421]Ibid., pp. 37-8.

[422]Ibid., p. 38.

ted a single theme: the grievous acknowledgement of the inadequacy
of human personality and the powerlessness of so-called individualism."[423] Samarin cited a number of specific examples to support his
claim that disillusionment with individualism was widespread in the
West. They included: the extensive condemnation of "society for egoism
and personal cupidity;" the demand after the July Revolution for a
"Strong, independent principle incorporating personality;" the rather
hasty repudiation of the revolutionary terms "freedom, personality and
equality," for terms like 'communion, brotherhood and others borrowed
from family and communal life;' the eulogization by George Sand, an
early devotee of unrestrained individualism, of family life and personal
self-sacrifice in her later works; and the "curiosity, sympathy and
expectation" that Mitskevich's work evoked for Slavic life in the
West.[424] On the basis of this evidence Samarin advanced the striking proposition that "if not the embryo, then the transition to the
future," lies in this line of thought emphasizing "communion," "brotherhood," "personal self-sacrifice," etc., and was the essence of Russo-
Slav tribal life as described by Kavelin himself:

> ...the Slavs were quiet, peace-loving, living in their place,
> not knowing the disastrous difference between mine and yours,
> living like members of a single family, having become con-
> scious of their relationship under the form of the family,
> having looked at slaves and foreigners not from the juridical,
> but from the family, blood point of view.[425]

---

[423]Ibid.

[424]Ibid., pp. 38-39.

[425]Ibid., p. 40.

Thus the essence of Russo-Slav life provided a vital example of the altruistic idea that contemporary Western society was looking for.

This being the case, Samarin went on to argue that the Slavonic world had nothing to gain from "inoculating itself with the one-sided Germanic principle."[426] Further, he maintained that a society based on the German principle could never be anything more than "an artificial, conditional association," because there was no logical process by which a principle which emphasized the critical importance of personality could produce the spirit of "reconciliation" essential for community life.[427] This proved, in Samarin's view, that personality was not itself an "absolute," but was limited by some other independent power; and that it was only "in combination with [this power] that personality could find justification."[428]

In Samarin's opinion Kavelin's work had a number of weaknesses which flowed inevitably from a single erroneous philosophical proposition. The weaknesses he summarized briefly. They were: "the incomplete definition of the historical influence of Christianity, the unbelievable one-sidedness of the view of the development of Western Europe, the prejudiced conclusion about the early life of the Germans and Slavs, the praise of

---

[426]Ibid.

[427]Ibid., pp. 40-41. cf. "... it is impossible to deduce from personality by means of logic an absolute norm, an unconditional obligatory law for each and everyone; consequently history will not deduce it." The Hegelian component in the latter statement brings to mind Herzen's accusation that "Hegelian formalism" was an important element in Samarin's analysis. See p. 167 above.

[428]Ibid., pp. 41-42.

Ivan the Terrible and the slander of his contemporaries...and the opin-

ion about the unconscious character of tribal life, and the consequence

flowing from it, that the Russians did not begin to live intellectually

and morally until the eighteenth century."[429] The single erroneous

philosophical proposition he identified as the idea that consciousness

is obtained by the route of personality as manifested in the experience

of the Germanic peoples. He illustrated what this meant in the follow-

ing fascinating exegesis of some passages from Kavelin:

> The principle of personality never existed among the Slavs'....
> Consequently consciousness did not exist either. Why? Because
> 'quiet and peaceloving, they...lived continuously on their
> territory. The family mode of life and relationships could not
> nurture in the Russian Slavs a sense of identity, of concen-
> tration, which forces man to draw a sharp line between himself
> and others.... Such a sense is born in primitive man by cease-
> less war, frequent clashes with foreigners, loneliness,
> danger, wandering.... The family mode of life works in the
> opposite way. Under it man dissipates somehow; his strength,
> not concentrated by anything, is deprived of resilience, of
> energy and dissolves in a sea of close, peaceful relation-
> ships. Under it, man lulls himself, abandons himself to peace
> and quiet, and slumbers in moral torpor. He is credulous,
> weak and as unconcerned as a child.' And so, there was no
> personality, that is there was no consciousness, because there
> was no collision between personalities.
>
> This picture of the childlike unconsciousness of the family
> mode of life is contrasted with the brilliant picture of the
> life of the Germans, 'their hostile collisions, wars, travels,
> inner turmoil and threshing about are signs of strength,
> seeking nourishment. All of this developed a deep sense of
> personality in them,' consequently of consciousness. 'It
> remained for them only to transform the historical personal-
> ity, which they brought with them, into human personality, but
> the Slaviano-Russians,' deprived of personality, 'had to
> create it,' i.e., at the price of eight centuries of effort
> and suffering to buy, what the Germans brought from their

---

[429]Ibid., p. 44.

forests. In other words, the task of the German was to fashion himself into a man; whereas, the task of the Russian was
first to make himself into a German, so that he could then
learn to be a man.[430]

Having completed his analysis of the theoretical part of Kavelin's

article, Samarin launched into an incisive commentary on the results

which Kavelin achieved by applying his theory to Russian history. Some

of this commentary has considerable political relevance. Certainly, the

critique of Kavelin's position on the commune (obshchina) provides a

good example of this.

Kavelin characterized the commune as a sterile, enfeebling organiza-

tion because it was not founded on "the personality principle," which he

described in one particular instance as "the primary, essential condi-

tion of all civility (grazhdanstvennost').[431] Samarin categorically

rejected this negative view of the commune, finding it to have been dis-

proven by a number of specific incidents: the calling of the princes,

the adoption of Christianity, the growing awareness of the need for

princely power, and the preservation of the "unity and wholeness of

Russia" in 1612. No, he emphatically maintained

The communal principle constitutes the foundation, the ground
of all Russian history, past, present and future; it is the
seed and root of everything great, which comes to the surface,
or is deeply buried in its fertile depths, and no undertaking,
no theory, which rejects this foundation will achieve its aim
or survive.[432]

Thus, Samarin claimed that the communal principle was a positive force,

---

[430]Ibid., p. 43.

[431]Ibid., p. 49.

[432]Ibid., pp. 50-51.

"the embryo of life and consciousness," having the ability to renew itself in different forms. Hence "it had survived in the cities and villages, and had manifested itself in physical form in the vyeches (town assemblies), and later, in the Zemskii Dumas (Land Assemblies)." Moreover, "illuminated and justified by the principle of spiritual communion which had been introduced to it by the Church, it had continuously expanded and grown stronger."[433]

Elaborating on these convictions, Samarin advanced a theory of the evolutionary development of Russian political institutions, which assigned decisive importance to the influence of Christianity and Byzantium as will be demonstrated.

At first community life in Russia was based on the blood unity found in family and tribe; then community life was based on the city, which offered a different form of organization, rooted in regional and later diocesan unity; and finally the all-Russian unified state commune (go sudarstvennaya obshchina) expressing land (zemskiv) and Church unity became the bases of community life. Although all these forms of unity differed from one another, they were in "substance" the same, being but "moments in the spread of a single communal principle, of a single demand to live together in agreement and love." This pivotal demand to live together in agreement and love had the status of "supreme law" throughout the community, and found "its justification in itself alone and not in the personal willfulness of each member." Thus communal life

---

[433]Ibid., p. 51.

"was not founded on personality...but presupposed the highest act of personal freedom and consciusness - self-denial."[434]

An important fact, in Samarin's view, about the growth of a more advanced political system in Russia was the way the communal principle continued to express itself at every stage in two mutually interdependent "manifestations." The tribal vyeche (assembly) or princely diet was parallelled by a tribal chief, the city vyeche by a prince, and the land vyeche or Duma by a Tsar. The first of these expressed "the common principle" uniting or "binding" the community together, and the second the principle of personality.[435]

As regards the relationship between the prince and the commune, Samarin maintained that the prince was both "the impartial representative of personality," and "the acknowledged defender (zastupnik) and mediator (khodatay) before the commune of every one of its members." Thus it was the prince's responsibility to satisfy "the deep, essential demand of the popular spirit...for sympathy towards the sufferer, for compassion, benevolence and free favour."[436]

In "calling" the prince to power, the commune expressed its "vital unity." Through this act each member repudiated his personal freedom and at the same time preserved his personality in the prince as "the representative of the personal principle."[437] The chroniclers,

---

[434]Ibid., p. 52.

[435]Ibid.

[436]Ibid.

[437]Ibid.

Samarin maintained, by their clear and repeated description of the
prince in these idealistic terms emphasizing unity, the preservation of
individuality in the person of the prince, and universal benevolence,
left no doubt that this was the political ideal which ancient and Kievan
Russia sought.[438]

Thus the prince was something more than a military leader, something more than an updated manifestation of the "patriarchal, pre-
varangian system of elders." Rather, he was a manifestation of the
superior Christian notion of individual responsibility, or the idea, to
express it more precisely, that a "free individual" has "moral obligations."[439]

Clearly, Samarin saw Christianity as a force, which had exerted a
powerful shaping influence on both personality and political relationships in Russia. His opinion of the importance of Byzantine influences
is not clear from the above summary; however, it was expressed at least
twice: once, when he stated that Kavelin "lost sight of the influence
of Christianity and Byzantium;" and once, when he marvelled that
Kavelin, who had said so much about "Christianity, Byzantium and the
Greek clergy," could have failed to see, "to what extent the preceding
religious unity and organization of a centralized hierarchy had helped
the realization of an unified territorial state."[440]

---

[438]Ibid., pp. 52-53.

[439]Ibid., p. 53.

[440]Ibid., p. 54.

Another comment of some political relevance focussed on the question of personality. Kavelin, obviously acting under the influence of nineteenth century individualism, argued that a sense of personality had not developed in Russia owing to the cumulative effect of the kinship principle; and that, therefore, Russia could neither expect to play a world-role nor to develop a sense of civility or civic-mindedness (grazhdanstvennost').[441] Samarin negated Kavelin's argument by demonstrating with three examples, that in fact a sense of personality was highly developed in Russia. First, there were the bogatyr's (folk heroes) created by "popular fantasy," but nevertheless reliable examples of the individual spirit thirsting for scope and expression in ancient Russia. Then, there was the prince, a "real phenomenon," acting in the military-political sphere; and finally, there was the monk, who "manifested personality in the spiritual sphere."[442]

Samarin made another point of political significance in commenting on Kavelin's claim that the relationship between prince and vyeche in Novgorod "revealed the absence of a clear conception of state life."[443]

---

[441]See pp. 170 and 175 above. Kavelin in "Otvet 'Moskvityaninu'," Sobranie sochineniy K. D. Kavelina, vol. 1 (Moscow, 1897), p. 89 wrote an interesting comment highlighting his regard for individualism: "The German druzhinas founded states and gave them their first form, which was then developed and molded; all the states or powers founded by the Slavic druzhinas, were destroyed, more from inadequate cement, than from external conditions. This very significant fact, brings us to the basic difference between the German and Slavic druzhinas: the first contained within itself the juridical element, the second did not; the first was based on the principle of personality, the second was permeated with patriarchalism which was definitely unsatisfactory for the development of the individual and consequently for a just community (pravil'noe obshchezhitie)."

[442]Sochineniya, I, 56.

[443]Ibid.

Citing the dissertation of S. M. Solov'ev, Samarin maintained that
Novgorodians strove to achieve a condition of "dual power," or a balance
of power between prince and vyeche Acknowledging that this political
ideal was seldom realized, he claimed that those "rare moments" "represented the apogee of Novgorodian life." Pointing out that the prince's
role was defined on the negative side by statements prohibiting certain
action in Novgorod's charters, and on the positive side by tradition, he
stressed that the essential "elements of Russia's future state structure, commune (mir) and personality, existed in Novgorod, and all of
Novgorod's history expressed the striving for their agreement." To the
obvious question, why did Novgorod fail to build up "a sound (pravil'-
noe) form of state," he answered: Novgorod was only a part of Russia,
and "the state could only appear as a juridical expression of the unity
of the whole land."444

Another political point, notable especially for its democratic
idealism, if not for its naivete, was made by Samarin in answer to
Kavelin's professed confusion about the way in which decisions were
reached by the vyeches. To Samarin, formal voting procedures involving
the recording of votes and resolutions taken by majority were unacceptable, because they "marked the division of society into a majority and a
decay of the communal principle," which was best expressed as "the
internal agreement and vital unity" of an unanimous decision. In this
context, Samarin claimed that the task of the vyeche which expressed the

---

444Ibid., pp. 56-7.

communal principle, was to preserve unity by reconciling contradictions by means of the principle of unanimity; and neither the commune, nor Russian history could be understood unless this point was grasped.[445]

Finally, Samarin was firmly convinced that moral imperatives were binding for all, including those who exercise political power. Ivan IV, for instance, could not be forgiven the ruthlessness and cruelty of his Oprichnina system, even if, as Kavelin seemed to argue, they were employed in the interest of desirable reforms because to paraphrase Samarin, there are no circumstances under which even the genius leader can employ monstrous methods against "the depravity" of his compatriots without having to bear the full weight of opprobrium under "the obligatory moral law."[446] Applying this maxim to the question of the leaders' role in implementing reforms, he maintained that the results were better when "healthy sentiments" (zdravoe chuvstvo) were determinative in changing the government.[447]

Being satisfied at this point that he had conclusively demonstrated the one-sidedness of Kavelin's argument, and so refuted his interpretation of the juridical life of ancient Russia, Samarin ended his critique by setting out the theses of his own position for comparison. Although, as he freely acknowledged, half of them were hypotheses only, they were succinctly stated and put Samarin's ideology in a clearer light. They are stated here in full because of their value:

---

[445]Ibid., p. 57.

[446]Ibid., p. 61.

[447]Ibid., p. 62.

1) That the development of the German principle, left to itself alone, has neither an end, nor an exit; that it is logically impossible to arrive at the idea of man, that is to the principle of the absolute union and subordination of individuals under a supreme law, by means of the exhaustion of the historical appearance of personality; therefore the analytical process will never become a synthetic process by itself;

2) That this principle (the idea of man, or more precisely the idea of people) did not appear as the natural fruit of the development of personality, but as a direct reaction to it and penetrated into the consciousness of the progressive thinkers of Western Europe from the sphere of religion;

3) That the Western World now expresses a demand for the organic reconciliation of the principle of personality with the principle of an objective and universally obligatory norm - a demand of the commune;

4) That this demand coincides with our substance; that in justification of the formula we bring byt (mode of life), and in this is the point of contact between our history and the West's;

5) That the communal mode of life of the Slavs was not based on the absence of personality, but on the free and conscious rejection of its sovereignty;

6) That Christianity introduced consciousness and freedom into the national mode of life of the Slavs; that the Slavic commune, so to speak, having dissolved, took into itself the principle of spiritual communion and became, as it were, the worldly, historical side of the Church;

7) That the problem of our domestic history is defined as the elucidation of the national communal principle by the communal Church;

8) That the aim of our external history has been to defend and to save the political independence of that principle for Russia, as well as for the Slavonic tribes, by the creation of a strong form of state, which neither exhausted nor contradicted the communal principle.[448]

---

[448]Ibid., pp. 63-65. These are the theses about which Khomiakov commented as follows: "...in them for the first time definite Slavophil theses have been set out and consequently the beginning to a positive science has been laid, and we have emerged from that negative tendency, in which the confusion of our readers has reproached us." "Pis'ma Khomiakova," p. 327.

Kavelin's opinion of Samarin's critique merits special attention. As one who applied the scientific method in his research, and who believed in the progressive evolutionary development of ideas and institutions, he found Samarin's analysis, rooted as it was in the application of a priori principles, quite unacceptable. Very properly, he was impressed by the "cleverness of Samarin's objections," as well as by the "consistency of his point of view;" however, confirming the above statement, he found his theories because they were based on ideals and not on careful observation of the real world, to be "foggy-mystical theories, beautiful to contemplate, but dead anywhere in reality."[449]

Nikitenko's article, "O sovremennom naprevlenii Russkoy literatury" (On the contemporary direction of Russian literature), provoked much less critical fervour in Samarin than Kavelin's article did. So much less, as a matter of fact, that Khomiakov reproached him for showing "excessive respect to an opponent."[450] Although the reason for Samarin's softness is not clear, it is possible that he felt some sympathy for Nikitenko as a man without "a systematic point of view" and "the ability to influence others."[451] Perhaps on the other hand it was simply that Nikitenko's views were inconsequential, never rising above the level of "a casual conversation between intelligent people," and so never presenting enough substance to challenge.[452] Nevertheless,

---

[449]Kavelin, "Otvet 'Moskvityaninu'" pp. 67-68, and 94.

[450]"Pis'ma Khomiakova," p. 327.

[451]Sochineniya, I, 65.

[452]Ibid., p. 66.

for whatever reason, Samarin's critique of Nikitenko's article contains
little or nothing of interest to the student of his political philosophy. His critique of Belinsky's article "Vzglayad na Russkuyu
literaturu 1846 goda" (A view of Russian literature for 1846) was a
different matter, however, as the following summary will prove.

As a critic Belinsky had deficiencies which Samarin could not
ignore. To begin with he rarely, if ever, appeared as his true self and
possessed only in the most marginal way the gift of "free inspiration."
While he possessed a good aesthetic sense as demonstrated in previous
work he failed to exploit it effectively; but the great shame, as far as
Samarin was concerned, was that Belinsky was perpetually under the
influence of someone else.[453] This was his norm because he was very
receptive to new ideas and 'novelties" without, however, having the
capacity to understand them in other than a superficial way. Because
ideas were never "assimilated deeply...he was not able to think independently." "In this," explained Samarin, one finds the reason for the
"extraordinary ease with which he changes his point of view...." It also
provided the clue to his exclusiveness and lack of patience towards
contrary opinions...." Finally Belinsky's receptiveness to new ideas

---

[453]D. S. Mirsky states that Belinsky's"education was acquired by
omnivorous reading and personal contact with fellow students....For his
philosophical information (the great thing in the Moscow circles of the
time) he depended on his better educated friends.... His articles were
inspired with a youthful irreverence for all that was old and respected
in Russian letters, and an equally youthful enthusiasm for the new ideas
of idealism and for the creative forces of the young generation. D. S.
Mirsky, A History of Russian Literature, ed. F. J. Whitfield (New York:
Alfred A. Knopf, 1958), p. 165.

explained his "extraordinary fecundity," for the work of others provided him with a ready "store" of "convictions."[454]

Having offered this assessment of the famous critic, Samarin then proceeded to an analysis of Belinsky's contribution to the first issue of Sovremennik.[455] Samarin concentrated his attention on two aspects of Belinsky's work - his "praise" of the "natural school" of literature, and his "characterization" of the "slavophils" or "old believers."[456]

An indirect method of criticism was used to deal with Belinsky's praise of the "natural school" and left the reader to apply his own judgement. The briefest summarization will suffice at this point for Samarin was much more concerned to right the injustices perpetrated against the slavophils in Belinsky's "characterization" of them.

In essence Samarin said, that "naturalism" traced its origins to Gogol "with whom it had only its content in common;" and to the "influence of the latest French literature." Because it was based on "imitation" it lacked "reality" and "independence." As a result it could be expected to disappear early, and Belinsky its supporter could be expected, as quickly, to reverse himself ridiculing and mocking it. "Naturalism," concludes Samarin, "...has not grown on our soil and will not fructify it. The living stream of our development flows by to the

---

[454]Sochineniya, I, 80-81.

[455]See B. G. Belinsky, Selected Philosophical Works (Moscow: Foreign Languages Publishing House, 1948), pp. 347-394.

[456]Sochineniya I. 81-82.

side...[Naturalism] is only reflected on its surface. ...not a single first-class talent has committed himself to naturalism."[457]

The Slavophil polemicist, Samarin, concentrated his heaviest fire on Belinsky's "characterization" zeroing in point by point. He first quoted Belinsky directly and then analysed the contents of the quotation. This method was uniformly applied. Samarin began by citing Belinsky as follows: "It is well known, that in the eyes of Karamzin, Ivan III was higher than Peter the Great, and Pre-Petrine Rus' was better than modern Russia. Here is the source of Slavophilism."[458] With a few well-chosen quotations from Karamzin, Samarin demonstrated that it is most unlikely that the great historian ever said any such thing. Noting "differences in the aims and methods" of the two rulers he did not express an unequivocal "preference" for Ivan.[459] In any case, Samarin went on to demonstrate that there was nothing in Karamzin "to serve as the source of any kind of system,"[460] least of all Slavophilism. Samarin's judgement seemed clear - Belinsky lacked scholarship as well as an adequate knowledge of his sources.

This conclusion was developed further when Belinsky's second attribution to Karamzin - the idea that "pre-Petrine Rus' was better than modern Russia" was examined. "Everyone," said Samarin, "who had read

---

[457]Ibid., p. 94. D. S. Mirsky reports that the "First great success of the new school was Dostoyevsky's maiden novel, Poor Folk" published in January 1846. Mirsky, Russian Literature, p. 173.

[458]Ibid., p. 94.

[459]Ibid., p. 95.

[460]Ibid., p. 96.

A fragment on ancient and modern Russia, knows that Karamzin saw progressive movement in Russian history; that in the approach of ancient
Russia to Europe and in the borrowing from her of military regulations,
of a diplomatic system, of a form of training or education, of social
manners - he saw a triumph of evident advantage and superiority over
ancient custom."[461] Then to clinch the argument Karamzin is quoted
directly, where he says, "Comparing all the periods of Russia known to
us, there is scarcely anyone among us who will not say that Catherine's
time was one of the happiest for Russia, and scarcely anyone among us
would not like to have lived then."[462] Thus Belinsky misinterpreted
Karamzin ,attributing imagined ideas to him; and further compounded his
error by tracing the origins of Slavophilism to him.

Samarin continued his analysis with a look at Belinsky's statements:
(1) that "the positive side of [slavophil] doctrines consists of some
sort of foggy, mystical presentiments of a victory of the East over the
West," which is patently false; and (2) that "the negative side of
Slavophil teaching merits much more attention," because it is critical
of "Russian Europeanism."[463] Although Belinsky chose to let the
positive side of Slavophilism pass unexamined, Samarin took the liberty
of pointing out that the words "East" and "West" should be understood to
mean "Slavonic-Orthodox" (definitely not Oriental) and "Romano-Germanic"

---

[461]Ibid., p. 96.

[462]Ibid., p. 97

[463]Ibid.

or "Catholic-Protestant,"[464] respectively. Further, he stressed that
the traditional and continuing West European fear of "Russia" and "the
Slavic tribes" gave sufficient credibility to Slavophil "presentiments
of a victory, of Eastern principles over western."[465] (Note the
careful insertion of the word principles giving a rather different
concept of victory than that suggested in the Belinsky quotation above).

As Belinsky chose to limit himself to a discussion of the "negative
side" of Slavophilism, Samarin limited himself similarly, at no time
attempting a systematic enumeration of Slavophil ideas. To a charge
that the Slavophils did not understand the West, he replied that "the
non-Slavophils [Belinsky's term] do not understand Russia, because they
measure it with a Western measure."[466] To a charge that having
diagnosed the impact of "Russian Europeanism" correctly[467] the
Slavophils failed "to examine its causes" with a view to finding a
solution, he answered that the charge was "unjust" because the recommended investigation was so large that it would consume the energies of
"more than one generation."[468] Then a more telling point was made.
Belinsky refuted "absurd ideas attached to the Slavophils"[469] [Russia

[464]Ibid.

[465]Ibid.

[466]Ibid., p. 98.

[467]Belinsky saw as correct the Slavophil contention that Russian
Europeanism stemming from the reforms of Peter had produced a duality
and a weakening of Russian nationality and character. See Belinsky,
Selected Philosophical Works, p. 359.

[468]Sochineniya, I, p. 98.

[469]Ibid., p. 99.

must go back to the social arrangements of Great Novgorod or Alexis Romanov][470] with the argument that "Russia has exhausted, outlived the epoc of [Peter's] reform...and the time has come for Russia to develop independently, from its very own self,"[471] an idea which was first advanced by the Slavophils. Again Samarin had caught Belinsky in a serious misrepresentation of his opponents.

Samarin discharged volley after volley at Belinsky's misrepresentations. The principal objective of any debate was the "development of conscious conviction," Samarin believed. But this could only be achieved under conditions of "mutual conscientiousness," yet Belinsky "set forth" and "repudiated" Slavophil ideas without due attention. "You refute us, very good; but why after that stuff up your ears?" How could he say that the Slavophils wanted to re-establish the social customs of Alexis Romanov, when every Slavophil had stated that this was an era of "corruption?" How could he accuse his opponents of believing that Peter's reforms had destroyed Russian nationality, when they had said that the "loss of nationality" was only "temporary" and "conditional." Finally Samarin asked, "Whoever thought to recognize the appearance of Peter the Great, his reforms and the following events to 1812 as accidental? Who has not recognized them as historically necessary?"[472]

[470]Belinsky, Selected Philosophical Works, p. 360.
[471]Sochinenya, I, p. 99.
[472]Ibid., pp. 99-100.

As illustrated above, Samarin was appalled by Belinsky's method of disputation, which was to attribute wrong ideas to his opponents and then "to refute them" with their own ideas. A few such ideas are cited from Belinsky:

It is time for us to stop seeming and to begin being; time we ...[stopped] taking European forms and externals for European-ism. ...it is time for us...to begin to love, respect and aspire to [what is European] only because it is human, and on this basis to reject anything which is not human.... We have received European enlightenment...as the fruit and experience of another more learned and brilliant life...to become acquainted with these new discoveries is...for Russia...a necessity; but to use one or another experience...is left to our choice.[473]

The inconsistencies and the faulty logic of Belinsky's statements were also a cause of concern to Samarin. How could it be argued at one point, Samarin asked, citing Belinsky, that "it is time for Russia to develop independently, from its very own self," and at another "we have a national life, we are ordained to give our message, our thought to the world; but about what message, what thought it is too early for us to be concerned:" when realization of what one's message and thought is pre-cedes any work of independent development?[474]

Referring to an earlier passage where Belinsky emphasizes the need to borrow only what is human, Samarin proceeded to point out how un-realistic it was to think that "the human" and "the national" could be easily separated. They bear no "labels" to assist selection, therefore recourse must be made to "internal signs," that is, one must "define the

---

[473]Ibid., pp. 101-102.

[474]Ibid., p. 102.

truth and virtue of every idea and institution."[475] Since Belinsky
made no attempt to do this he set an impossible task for his followers.
"Instead of playing with the words national and human, it would be
better to indicate the norm or sign of what is human, compile a code of
human charactistics...until that is done you have presented us with a
conditional expression under which anything desirable can be understood."[476]

The line of argument presented at this point is worth pursuing for
it reveals at least three interesting ideas of Samarin. One of these is
that "essential human principles" cannot be separated, for "as an expression of human reality, they must constitute a single whole permeated by
a single spirit." Another is that formulating these basic principles
must be followed by applying them to every "sphere of life," an arduous
and "continuing task for all ages." Still,a third is that this line of
reasoning made understandable the Slavophils' respect for "old Russia,
not because it was old or because it was ours, but because we saw in
it an expression of those principles which we considered human or
true."[477]

As much as anything Samarin was disturbed by the superficiality
of Belinsky's treatment of Slavophilism, never coming to grips with
"basic questions" and always expounding Slavophil ideas "after his own

---

[475]Ibid., p. 103.

[476]Ibid., p. 104.

[477]Ibid., p. 104.

fashion."[478] This is revealed in what has gone before; it is also revealed in Samarin's comments on the statement that Slavophils for reasons of nationality rush to the defense of ancient customs and practices like "the chimneyless and dirty peasant hut, radishes and kvas, and even raw brandy."[479] "The Slavophils," Samarin objected, "respect the house, in which the Russian peasant lives, no matter what it is like, and the food, obtained by his work, no matter what it is... [however] they no less than others sense the discomfort of a chimneyless hut, of the deprivation and temptations, to which the peasant is subjected."[480] Where they differed was in their conviction that "irony and mockery" were hardly likely to produce an improvement.[481] It is also revealed when he takes Belinsky to task for mocking the Slavophils because "they pointed to humility as an expression of Russian nationality, "even going so far as to equate it with national character.[482] In essence Samarin saw no reason why "an essential human characteristic" like "humility" could not be an expression of Russian "national character," just as "individuality" another "essential human characteristic" was an expression of German national character.[483]

---

[478]Ibid.

[479]Ibid.

[480]Ibid., pp. 104-5.

[481]Ibid., p. 105.

[482]Ibid., p. 105.

[483]Ibid., pp. 105-6.

Belinsky's objection to recognizing love as a principle of Russian life provides Samarin with the last question on which to test his debating skill. In accord with his general method he began by citing his opponent:

> The Slavophils explain love as a national principle belonging exclusively to the Slavic tribes.... We on the contrary think that love is a property of human nature in general and cannot be the exclusive property of a single people any more than breathing, vision, hunger, thirst, mind or speech.... The mistake here is that the relative has been taken for the absolute.[484]

Samarin took as his jump-off point the last statement:

> The mistake is that you...have inserted a single superfluous word: exclusive...it perverts the opinion to which you are objecting. Love is a general human characteristic, accessible to every individual, but which can be much more developed in one tribe than another...what is much more important, one tribe can believe firmly in the creative force of love and strive to found a social order on it; another tribe can have no faith in it at all, and...found its well-being on law and compulsion. Whether the Russian people are distinguished by the predominance of love and faith in it is another question. The critic has not proven the opposite, because the aspiration of a people is not proven in ten lines, by examples, snatched from its history. From the fact that a law has been broken, it does not follow, that it is not recognized as obligatory.[485]

In this manner Samarin sought to prove "that any people can or cannot have any national characteristic."[486]

The article was concluded by an orderly summarization of all that Belinsky had said about the Slavophils. Listed first were all the

---

[484]Ibid., p. 106.

[485]Ibid.

[486]Ibid., p. 107.

"absurd" ideas which had been "arbitrarily ascribed" to them:

> The reforms of Peter destroyed in Russia nationality and every breath of life.
>
> Russia for its salvation must turn to the customs of the epoch of Alexis Romanov or Novgorod.
>
> The characteristic of humility (smirenie) is a national Russian principle.
>
> Love is a national principle, belonging exclusively to the Slavic tribes.[487]

Listed second were ideas which Samarin described as "completely just." They were the Slavophil ideas which Belinsky used in his refutations. Some of them were ideas "first advanced" by the Slavophils and others of them were self-evident:

> Russia has overcome the epoch of [Peter's] reform, and the time has arrived for her to develop independently, out of herself. It is impossible to pass, to jump over the epoch of reform. The reform of Peter could not be accidental. It is time for us to stop seeming and to begin being; It is time to respect and to love only the human and to reject everything which is not human be it European or Asiatic.
>
> A strong political and state organization is the guarantee of the peoples' internal strength.
>
> Humility (smirenie) and love are the essential property of human nature in general.[488]

As characterized in this Belinsky was a critic with a good aesthetic sense, who was prolific and articulate, but dependent on others for his ideas. This latter characteristic made him changeable and impatient towards his opponents. As a critic of the Slavophils he was shown to be

---

[487]Ibid.

[488]Ibid., pp. 107-8. The italics are Samarin's.

arbitrary and uninformed. But that is not all; he was also shown to be unscrupulous, unrealistic, inconsistent, if not illogical and superficial. That, in substance, was Samarin's criticism of Belinsky. Whether or not his criticism can be allowed to go unchallenged, even when the internal evidence seems so conclusive, is hardly an issue in this case, because it contributes so much to an understanding of his political philosophy.[489]

The other major work from this period Pis'ma iz Rigi (Letters from Riga) was written in May-June 1848.[490] It was written after Samarin had worked as an official on two special committees struck by the Department of External Affairs to draft a peasant reform for Livlandia (Latvia) and Estlandia (Estonia).[491] Samarin's specific assignment was to help Ya. V. Khanykov, the executive director (proizvoditel') of this important project.[492]. In this capacity, Samarin compiled Istoricheskiy ocherk unichtozheniya krepostnogo sostoyaniya v Liflandii (An Historical Outline of the Abolition of Serfdom in Livlandia), and wrote

---

[489]In support of Samarin's general criticism of Belinsky, it seems worth noting once again that Mirsky stated that Belinsky was not a systematic scholar, and was very dependent on "his better-educated friends for his philosophical ideas." Mirsky, Russian Literature, p.165. Also, when the author presented Samarin's criticism of Belinsky to a session of the Canadian Association of Slavists (June 15, 1968) the discussant, Professor F. D. Walker of the University of Windsor, reported that Professor D. Chizhevsky had found Belinsky to be "ignorant, narrow, intolerant and of bad judgement."

[490]See above, p. 148.

[491]Sochineniya, VII, IV.

[492]Ibid., p. XVIII.

a detailed comparative outline of the peasant statutes introduced in
Livlandia during the reforms of 1804, 1809, 1819 and 1843. Besides this
he helped to draft detailed protocols for the committees and translated
many working documents from German into Russian and vice versa for the
committee members.[493] Subsequently, actually living in Riga, while
working under Khanykov on a commission established to draft a reform of
the civic organization of that city, he wrote Istoriya Rigi (A History
of Riga), a major work which he himself described as "a scholarly
investigation, rather than a compilation of ministerial notes."[494]
Pis'ma iz Rigi, a passionate denunciation of Russian government policy
in the Baltic provinces, burst forth under the impact of these experiences.

However, the passion of Pis'ma iz Rigi could hardly have been anti-
cipated by those familiar with Samarin's early enthusiasm for his Baltic
assignment. In early 1846, he was clearly ripe for just that kind of
work.[495] For instance, in telling Khomiakov (1 January 1846) about
his projected reform activities, he said that "it was good work, such
that a person could take part in it without hesitation, without the
slightest misgiving."[496] That the reform aspect made the work

---

[493]Ibid., p. XX.

[494]Ibid., p. XXXIV. In effect, Samarin worked primarily as an
historian while in Riga. Glynn Barratt, writing about Samarin's later
work Okrainy Rossii (Russia's Borderlands), observed that it was the
work of "a serious historian." Glynn Barratt, The Rebel on the Bridge
(London: Paul Elek, 1975), p. 227.

[495]See pp. 157-159 above.

[496]Sochineniya, XII, 415.

appealing to him is clear from his setting up of the problem: "to eman-
cipate the lower classes, or better, all classes (excluding the highest
class), from the exclusive domination of the aristocratic class," and
also, just as important, "to free the people from the slavery, which had
been concealed by legalisms, and to give them (1) inalienable property,
(2) the right to move to neighbouring provinces under certain conditions, (3) the right to obtain land and (4) for Russians, the right to
settle under certain conditions on the estates of Latvian and Estonian
landlords."[497] Samarin also had some other things to say which con-
firms this thesis, while at the same time elucidating his political
philosophy. In another letter to Khomiakov (February-March, 1846), he
lamented the fact that "good initiatives" (dobryya nachala) had to be
defended against "revilers" and "perverters," and that he was being
widely condemned for his decision to participate in the Baltic reform
drafting programme. Then, undeterred by this condemnation, he observed:

> My participation in this work, has more importance than I my-
> self assumed. Everyone knows that I am acting from conviction,
> consequently deep down I agree with the government's aim, if
> not its separate measures. ...Finally, I am encouraged about
> the success of this enterprise now begun, by a (perhaps)
> superstitious premonition, that the Russian government, in
> spite of all its inadequacies, has been stamped by some
> character indelebilis, which as the theologians say, it cannot
> fully lose; there is some kind of rational power, which is not
> manifested in anything in particular, but which, being depri-
> ved of representatives and organs, in any case, in spite of
> everything, determines a known form of action, a known posi-
> tion of the government. So it has been in the past, so, I
> think, it will be in the present circumstance.[498]

---

[497]Ibid., pp. 414-15.

[498]Ibid., p. 420.

In spite of his optimism, however, Samarin's hopes were dashed, partly by the crass unprincipled manipulation of politics,[499] but especially by the harsh confrontation between the policies and actions of the Russian government and Baltic German nationalism. The passion of Pis'ma iz Rigi expresses his anger and frustration, as the following quotation from a letter to Konstantin Aksakov (April, 1848) attests:

> The systematic repression of the Russians by the Germans, the hourly insult to Russian nationality in the face of its relatively small number of representatives stirs my blood, and I work with the sole aim of bringing this fact to everyone's attention.[500]

However, Samarin's anger is not apparent in the first lines of Pis'-ma where he states his objective - to inform by bringing several new

---

[499]Commenting on the political process to A.O. Smirnova (22 January 1848) Samarin said: "I can't describe what revulsion this kind of public work (deyatel'nost') has evoked in me. The unscrupulous reservations, the calculated distribution of unrealizable promises or future threats, the conscious injustices by way of example, finally, the view of things which completely sets aside the conception of true and false, right and wrong, the view of the soul-less administrator, who sees in the world only means and obstacles to the accomplishment of somebody else's idea...all this is not personal vice or inadequacy, but the unavoidable condition of public work. This is what is so terrible! It is terrible that the best principles triumph by these means, that a sacred work will not be accomplished without these machines (stanok). At least, in our time...only the action of one person on another, words to the soul can be pure and kind-hearted." Ibid., p. 363.

[500]Ibid., p. 200. In a letter to Pogodin (April, 1848), Samarin wrote: "I am also preparing several letters about the Baltic region which I will send to Khomiakov in order that he can put them into circulation. You would not believe how angry I have become from all I have seen and heard." Ibid., p. 258. In another letter to Pogodin he said, "Everything here breathes hatred for us, the hatred of the weak for the strong, of the beneficiary for the benefactor...The whole environment is such that every minute you recognize yourself as a Russian, and as a Russian, you take offence. My work is purely literary, but even here it takes a terrible effort to preserve in oneself scientific objectivity and not to allow bilious impulses." Ibid., pp. 255-6.

facts to light and to publicize the Slavophil point of view. His anger
is even less apparent because he stresses the importance of cool objectivity and dispassionate analysis.[501] As was so characteristic of
him, he rooted his analysis of the Baltic situation in a study of the
region's history, and documented his conclusions with numerous examples.

Thus he began by noting that although Russia seemed destined to
occupy and to develop the Baltic region in the twelfth century, it was
conquered by the Germans, who established a feudal regime based on
feudal service there. This latter fact was of more than passing
interest to Samarin because it explained the difference between "the
slavery," which existed in the Baltic region until the early nineteenth
century, and Russian serfdom. There "the farmer, his house, his wife
and his land" were taken by conquest, whereas in Russia the land was
given to the landlord (pomeshchik) as a reward for state service
(Kormlenie). Thus in Russia the land belonged to the peasant farmer and
his rights to it collided with those of the landlord, which "were conditioned by service and strengthened by government force." Although the
peasant lost his freedom out of this confrontation he refused to be
separated from the land,[502] and so escaped the fate of his Baltic
counterparts.

The German conquest of the Baltic region with its inevitable con-
comitants of force, violence and suppression of the native inhabitants,

---

[501]Sochineniya, VII, 3.

[502]Ibid., pp. 4-6.

produced perhaps a deeper more unbridgeable gulf of hatred between the natives and their conquerors than anywhere else in the world. As a result, the natives were never able to form "a vital union of all classes in a free communion," that is, "give political definition to their national life or form an independent state."[503] This outcome, Samarin maintained, was the principal result of the history of the region, and was a "moral evil" perpetuated to the present and even worsened by the fact that the present German rulers were oblivious to the evil which their ancestors had wrought.[504]

As for the Germans, Samarin concluded, that they also were disunited, in spite of their "common origin, faith, language and...interests." There was an essential difference, however, for they were disunited as a result of class antagonisms. Nevertheless the end result was the same for they failed to adopt the idea of a "supreme power" responsible for providing "administrative unity, the social well-being of all, and the rule of law." Thus their political development had never grown beyond the stage of "medieval anarchy."[505]

Therefore, no absolute political authority having local origins ever appeared in the Baltic region, and this explained why in times of crises the Baltic Germans (ostzeytsy) failed to reach beyond considerations of "self-preservation and class interest" - to the idea of "self-sacrifice"

---

[503]Ibid., pp. 6-8.

[504]Ibid., p. 8.

[505]Ibid., p.9.

on behalf of the larger community or "fatherland."[506] Thus, unable
to develop a unified political state from its own resources the region
fell easy victim to outside control towards the end of the sixteenth
century.[507]

From this time forward, cut off from Germany and refusing to
reconcile herself to either Polish or Swedish control, the Baltic region
was doomed to stagnation. Henceforth the actions of the Baltic classes
became entirely negative. The hallmark of this period of the history of
that area was "continuous opposition to the spirit of the times, stubborn rejection of historical demands in the name of an obsolete past,
and a battle of provincialism and the class principle of separation with
state and national principles."[508]

The reasons which Samarin advanced to explain the failure of Poland
and Sweden to take over the Baltic lands merit attention, especially as
they contrast so strikingly with the reasons which he advanced for Russia's later successful conquest of the region. Beginning with the summary statement that Poland and Sweden had failed because they lacked
both "calling" (prizvanie) and "sufficient power," he made the following
points by way of explication. Firstly, neither power had a legal historical claim to the area (the grounds for this conclusion will become
clear later). Secondly, both powers scorned the local inhabitants and

---

[506]Ibid., p. 10.

[507]Ibid., p. 11.

[508]Ibid., p. 12.

introduced their own subjects to the area as administrators and settlers. Thirdly, Poland tried to restore the Catholic Church in the
area. Fourthly, Sweden plundered the region for her own purposes. And
fifthly, both powers pursued their own interests irrespective of local
needs and so failed to advance a theory of state to which the local
inhabitants could rally.[509] On the positive side, Samarin noted,
that Poland and Sweden had undertaken several advantageous measures:
they had taken the very difficult first steps towards the organization
of a unified state structure, they had reduced the level of class
anarchy by publishing "various statutes and charters," and they "had
always been true to their appointment - to be the defenders of the
common people."[510]

As stated above, Samarin's conclusions about Russia's role and
position in the Baltic region were quite different: "the union of the
Baltic provinces to Russia was...an historically-necessary event" made
inevitable "by the past fate of both lands and by their geographical
positions."[511] On historical grounds he argued that Russia's claim
rested on the fact of "first occupation." On economic grounds he argued
that she was the source of the region's wealth, because she provided its
"objects of trade." On geopolitical grounds he argued that the Baltic
littoral was Russia's "natural frontier," and that its occupation by

---

[509]Ibid., p. 16.

[510]Ibid., pp. 16-17.

[511]Ibid., p. 18.

Russia was as inevitable, therefore, "as the manifestation of an historical law." Moreover, he concluded, the German colony, by deliberately
hindering Russian attempts "to borrow the fruits of Western enlightenment," by preventing the free movement of "scientists, artists and
craftsmen" into Russia from the fourteenth century onwards, created a
situation which Russia could legitimately try to end.[512]

However, if Russia had clearly defensible "historical and natural
rights" to the Baltic region, she had, by that very fact, obligations to
it, which neither Poland nor Sweden had. Those obligations were to
embrace it as an integral part of Russia, "once lost, but now restored
to her," and accept its people into the Russian state as full and equal
partners. This "historically-predestined" development was accomplished
by Peter, even to the extent of granting all the rights requested by the
inhabitants of the region, and "to inviting them to participate in the
political and social life [of Russia]." Thus Russia, unlike Poland and
Sweden, was "more than just" in her treatment of the Baltic Germans.
"But were they just in their relationship to Russia?"[513] Samarin
thought not. He found the proof of this latter assertion in the history
of "the relationship of the Baltic German classes to the state," on the
one hand, and in the history of "their mutual relationships," on the
other.[514]

---

[512]Ibid. These ideas are developed at somewhat greater length
in Istoriya Rigi, VII, 252-253.

[513]Ibid., pp. 18-19.

[514]Ibid., p. 20.

On "the relationship of the Baltic German classes to the state,"
Samarin found that the classes, although ready enough to accept the pro-
tection of the state, systematically opposed its objectives and policies. To do so they used many different devices: they tried to act
independently of the state's authority; they worked to prevent it from
interfering in regional affairs; they imposed a ban on all local
initiatives; they restricted financial arrangements with the state, and
they boycotted foreign officials and settlers in the region.[515]

The means used to realize these objectives by the local inhabitants,
and by the Germans in particular, were the privileges, which had been
either granted or ratified by successive governments. But what were
these privileges? In Samarin's broad definition they included "any
agreement, regulation, decree, legal decision, in general, all written
acts, serving to define the juridical position of a province, city,
class or person, supplemented necessarily by the addition of custom or
antiquity."[516]

By converting these privileges into a legal weapon, and by reinforcing them with the liberal use of bribes, the Baltic Germans (Ostzeytsy)
were able to obstruct the will of their governments, and even to forestall normal political progress. The measure of their success in
Samarin's opinion was the fact that the Baltic region was still at
that very time (1848) a medieval society.[517]

---

[515]Ibid., p. 21.

[516]Ibid., p. 23.

[517]Ibid., pp. 22, and 26.

Samarin demonstrated his second point that "the history of mutual relationships of the classes" proved that the Ostzeytsy were not just in their relationship to Russia by demonstrating that "internecine quarrelling" and persistent opposition to the relocation of foreign elements in the region were constant features of Baltic life.[518]

Thus Samarin concluded:

The Baltic region opposed the state principle in the name of its political independence; but is it not evident that carrying in itself the seeds of discord and without a single principle of reconciliation, it would have become the sacrifice of internecine war, if the ruling power had turned away from it and left it on its own for a moment?

The region fenced itself off from foreigners in the name of German nationality; but what right has a handful of settlers to call itself a nation, when it has pressed a foreign people under foot, and at the same time bowed its head before another people, which has spread its dominion to it? Can any stump, without roots and a top, justly assume the status of a nation? We will reach the point where the German club in Moscow speaks of its nationality.

Thus, neither of the principles, upon which the Baltic region founded its pretentions, contained in them anything positive, any embryo, any future.[519]

What Samarin found among the Baltic Germans was "a hostile and systematic" will to gain their independence from Russia.[520] He had no sympathy for their will to independence, because "the Baltic region belonged to Russia."[521] But instead of accepting this fact and re-

---

[518]Ibid., pp. 27-29.

[519]Ibid., pp. 30-31.

[520]Ibid., p. 37.

[521]Ibid., p. 32.

cognizing Russia as their native country they (Ostzeytsy) blindly opposed fate and the will of history. And sadly, they made this error even though they had no country in the true sense, being inspired only by an "abstract," and therefore, "fruitless and impractical" vision of the German world; and even though the Russians had taken them in without reservation or restraint as full and equal partners.[522]

Samarin recognized that there was no easy answer to this "strange phenomenon." Nevertheless, he sought one and found it in historical and psychological factors. The root cause was "discontent" stemming from the failure of the "descendants of the Livonian knights" to live up to the glories and promise of their past. Thus, conscious of their failure and lacking the realism and strength of character "to submit to a just fate," they found escape "in a sense of tribal pride, unjustified boast-fulness, and laughable contempt for Russia and every Russian."[523]

Yet the Ostzeytsy themselves were well aware that "their archaic middle age institutions, privileges and class interests," were too weak to survive without Russian help, or expressed in a more general way, that "their only hope [for survival] lay in the well-meaning unconcern and trustfulness of [the Russian] government."[524]

Samarin felt that the Ostzeytsy attitude was a reprehensible betrayal

---

[522]Ibid., pp. 32-33.

[523]Ibid., p. 37.

[524]Ibid., p. 37.

[525]Ibid., p. 41.

of Russia;[526] however, he also felt that it gave rise to a bad political theory, especially when equated to the needs of a viable state.
He felt that the Ostzeytsy expressed the theory most clearly in the
words: "We are subjects of the Russian Emperor, but we don't want to be
confused with Russia."[527] Samarin interpreted this to mean: "We
will do business exclusively with the government, but we don't want to
do business with Russia." In Samarin's opinion the absence of a strong
commitment to country, so apparent in this statement, pinpointed the
deficiency of the theory, for it was commitment to country which made
unselfish service possible. He exemplified the kind of commitment which
he meant by citing the love which Russians bore for their "best possessions - people, language and Orthodoxy," for these provided the real
strength of the Russian government and the raison de'être of the Tsar,
who was "the first man of the Russian land and the first son of the
Orthodox Church."[528]

Because, Samarin continued, "the idea of service and its meaning is
derived from the idea of the relationship of private individuals to the
supreme power," the Russians with their high commitment to country
served as a matter of duty. However the Ostzeytsy, who had no real
native land and refused to make such a commitment to Russia, served as a
matter of class interest.[529] And so, the Ostzeytsy "systematically

---

[526]Ibid., p. 43.
[527]Ibid., pp. 41-42.
[528]Ibid., p. 42.
[529]Ibid., pp. 42-43.

opposed government measures" just as they had in the sixteenth and

seventeenth centuries, and they even used the same devices: "citing

their privileges and explaining them in an unscrupulous manner, procras-

tinating and offering bribes."[530]

Samarin concluded that the relationship of the Baltic provinces to

Russia and her government could only be understood if they were seen as

a war:

> There is not another corner of Russia, where the government is
> so powerless for good; because in the Baltic region the govern-
> ment is not met by personal passions and advantages, always
> and everywhere unavoidable, but by general, systematic opposi-
> tion, stemming from rooted conviction about the relationship
> of the region to the state. The local German society per-
> ceives this relationship as an eternal lawsuit. The state on
> one side, and the Baltic region, or more precisely the pri-
> vileged classes on the other; both camps positioned one
> against the other, and between them war.[531]

The position of individual Russians in the Baltic region was also a

question of vital importance to Samarin. Once again historical investi-

gations provided the evidence upon which he based his conclusions. They

revealed that the highly Germanized Baltic nobility had pursued a very

successful programme of aggrandizing itself at the expense of all

classes for centuries.[532] Very early it won "the essential privi-

leges of land ownership and access to administrative and service

posts."[533] Thus, the Russians were excluded from these privileges and

---

[530]Ibid., p. 44.

[531]Ibid., p. 53.

[532]Ibid., pp. 65, 73, 74.

[533]Ibid., p. 65.

successfully prevented from acquiring them by skillful lobbying after-
wards. So skilful was the lobbying of the Baltic nobility, as a matter
of fact, that the Russian government sacrified its right to reward
Russians in the area from state rents and "legalized measures" which
had been adopted "to prevent Russians from settling in the Baltic
region."[534]

Samarin also established that Russians living in Baltic cities
endured the same kind of abuses. Generally they were treated as out-
siders and had no privileges. During the eighteenth century, however,
the situation improved, because the government supported them and
Catherine II issued a City Statute in 1784 which placed them on equal
terms with the Germans.[535] This improvement was short-lived, however, for Paul abrogated their rights in 1796 and hatred for them increased two times over, so that "their position [in the cities] became
intolerable."[536]

To summarize, Samarin said that the position of individual Russians
in the Baltic region was intolerable, because they had "to endure the
insults of their enemies and the indifference of their government, because they had "to reject bribes and incitement to treason..." rooted
in "hatred for the whole Russian tribe," and because the region was
"gradually being conquered by the Ostzeytsy" even though it belonged to

---

[534]Ibid., p. 71.

[535]Ibid., p. 78.

[536]Ibid., p. 86.

Russia. Finally, he said that a major cause of their intolerable position was "the German party," which was driven by "a systematic hatred of
Russia."[537]

On the basis of the above analysis, and the heavy component of hard
factual data with which he buttressed it, Samarin felt justified to
state. "that the present organization of the Baltic provinces contradicted the basic political and social principles evolved by recent
history, the dignity (dostoynstvo) and advantages (vygoda) of Russia,
and finally, the interests of the region itself."[538] Further, he
maintained that because its organization was "decrepit, burdensomely
complex and artificial" (not the product of organic development) it was
only able to survive with Russian government support. But it was the
aim of the provinces' "privileged classes" to manipulate, and ultimately, to control the Russian government which disturbed Samarin most, for
it threatened Russian power in the region: "I repeat," he said, "one of
two things: either we will be masters, or they will be."[539]

In order to win the support of the government and to forestall all
attempts at reform, the Oztzeytsy advanced the doctrine that their privileges were "untouchable." At the same time they soothed the govern-

---

[537]Ibid., pp. 95, 97 and 105. In a letter to K. Aksakov (April
1848) Samarin said: "The systematic suppression of the Russians by the
Germans, the hourly humiliation of Russian nationality in the person of
many of its representatives stir the blood in me now, and I work only to
bring this fact to everybody's consciousness." Sochineniya, XII, 200.

[538]Sochineniya, VII, 106.

[539]Ibid., p. 106.

, ment with "pledges of loyalty" and boasted about the superiority of the legal order in their region.[540] Clearly Samarin was very disturbed by the great success the Ostzeytsy had had in propagating these ideas throughout Russia. Noting that they had been accepted in all classes[541] he subjected them to careful scrutiny with the aim of demonstrating their falseness.

"Loyalty," Samarin stipulated, "only had value when it was freely given by autonomous individuals."[542] Therefore, the loyalty professed by the Ostzeytsy was quite unreliable or a sham, because it "was compelled by the sense of self-preservation" and "conditioned by an implied contract: [if you are a passive government and do not touch our privileges, we will be loyal]."[543] In any case, he asked in a philosophical vein "can unconditional and freely given loyalty, readiness for sacrifice" be expected from a society which does not have a "fatherland," and does not know the deeper springs of human motivation.

> The consequences of love and hate cannot be identical. If the foundation of the inner and outer life (byt) of a whole society is not love, but egoism and disunity, if long service to class self-interest has dried up its soul and made it incapable of free sympathy and uncalculating enthusiasm, it is possible and one must be sorry for it, but it is impossible to blame private individuals or a generation for the historical crime of a whole society.[544]

---

[540]Ibid., pp. 107 and 110.

[541]Ibid.

[542]Ibid., p. 112.

[543]Ibid., p. 114.

[544]Ibid.

Samarin began his scrutiny of the Ostzeytzy boast that they possessed a superior legal order by defining "legality." "The first condition of legality was the existence of laws." But that was not enough to guarantee legality. Certain other conditions had to be met: first, there had to be enough laws for the successful adjudication "of all existing relationships and juridical questions;" second, the laws had to be applicable to current needs; third, there had to be "a clear delimitation of the laws in force from the laws which were not;" and fourth, it was "essential that the laws be accessible to all."[545] Samarin found that these criteria were not met, and that even though local officials were well-trained in the law, the practice and administration of justice was defective. Therefore, he concluded, "strict legality" did not exist in the Baltic provinces, and the Ostzeytsy boasts were hollow.[546]

One Ostzeytsy argument to which Samarin took particular exception was the traditionalist argument that old links with the Hanseatic towns and the countries of Poland, Sweden and Denmark made it impossible and undesirable to unify their legal order in the new era of Russian control. While specifying that "unconditional external unity" of the law was not essential, Samarin countered with the reformist argument that changing historical conditions including the Russian presence, required that both the law and legal administrative practice be updated.[547]

---

[545]Ibid., p. 115.

[546]Ibid., p. 124.

[547]Ibid., pp. 126-7.

Samarin examined the last Ostzeytsy claim that their privileges were "untouchable" on the basis of the historical record, and found that the privileges had been regularly altered as both "the supreme power and the classes" had adjusted "to changing historical circumstances."[548] From this, he argued that "if the supreme power had enjoyed the right from olden times to change and to improve, subjecting private interests to the social benefit" and "if the nobility considered it permissible to violate the privileges of the middle-class...for their own advantage", then it was fallacious to argue that the privileges were "unconditionally-untouchable" in the present. Implicit in this statement is Samarin's firmly-held view that governments existed to serve the interests of the whole people.[549]

Samarin also examined this last Ostzeytsy claim from the juridical point of view. In this test he found their case to be equally fallacious, on the basis of the argument that a privilege is "an act of free favour" granted by "the supreme power" and subject to alteration or abrogation by that power as changing circumstances dictate. In the Ostzeytsy case when the Russian government took power it ratified the privileges in their totality but did not by that act give up its right as supreme power "to change and to abrogate the privileges as seemed proper."[550] On this latter point concerning the rightful and neces-

---

[548]Ibid., p. 130.

[549]Ibid., p. 131. On this very page Samarin posed the question: "Does government really exist to serve as a submissive weapon of the whim of a single class?"

[550]Ibid.

sary authority of the supreme power Samarin said:

> The first condition of the existence of a state union is the submission of all rights and private interests, both local and class, to social uses, and to the right of the supreme power, no matter in what form it is expressed, to decide without appeal all questions related to social use and to implement those decisions. The destruction or the bifurcation of the state would be inescapably linked with the concession or division of this right.

Thus he concluded:

> It is possible to argue about whether it is necessary or useful to abolish the privileges; but it is ridiculous to object to the proposed reformation on the basis of the untouchability of the privileges and to turn administrative and political questions into legal ones; it is ridiculous even to believe in the possibility of the untouchability of the privileges, before a way has been found to stop history, to prevent the growth of population, and to stop the development of trade and industry.[551]

To sum up, Samarin argued that the doctrine of the "untouchability of the privileges" in the Baltic provinces could not be supported from the historical or juridical points of view.

The religious question also provoked a crisis to which Samarin responded. The crises erupted in the forties when peasants began to convert to Orthodoxy. The main protagonists were the peasants, the Lutheran pastors, the largely German nobility, the Orthodox priests, and the Russian government. The antagonism, spawned by the controversy, affected relationships as far away as Moscow and St. Petersburg "where ignorance, the credulity of Russian society and total security provoked fictions and exaggerations," and spurred Samarin to explain how the crisis should be viewed.[552]

---

[551]Ibid., pp. 132 and 133.

[552]Ibid., pp. 134, 144 and 148.

What Samarin railed against was a plot by pro-Lutheran landlords and pastors against Orthodoxy, aided and abetted by Russian government responses aimed at placating the Germans. By way of example the government first applied only "negative measures" that set limited controls on Protestant enterprises and punished only those who were guilty of extreme attempts to suppress Orthodoxy.[553] Later, in 1845, the government applied more pro-German measures, putting Orthodox priests under police surveillance and prohibiting them from propagating the faith among Latvian peasants.[554]

Clearly Samarin was incensed because his government had not only been duped into obstructing the conversions, but even seemed prepared to accept the nobility's claim that these conversions were caused by material considerations and not "religious convictions."[555] He found this galling because his investigations showed that the religious impulses of the Latvians were very real. Without depreciating the importance of material considerations (the demand for better living conditions) one iota, he stressed that both Protestantism and Catholicism had failed to satisfy the inherent religious demands of the Latvians; thus

---

[553]Ibid., p. 142.

[554]Ibid., p. 146. It was especially galling to Samarin that Governor-General Prince Alexander A. Suvorov (1804-1882), a grandson of the illustrious General Suvorov, was offensively pro-German from the moment of his appointment (February, 1948). See his letter to M. P. Pogodin (April 1848), Sochineniya, XII, 256-258, plus the long following letter called "The Relation" in which he outlines Suvorov's actions while summarizing his own view of the Baltic question as set out in Pis'ma. Ibid., pp. 258-265.

[555]Ibid., p. 148.

a genuine religious impulse to convert to Orthodoxy was being frustrated by "an administration which had undertaken to serve as the humble tool of the passions and hatreds of the German community."[556]

This whole "unnatural" situation demanded urgent reform, Samarin concluded, because the government's stature and credibility was daily being undermined by lies and abuses, and because the future prospects of both the Russians and the Ostzeytsy were being threatened. But such a far-reaching reform could not be achieved unless the government had at least the sympathetic support of Russian society, which in turn required an end to the untruths being spread in St. Petersburg and Moscow. There will be no improvement until these lies "about the Ostzeytsy, about the rule of law in their region, about the sanctity of the privileges, about the scurrilous" behaviour of Russians including their clergy, are set right, and the Ostzeytsy "repent...their sins." "Their and our under-standing must change, if the great storm predicted by the dying Lomono-sov is not to be kindled at some time."[557]

Samarin made at least six points of relevance to any study of his political philosophy within the framework of Pis'ma iz Rigi, which require separate mention. One of these points, made in the seemingly contradictory process of blaming the Ostzeytsy for resisting the opportunity to join Russia, was that "the spirit of class and national exclusiveness was [intrinsically] negative and fruitless."[558] A

---

[556]Ibid., pp. 156-158.

[557]Ibid., pp. 159-60.

[558]Ibid., p. 32.

second, was the Hegelian-sounding point that since fate determines the
course of history, the strength of "organisms," including "societies,"
is determined by their ability to understand themselves, and "to submit
to a just fate", that is, to accept reality.[559] A third point was
that love of country rooted in common experiences, language and religion
provided the Russian government with its real strength and was the
source of every Russian's personal commitment to service.[560] A
fourth, actually a corollary of number one, was that it would be a
mistake to establish a court system upon "the principle of class repre-
sentation."[561] A fifth point, another corollary of one, was that
the role of government was to serve the interests of the whole society,
irrespective of the needs or advantages of a particular class.[562] And
finally, a sixth point was that the Russian government had to have the
"cooperation" or "at least the sympathy of society" in order to be
effective.[563]

---

[559]Ibid., pp. 33 and 37.

[560]Ibid., pp. 42-43. Commenting on this point in a letter to
Pogodin (April, 1848) Samarin observed that the Hungarians exemplified
the sad political result of replacing love of country with simple
personal regard for the sovereign. "Not long ago," he said, "the
Hungarians were aflame to die for Maria-Theresa, but now they are the
main villains in the fall of Austria." Sochineniya, XII, 264.

[561]Ibid., p. 124.

[562]Ibid., p. 131.

[563]Ibid., p. 159.

As indicated above the decision to write Pis'ma iz Rigi was prompted
by a number of factors - German opposition to Russian rule, the obstruc-
tion of the conversion of Latvians to Orthodoxy, the iniquitous position
of Russians in the Baltic Provinces and the pro-German policy of the
Russian Government; however, to these must be added another, the fact
that Samarin made an important political decision before going to Riga.
That was the practical decision to help the government to resolve
difficult problems wherever and whenever they might occur providing its
"aims coincided with Slavophil principles and objectives."[564] Even
though this decision brought him into direct conflict with his friends
in Moscow including Konstantin Aksakov, who favoured a policy of non-
collaboration with the government whatever its intentions, he persisted
in it. Clearly, Samarin's rejection of this "basic Slavophil principle" provoked the fury of many in the movement and prompted him to defend himself in Pis'ma.[565]

It is instructive to note that Khomiakov sided with Samarin in this
dispute. Confused and upset by the opposition of his friends on this
basic question of orientation towards the government, he sought out
Khomiakov's opinion. Samarin was gratified and encouraged by the
response, which stated in part:

> ...a twofold work, which I look upon as a positive obligation,
> stands before us: the work of expounding theory in a scienti-
> fic way...and the work of practical application...Our epoc...

---

[564]Ibid. p.XXXVII-XXXVIII.

[565]Ibid. p.XXXVIII and XL.

demands practical application. The questions have been
raised, and because these questions are historical, they can
only be decided by historical means, that is by real appearance in life.[566]

Thus Khomiakov gave his authoritative support to Samarin's policy of

helping the government to realize those reform initiatives and pro-

grammes which promised to bring Slavophil objectives closer.

While practical political considerations like these, supplemented

certainly by the conviction that at least one Slavophil had to master

the intricacies of Russia's government,[567] contributed to the adoption

of this service-oriented policy by Samarin, it is clear from his corres-

pondence that deep-seated psychological and religious factors helped to

strengthen his commitment to it. For instance in January 1848, a few

months before Pis'ma iz Rigi was written, he expressed a strong general

desire to serve his country and people:

> It is only possible to find personal bliss in self-sacrifice,
> in the submersion of one's self in deeds, in work, begun for
> the benefit of our country, in the awareness of the vital
> union of our personality with living reality, with the people,
> to whom we belong.... Only the consciousness of duty, which re-
> sides in us, can tear man from the charmed circle of personal
> concerns, personal worship and empty conversations with him-
> self about himself.[568]

Fifteen months later, after his arrest for writing and circulating Pis'

ma, he revealed the same factors in another letter. Deeply impressed by

---

[566]Ibid., p. XXXIX. The Samarin letter referred to has not survived. The Khomiakov letter is found in Pis'ma Khomiakova, p. 331. In
passing Khomiakov observed that Aksakov was not capable of practical
work. Ibid., p. 330.

[567]Letter to K. Aksakov, Sochineniya, XII, 211.

[568]Letter to his brother Michael, Ibid., p. 352.

everything that had happened to him since that event, and profoundly

moved by the personal reprimand which Tsar Nicholas had bestowed upon

him, he committed himself anew to his policy of supporting the govern-

ment:

> I have ceased to fear misunderstanding, suspicion and slander
> ....I have thrown aside a multitude of doubts, which confused
> me, and am prepared to work in the last rows, silently and
> humbly, not doubting success, but not running after it. So it
> has been arranged by Providence itself, that in Holy Russia no
> work, conceived under the influence of passion or strained
> pride, can have success. Now, having seen an open road before
> me, it would be sinful to stop or to digress to the side ....
> Therefore my choice is made, I will accept the hate and the
> injuries of society and give myself freely to the government.[569]

However Samarin had no illusions about the government in making this

commitment. In fact, his policy stands in sharp contradiction to his

low opinion, some would say realistic assessment, as he was commenting

on a perennial bureaucratic problem, of the government's integrity and

capacity to act. His opinion was recorded in a memorandum which he

wrote to himself on July 1, 1848 just before leaving Riga for good. In

this document, he said that the government was "inconsistent" and pow-

erless"; that it was "inconsistent" because it was "powerless"; and that

it was "powerless" because of "an inner flaw" and not because of "exter-

---

[569]Letter to A. O. Smirnova, Ibid., pp. 380 and 386. By this
time Samarin's concern about the response of his friends had been re-
placed by a deep concern about the hostility of "disinterested guardians
of order and conservative principles," who had recently attacked Pogodin
for his article "Tsar in Moskve" (Moskvityanin, no 8, 1849), and who had
also attacked the Tsar for his "magnanimous" treatment of the Aksakovs
The Aksakovs had been arrested for defending Samarin's actions, but
were soon released. In general Samarin felt that these reactionaries
were saying outrageous things against the Slavophils. Ibid., p. 386.

nal obstacles." The critical flaw he defined, as an "inner emptiness or sort of senselessness." Thus ministries operated without "conscious direction, proceding from conviction," so that government policy and action was shaped by "personality, whim and chance." Thus the government could not be relied upon, as it had demonstrated in the Baltic provinces, where it had initiated reforms five times without ever pushing them through to a successful conclusion. Yet in spite of this negative assessment, Samarin optimistically concluded:

> ...I have not lost the desire to serve, on the contrary, I have decided to serve, because I have concluded that it is too late to choose another path. The very senselessness and powerlessness of the government provokes thought and vouches for its success, when it has reached sufficient ripeness to appear not in a polemic and not even in dogmatism, but in an authoritative form, when it can be said to the government: you are standing in a blind-alley, do these things, and here are people who are experienced, and who have trained themselves to work for it.[570]

This result, in point of fact, was one of the two convictions which Samarin took with him from Riga. The second, made so forcefully in Pis'ma, was that the Russophobia of the Baltic Germans was so bitter and deep that they were bent on inflicting "terrible harm" upon the Russians and that it was, therefore, "the duty of every Russian...to oppose the Ostzeytsy."[571]

As already demonstrated Samarin's correspondence is an important source of information about his politicl ideas. Therefore, no discussion

---

[570]Sochineniya, VII, XLIII-XLV.

[571]Ibid., p. XLV.

of this period could be complete without devoting some space to the pot-
pourri of ideas expressed and frequently elaborated upon in letters
written to his friends as events unfolded.

In a letter to his father of 12 March 1848 he expressed sympathetic
understanding for the February Revolution in France, and had a number of
very interesting things to say about it. To begin with, he said that
social and not political factors were at the bottom of the revolution,
because the repeatedly frustrated demands of the working class had done
more to provoke the uprising than had the form of government.[572] The
full extent of working class suffering especially as a result of their
being uprooted by the new machines was incalculable. Continuing, he
pointed out that "the word communism," which was presently being used to
frighten everyone, "was only a caricature of a splendid and fruitful
idea, about cooperative work in agriculture and industry for the mutual
benefit," just as "tyranny" is a caricature of "monarchy," just as "the
reign of Ivan the Terrible" was a caricature of "tsarist power."[573]

Further, he observed that scientific study of the experience of
England and France had conclusively proven that "under the conditions of
the contemporary disorganization of agriculture and industry, of the
dominance of unrestricted combination, and of the theory of laissez
faire, the value of capital (land and money) inevitably rises in propor-
tion to the decline of the working wage," and that the inevitable result
of such a system is "hunger or the eviction of the masses."[574]

---

[572]Sochineniya, XII, 328.

[573]Ibid., p. 329.

[574]Ibid.

Characteristically, it seems fair to say at this point, Samarin saw

the solution to this intolerable result in a basic reform carried to

completion in the establishment of a "lawful (pravomernyi) order."

Hence, he believed that communism could only be conquered by this path

of reform. Furthermore, he was very optimistic of ultimate success

because of his progressive view of historical development:

> If the demand for the organization of agriculture and industry
> is natural and necessary, then it is therefore realizable
> (osushchestvimo). To us it seems an impossible dream, but in
> a hundred years it will seem simple and ordinary. Remember
> that everything in the world developed in this very way. There
> was a time when every landlord-baron was the supreme judge of
> his vassals and supervised the administration of justice as
> his own personal prerogative; subsequently they grasped that
> there could not be as many laws and as many courts as there
> were people, that the court is not a personal matter, that the
> court and the law must be the same for everyone, that it is an
> affair of state and not a personal affair. In precisely this
> way with the passage of time, trade, agriculture, and indus-
> trial production will assume the character of a social ac-
> tivity.[575]

A letter which was written to A. O. Smirnova on 25 May 1849 provides

an enlargement of the opinion expressed above about communism and re-

veals once again what weighty components religion, family and national

instinct were in his thought. The event which occasioned Samarin's com-

ment was the arrest of some twenty members of the so-called Petrashevsky

group for plotting against the Tsar.[576] After first describing this

---

[575]Ibid.

[576]Ibid., p. 387. The members of the Petrashevsky group met
regularly on Friday evenings at the St. Petersburg home of the young
nobleman Michael Butashevich-Petrashevsky. About 20 strong, they were
Fourierists (moderate socialists) who protested against Nicholas' rule.
See Riasanovsky, A History of Russia, p. 405. They came from a lower
social-stratum than the Slavophils.

conspiracy, about which he had heard only rumours at the time of writing as "lunacy," Samarin went on to observe that "the revolting absurdity of the communist idea" was not so disturbing as the "absolute spiritual and intellectual void which the adoption of [communist] ideas presupposes." Then acknowledging that he could understand how "this void could result from the atheism of the eighteenth century, the storms of the revolution, and the cult of materialism under the reign of the bourgeoisie and Louis Philippe," he said that he was dumbfounded that "a Russian on graduating from school could stand at the same point at which he entered life, disencumbered of all religious notion, of all respect for the family, and of all national instinct."[577]

Samarin also had a number of interesting things to say about the study of political economy based on a concentrated study of that subject, which he undertook between May and August 1849. In a letter written to Khomiakov in mid-August, he professed "to having swallowed up to fifteen fairly thick volumes."[578] From this he reached the conclusion that political economy deserved neither the animosity which it received from many authorities, nor the great respect which it received from others "who saw in society a company of shareholders, in national life a trade enterprise,and in the life of man a digestive process." In point of fact, he concluded that political economy was a "necessary" and "perhaps useful" science with the potential of helping in Russia, pro-

---

[577]Ibid., p. 388

[578]Ibid., p. 430.

viding it was studied as a method for examining frequently ignored but nonetheless important aspects of the national life; and not as a system of directives, because many of its basic propositions such as "the superiority of free labour over compulsory, the advantage of free exchange, and the harmfulness of artificially stimulating industrial activity" were simply not applicable to Russia.[579]

He demonstrated what useful insights this method of posing questions could lead to by citing the example of the harsh criticism which French and English economists had levelled at the "ateliers nationaux" and the general socialist "idea that man works according to need and desire." The essence of their criticism - "need presupposes the necessity to guarantee oneself and one's family by one's own means; and desire pre-supposed the free disposition of one's strength and a guarantee of the right of ownership to the results of one's labour" - was greeted enthus-iastically by Russian society for their correctness. However, ques-tioning by the methods of political economy gave cause for concern, because these criticisms were as devastating for serfdom as they were for the "ateliers nationaux", for the Russian peasant was protected from need by the landlord's obligation to feed him, and the peasants' desire to work was sapped by the landlord's control over the product of his labour.[580]

He took as another example contemporary political economies' claim that a "disideratum" for any society was: "on the one hand, la partici-

---

[579]Ibid.

[580]Ibid., pp. 430-31.

pation du plus grand nombre possible aux bienfaints de la propriété
territoriale; and on the other, l'emploi des procédés de la culture
en grand." Then, noting that "the idea of personal property" had become
so entrenched in the West that there was no middle ground between "infinite fragmentation of the land and proletarianization," he posed the
question, a very significant one, for any Russian: "Is not the desired
reconciliation found in communal ownership?"[581]

So, Samarin concluded that the study of political economy could be
useful if conducted within the limits described above. If he had any
regret at all to express about having devoted so much time to studying
the subject (about 6 months), it was that he had little prospect of
getting an article which he wanted to write about "the contemporary dis-
orderliness" of Western Europe published. What he wanted to demonstrate
in such an article was that there was "the closest, most legitimate connection...between Hegelian philosophy and French communism."[582]

All things considered, it is very appropriate that Samarin's last
published letter to Khomiakov (August 1850) should contain a personal
reaffirmation of his belief that "the spiritual principle" provided the
only cure for the "ailment of contemporary society."[583] What was this
ailment? Experience had taught him, first, that Khomiakov was correct
in diagnosing the ailment as "course, conscious materialism," and
second, that the characteristics of the age could only be explained on

---

[581]Ibid., p. 431.

[582]Ibid., p. 432.

[583]Ibid., p. 434.

the basis of this perception. Since society, including the government, was falling more and more under the spell of materialist thinking, Samarin was forced to give up many of his "hopes" and "expectations." The practical conclusion which he drew from everything around him was "that nothing more remained to be done, except to constantly remind people...of the spiritual principle." Understandably, his interest in governmental service had declined by this time, although he did not reject it - as a "helpful means," at least for the present.[584]

Finally, Samarin recorded some of his thoughts on the Ukraine shortly after his appointment to the office of General Bibikov in Kiev. These comments were not exhaustive on any point, nevertheless taken together they make a valuable contribution to this reconstruction of his political philosophy. For instance in discussing the problems of the Ukraine after the War of Liberation fought under the leadership of Hetman Bogdan Khmel'nitsky (1648-54), he pointed out that an improvement in the quality of Ukrainian life at that time required the reattachment of the peasants to the land [the reintroducion of serfdom]. Because neither the Cossacks nor the nobility had sufficient power to accomplish this essential task, he continued, an "external, autocratic power, beyond the control of the courts - a monarchical power was necessary."[585] Even

---

[584]Ibid., pp. 434-435. On this last point he likened a service position to "a scaffolding from which a speech goes forth clearer and farther." Ibid., p. 435.

[585]"Iz dnevnika vedyonnago Iu. F. Samarina v Kieve v 1850 gody," Russkiy Arkhiv, Bk. 2, 15, 230. It appears that these thoughts were noted down after a reading of Povest' ob Ukrainskom narode. Napisal dlya detey starshago Vozrasta Kulesh. (St. Petersburg)1846.

after making allowance for the time and the particular circumstance, this statement seems to reflect a preference for government by a sovereign or autocrat. The impression is re-enforced when this statement is considered along with the general comment which follows immediately after it about the inadequacies of "an elected power":

> An elected power is not strong enough, to defend the people, to put an end to the battle between classes and to bridle the nobility, because it is timid before those who have elected it.[586]

At another point, he noted that Ukrainian hatred for Polish domination became so intense that they rejected both "a particular Polish government" and "the condition of state power" in general. In fighting for their freedom they lost sight of the fact that accepting limits on personal and class freedom "constitutes a necessary condition for the existence of any state." In the end, many Ukrainians and the Cossacks in particular, "recognized the necessity for Moscow's supreme power, but feared and could not become accustomed to its demands."[587]

Finally his concluding remarks about the relationships of the Ukraine to Moscow are instructive, especially as they echo his complaint against the Baltic Germans who were caught in a similar situation, for not being "just" in their response to Russia:[588]

---

[586]Ibid.

[587]Ibid., p. 231.

[588]see pp. 206-209, above.

...the Moscow state saved the material existence of the common
people of the Ukraine and has now improved it significantly by
the introduction of inventories; it ended the pretensions of
Poland, saved Orthodoxy and expelled hateful Uniatism. The
Ukraine could not do any of these things for herself.

Let the Ukrainian people preserve their language, their
customs, their songs, their traditions; let them in brotherly
cooperation, hand in hand with the Great Russian people,
develop in the field of science and art, for which nature has
so liberally endowed them, and develop their spiritual uniqueness in all of its natural originality; and let the institutions, which have been created for them, be adapted more and
more to their local needs. But at the same time let them
remember, that their historical role is within the limits of
Russia, and not outside of her, in the general composition of
the Moscow state, for the building and extolling of which the
Great Russian people have worked so long and stubbornly, for
which the Great Russian people have made so many bloody sacrifices and have endured suffering, unknown to the Ukrainians;
let them, in a word, guard, unspoiled, the legacy of their
history and study ours.[589]

That Samarin was an exceptionally dedicated man is beyond question.

That he was driven by a sense of mission is clear both from his corres-

pondence and his jottings. He frequently called government service a

"school," and he certainly felt that everything he had thought and

written up to 1848 was only training for some major task. Nowhere is

this expressed more clearly than in the memorandum which he wrote as he

was preparing to leave Riga. Musing about these things, he noted that

he had not worked on a single really important project, and that no

assigned task had really suited his abilities. He wondered also if his

---

[589]"Iz dnevnika," Russkiy Arkhiv, p. 232. Samarin's comments
in a letter to A. O. Smirnova (February 7-10, 1850) enlarge on the
opinions expressed here. Briefly, he said, that "the individual principle" developed in the Ukraine "in preference to the northern communal
(obshchinnyi) principle;" that the Ukrainians failed to develop the
capacity for "united consistent action;" and that Moscow saved the
Ukraine from being "exhausted by fruitless Cossack uprisings and disputes with the Jesuits." Sochineniya, XII, 391.

conviction that a major task awaited him was "youthful pride" or a genuine premonition, and he prayed to God for guidance.[590]

Ruminating gloomily on this question almost a year earlier in a letter to A. O. Smirnova (May 21, 1847), he moaned: "Can I really not find a satisfying task for myself in the whole kingdom of Russia? I mean a task which would demand all of my abilities, all of my time and all of my concentration."[591] In his ruminations he indicated that university teaching - teaching "live ideas to live people," would have satisfied him; but that the practical work of service could not: "Instead of life - affairs (that is <u>des dossiers</u>), instead of living people - your supreme excellency, your highest lordship, instead of action - editing the ideas of others." However, from this letter it becomes clear that he already knew of one such task, one task to which he could dedicate himself with the certainty of achieving positive results. That task was "the abolition of serfdom."[592]

In point of fact Samarin had already gained direct personal experience of the peasant problem in 1846, when he had served as the assistant to the executive director of the Livlandian Committee. That this experience made a lasting impression on him is clear from the record. He became acquainted with the pitfalls of peasant reform, and was able to divide the problem into its component parts.[593] He saw that the

---

[590]<u>Sochineniya</u>, VII, XLII.

[591]<u>Sochineniya</u>, XII, 373.

[592]<u>Ibid</u>., pp. 373-374.

[593]<u>Sochineniya</u>, VII, XXV.

peasant problem could be solved "by legislative and administrative measures.[594] He concluded that it was the most critical problem facing Russia, and according to Khomiakov formulated the juridical formula which best explained the essence of Russain serfdom: "It comprised the existence of two equally firm and sacred rights: the rights of inheritance to property, and exactly the same rights of inheritance to use."[595] Finally, he first formulated the idea, which he pressed so relentlessly in his compositions and in his work thereafter, i.e., the idea that "the peasants had to be freed with land.[596]

Subsequently, while helping to prepare economic and administrative reforms for the city of Riga, Samarin became convinced that the Slavophils had to become involved in the practical work of applying their theories.[597] And in the fall of 1848 after his return from Riga, he deliberately avoided theoretical arguments, and concentrated more and more on applying his ideas to the solution of practical problems: for as he said to Popov: "I do not understand how it is possible to find pleasure in [theoretical discussion], after a man has established his own convictions, and lost the hope of convincing others."[598]

Thus, Samarin became absorbed by the problem of peasant reform in

---

[594]Ibid.

[595]Pis'ma Khomiakova, p. 331.

[596]Ibid. This comment was made by I. Aksakov in a footnote.

[597]See above pp. 220-221.

[598]Sochineniya, XLVI.

1846, and already sensed in 1847, while working on economic and administrative reforms for the city of Riga, that this problem represented a task to which he could devote himself heart and soul. Also by 1848, he was firmly committed to a well-developed theoretical system, and was equally firmly committed to applying the principles of that system in reform programmes at every opportunity. Thus, late in 1849, after the crisis produced by Pis'ma iz Rigi had subsided, and after he had been appointed to Bibikov's chancellery in Kiev, centre of the fertile Ukraine with its restive peasant population, Samarin was ready to devote all his strength of mind and body to the practical task of abolishing serfdom. Is it too much to say, that the abolition of serfdom was to become a laboratory test for Slavophil principles?

CHAPTER V

The Laboratory of Serfdom

Vladimir Klyuchevsky described the peasant problem as "the most
difficult question ever resolved by the Russian people in the whole
course of their history."[599] The Great Emancipation of 1861 which
'resolved' the problem was described by Terence Emmons, a less illustrious but nevertheless competent present-day American historian, as
"an epochal event in the life of the Russian state and ... in the
history of human bondage," at one point, and at another, as "probably
the most ambitious piece of social engineering in the history of modern
Europe to the twentieth century."[600] The condition of serfdom
abolished by emancipation was a rigid system of control over the
peasants which had evolved over five centuries. At critical junctures
in its evolution, such as 1497, when Ivan III restricted the peasants'
right to move, and 1649, when Tsar Alexis issued a statute placing the
peasants in bondage, legislation was promulgated to confirm conditions
which already existed in fact. By 1856 the iniquitous situation
created by serfdom threatened a horrendous social catastrophe, so that
the autocratic government of Axexander II acted deliberately to forestall it by legislative measures designed to establish entirely new
conditions between landlords and peasants. Samarin and other enlightened and progressive noblemen like him, conscious of the inefficiencies

---

[599]V.O. Klyuchevsky, "Krepostnoy vopros nakanune ego zakonodatel
'nogo vozbuzhdeniya. Razbor vtorogo toma sochineniy Yu. F. Samarina,"
Sochineniya (Moscow, 1959) VII, 114.

[600]P.A. Zaionchkovsky, The Abolition of Serfdom in Russia, ed.
and trans S. Wobst, Intro. Terence Emmons (Gulf Breeze, Florida: Academic International Press, 1978), p.vii and viii.

and injustices of serfdom and fearful of a violent revolution if timely changes were not made, played an important role in drafting this legislation.[601]

Samarin brought wide experience and great knowledge to the task of destroying serfdom. He had studied the question of peasant reform in Latvia. He had studied peasant-landlord relationships in the Ukraine when inventories were being introduced to regulate those relationships. Personal service in both of these regions had helped to broaden his experiential base, as had administering his father's estates in the Samara region. As a scholar he had devoted serious study to the political and economic aspects of reform, and in addition he had a firm ideological commitment to freeing the peasantry. Undoubtedly, this preparation made it possible for him to speak out as an authority and promoted his career as an agent of peasant reform.

A simple measure of Samarin's commitment to reform is the extensiveness of his writings on the subject. They comprise three volumes of his Sochineniya, and encompass 1,534 pages of text. His first pieces were written while he was compiling a report, Istoricheskiy ocherk unichtozheniya krepostnogo sostoyaniya v Liflandii (An Historical Out-

---

[601]Klyuchevsky calls Samarin "an educated and intelligent landlord, who long before the legislative solution of the peasant question thought much about how to resolve it ... it forced him, a philosopher and theologian, to become an agricultural boss (khozyain)." Klyuchevsky "Krepostnoy vopros," p. 107. Zaionchkovsky, the outstanding Soviet historian, identifies the Slavophils K.S. and I.S. Aksakov, I.V. and P.V. Kireyevsky, A.S. Khomiakov, and A.I. Koshelev as liberal thinkers and states that "pre-reform liberalism was undoubtedly a progressive ideology." Zaionchkovsky, pp. 32-33.

line of the Abolition of Serfdom in Livlandia) for two special committees preparing peasant reforms for Latvia and Estonia in 1846. The
conclusion of this report is noteworthy because it contains a clear
statement of the liberal idea which underpinned all of his subsequent
work on the peasant question, that is, the idea that the peasant had to
be liberated with land.[602]

Thus Samarin's Baltic experience convinced him that a durable land
reform could not be achieved unless the peasants were given a land
allotment. Subsequently his historical investigations led him to
buttress this conviction with the juridical perception that peasant
farmers owned the land, but that their rights to it collided with the
governmentally enforced service rights of their landlords.[603] Khomiakov, to whom Samarin outlined his idea, probably in March 1848, was
impressed by its accuracy, "clarity and preciseness," and gave it the
following formulation in one of his letters:

> [Russian serfdom] comprised the existence of two equally
> firm and sacred rights: the [peasants'] right of inheri-
> tance to property, and exactly the same [landlords'] rights
> of inheritance to use.[604]

Thus Samarin originated an historically based juridical argument for
defending the peasants' right to land.[605]

---

[602]Sochineniya, II, VI. Zaionchkovsky, who referred to Samarin
as "the famous liberal public figure," said that opposition to serfdom
was one of the distinguishing marks of a Russian liberal in the 1850's.
Zaionchkovsky, pp. 32, and 108.

[603]Sochineniya, VII, pp. 4-6, and above, p. 233.

[604]Pis'ma Khomiakova, p. 331, and above, p. 233.

[605]Nol'de calls it "a daring and original perception of great
practical value." Nol'de, p. 53.

Somewhat later, while observing the introduction of inventories in the Kiev region, Samarin used his idea as a yardstick for evaluating them. But first, what were the inventories? They were precise official calculations of peasant obligations to landlords, determined on the basis of their mutual land relationships. Introduced in the southwestern region in 1848, they were in full swing when Samarin was assigned to Bibikov's chancellery. Samarin saw the inventories as a positive first step towards recognizing the peasants' historical right to the land, which he defended in one of his notes as follows:

> The peasant must work for the landlord (pomeschchik); the landlord must provide his peasants with a land allotment. Therefore their mutual relationships must be inviolable and founded on justice. At present they are based on force and on the almost unlimited arbitrariness of the landlord, and are therefore oppressive to the peasants. When they have been changed, either as a result of voluntary agreements between them, or on the basis of norms, introduced by the government, a legitimate order, flowing from the conditions of our historical development will have been established. At its base will lie, it seems to me, the conception of the inseparability of the farmer from the land, a conception which is completely foreign to Western Europe. This inseparability manifests itself in a dual form: as the dependence of the farmer on the land - serfdom (krepostnoe pravo), and as the dependence of the land on the farmer, i.e., a mutual relationship the realization of which has been left to the future.[606]

In this context the inventory system was a good system, because it headed peasant reform in the right direction. In spite of its incompleteness, therefore, it was a sound building block in the edifice of reform and Samarin, with practical common sense and patient optimism, proceeded to build on it.

---

[606]Sochineniya, VII, 15. Italics in the original.

He proceeded to shape that building block in an extensive memorandum entitled <u>O krepostnom sostoyanii i o perekhode iz nego k grazhdanskoy svobode</u> (On the Peasant Condition and the Transition from it
to Civil Freedom), which he began to write in 1853, soon after he
retired from the civil service, settled in Moscow and undertook to
administer his father's estates.

This memorandum was conceived and written at a time when there
seemed to be little prospect of successfully abolishing serfdom. However, when Russian failures in the Crimean War (1854-1856) compelled a
new hard look at serfdom, Samarin was ready. Quickly reworking his
memorandum <u>O krepostnom sostoyanii</u> he put it into circulation in Moscow
and St. Petersburg. Passing from hand to hand, it helped along with
other memoranda by other progressive authors like Koshelev and Cherkassky, to convince public opinion of the need for abolition.[607]

When Samarin's memorandum began to pass around, Russian society
was "deeply agitated" and in a quandry about how to resolve the problem
of serfdom. In 1856 the government had still not committed itself to
any course of action and even the "most timid word, spoken in favour of
liberation" brought a two-fold threat of reprisals: on the one hand,
from those who condemned the speaker as a self-seeking agent of the
government, and on the other, from those who condemned him as an "enemy

---

[607]Klyuchevsky, "Krepostnoy vopros," p. 108. Klyuchevsky
quotes Samarin as writing: "My memorandum has gone into circulation
and is having great success." <u>Ibid</u>. Nol'de claims that "everybody
wanted to obtain and read it, everybody discussed it and Samarin's name
was on everybody's lips." Nol'de, p. 74. See above, p. 21 for brief
notes on Koshelev and Cherkassky.

of the government and order." In 1857 it was still an offence against censorship laws to print anything about the peasant question. It was August of that year before a secret committee decided to collect information of possible legislative value about the serfs, and it was 1858 before the government committed itself to emancipation.[608]

O Krepostnom sostoyanii is not a scholarly treatise, but a political tract, designed to achieve a political objective. It contains only those things which would, in Samarin's judgement, contribute to his purpose of convincing the government and the serf-owning class, his own class, of the need to abolish serfdom,[609] as he said:

> In first place among the contemporary domestic problems, with which we must be concerned, standing as a threat to our future, and an obstacle in the present to every essential improvement whatsoever, is the question of serfdom. From whatever point our domestic renewal begins, we unavoidably meet it. We cannot escape it and we must not shirk a resolution of it.
> This memorandum has been prepared with the sole aim of calling all sides to a calm sincere discussion, in full confidence, that the question of serfdom has developed to complete maturity; that the resolution of it demands not only firm will on the government's part, but in addition and to advantage, clear consciousness and candid cooperation on the part of the class, which is most interested in a peaceful resolution of it.[610]

Samarin began his memorandum by noting that the Crimean War, which had cost Russia her "political and military primacy," had exposed the real measure of her "internal disorder and powerlessness."[611] After attacking the status quo with this harsh object lesson, he began a sys-

---

[608]Klyuchevsky, p. 108.

[609]Nol'de, p. 67, and Klychevsky, p. 110.

[610]Sochineniya, II, p. 19-20.

[611]Ibid., pp. 18-19.

tematic cataloque of the moral, political and economic harm which serfdom had done to Russia. On the moral side, he said, to summarize his
analysis, the unjust relationship between the peasant and the landlord
stimulated pretense and connivance between the classes themselves as
well as between them and the government, producing a dishonest society
split against itself.[612] The results on the political side were
alarming:

> Three hundred thousand landlords, with reason frightened by
> the expectation of a terrible revolution; eleven million
> peasants, firmly convinced of the existence of a silent,
> longstanding plot of the landlords against the Tsar and the
> people, and at the very same time considering themselves at
> one with the Tsar in a defensive conspiracy against their
> common enemy, the nobility; laws, in which the people do not
> recognize a genuine expression of the Tsar's will; a govern-
> ment, which suspects the people of treason, and does not
> inspire any faith - this is what we are obliged to serfdom
> for in our political relationships.[613]

His assessment of the economic impact of serfdom was no less harsh:

> ... it ties [the peasant] hand and foot ... he gradually
> loses the ability to use his own mind. Little by little his
> personality, as a master (khozyain) and family man, loses,
> together with his natural rights, his native abilities and
> is reduced to the level of a soul-less working unit and is
> swallowed in the mechanism of the landlord economy.[614]

Thus Samarin demonstrated serfdom to be immoral, politically dangerous
and economically harmful.

In the second part of O krepostnom sostoyanii, Samarin developed
his plan for making the "transition" from serfdom to "civil freedom."

---

[612]Ibid., pp. 21-30.

[613]Ibid., p. 36.

[614]Ibid., pp. 57-58.

His plan was "unusually moderate...almost timid," according to Nol'de,
who explained it as a politically motivated decision inspired by
fear of provoking opposition by enunciating "far-reaching radical
demands."[615] The moderateness of Samarin's plan lay in its recommendation that the peasants be helped to freedom and independence with
land over a number of years by means of voluntary agreements negotiated
between themselves and their landlords. Voluntary agreements were
preferred, he maintained, because they would automatically reflect
local conditions, while at the same time guaranteeing the negotiation
of both "applicable" and "mutually satisfactory" terms of settlement.
In general these agreements were to transform the peasants into independent tax-paying farmers, on the one hand, and to compensate the
landlords for their loss of land and labour, on the other.[616]

Samarin was well-prepared for a "significant role" in liberating
the peasants.[617] The circulation of his memorandum established him,
both as one of the country's foremost experts on the question, and as a
leader among those in Moscow and St. Petersburg who stood for reform:

---

[615]Nol'de, p. 67. It did not occur to Klyuchevsky that political calculation could have determined the character of Samarin's
reform proposal. He attributed its moderateness to indefinite causes:
"perhaps, fear of frightening the landlords by definite measures; perhaps inadequate personal decisiveness; more likely - a view of the problem, which did not correspond to reality." Klyuchevsky, p. 113.

[616]Sochineniya, pp. 133-136.

[617]Semevskiy, V.I., Krest'yanskiy vopros v Rossii v XVIII i
pervoy polovine XIX veka, Vol. II Krest'yanskiy vopros v tsarstvovanie
Imperatora Nikolaya, (St. Petersburg, 1888), p. 417.

"For the majority of them Samarin was a teacher with enormous authority, who they not only respected, but also feared. Thus the peasant
reform was conducted under the fascination of his mind and spirit."[618]

At the beginning of 1857 Tsar Alexander II established a secret
committee for "the discussion of measures regarding the status of seig-
norial peasant conditions."[619] In early August Grand Duke Konstantin,
Alexander's brother, was appointed to the committee for the express
purpose of speeding up the preparations for reform.[620] On August 1
and 17 the committee recommended a moderate three-stage programme of
reform. The first stage would be "preparatory." During this period
the government would do all in its power to improve the lot of the
serfs, permit the landlords to free their peasants on the basis of
mutual agreements, and collect evidence relevant to the drafting of
reform measures. The second stage would be "transitional." During
this stage the regime would force the emancipation of the serfs on "a
step by step" basis. In the third, and "final" stage, the peasants
would acquire both "personal rights" and the status of "free individuals in their dealings with landowners."[621] Alexander II approved
the committee's proposal on 18 August 1857 - the great peasant reform
had definitely begun.

---

[618]Prince V.P. Meshchersky, as quoted in Nol'de, p. 83.

[619]Zaionchkovsky, p. 44.

[620]Ibid., p. 51. On Grand Duke Konstantin, see p. 23 above.

[621]Ibid., p. 52.

Samarin must have been pleased by Alexander's decision for it was
the one he had hoped for when he put <u>O krepostnom sostoyanii</u> into
circulation. Furthermore, his expertise earned him an opportunity to
play an active role in the work of the secret committee from this time
onward as an advisor to Grand Duke Konstantin, who called him to St.
Petersburg to prepare memoranda for his consideration.[622]

Now Samarin, always the practical politician, began to spell out
the details of his plan for reform in precise, unequivocal memoranda.
Such were <u>Chetyre zapiski po krest'yanskomu delu</u> (Four memoranda on the
peasant question), which he presented to the Grand Duke Konstantin in
August. They were devoted to the "central questions" confronting the
reforming autocracy.[623]

In the first memorandum, <u>O prave krest'yan na zemlyu</u> (On the right
of the peasants to land), he developed once again his theory about
peasant land rights:

> ... the historical development of land relationships in
> Russia and the contemporary national consciousness, the
> living fruit of this development, points us to the undis-
> putable existence of mutually-limiting rights to the land:
> the right of ownership to the land, belonging to the pea-
> sants, and the right of property on the land, belonging to
> the landlord (<u>votchinik</u>).[624]

From this theoretical base, Samarin argued, that the peasantry must be
freed with land.

---

[622]Nol'de, p. 78.

[623]<u>Ibid.</u>, p. 79.

[624]<u>Sochineniya</u>, II, 153.

The second memorandum, <u>Chto vygodnee: obshchinnoe mirskoe vlad-enie zemley ili lichnoe?</u> (What is more advantageous: communal or personal ownership of the land?) as the title suggests was devoted to a defence of the commune (<u>obshchina</u>), which was under attack from "the more conservative members of the committee who favoured personal land ownership."[625] His defence included historical, economic and practical arguments, which coalesced to produce a strong plea for preserving communal land ownership. Historically, the commune had protected the integrity of Russia and defended her against the scourge of revolution. Economically, it had been a guarantee of rational and just use of land commensurate with individual skills and needs.[626] Practically, he concluded:

> Intelligent conservatism demanded that we restrain ourselves from the premature transference of the question of land ownership from the province of national custom to the province of legislation and administration.[627]

The third memorandum, <u>Mozhno li dopustit' srochnye dogovory?</u> (Can temporary agreements be allowed?) and the fourth, <u>Proekt ukaza o poly-ubovnykh sdelkakh mezhdu pomeshchikami i pripisannymi k ikh imeniyam krepostnymi lyud'mi</u> (Project of a decree on mutual agreements between landlords and the peasants attached to their estates), dealt with decisions taken by the secret committee 14 and 17 August. Both provide valuable insights into Samarin's thinking. <u>Mozhno li dopustit'</u> attempts

---

[625]Nol'de, p. 81.

[626]Ibid.

[627]Sochineniya, II, 171.

to prove that the government must use its authority to complete the
drafting of agreements between landlords and their peasants:

> The government ... cannot allow the two interested sides to
> part without an agreement. By one means or another. by
> amicable agreement or by legislative act, the mutual rights
> and relationships of the sides must be established without
> fail, because the sides cannot part without loss by a whole
> class, or perhaps, by both, of the most essential condition
> of their strength and independence. In this situation an
> agreement bears the character of a private deal only in its
> origins and form, but in its nature it is a legislative act.
> From this point of view its permanency and its inviolability
> is fully justified.[628]

In Proekt ukaza an attempt was made to prove that a law on voluntary
agreements must require, without fail, the granting of "settlement land
to the peasants, and recognize it as having the character of 'communal'
(mirskoy) land."[629]

The decisions of the secret committee which were approved 18
August by Alexander II parallelled very closely Samarin's ideas as
elaborated up to that time. Even on the critical question of how the
government should use its authority to accomplish a reform, Samarin
seemed to favour a role for it as instigator and organizer. Certainly,
he preferred the negotiation of mutually beneficial voluntry agreements
over legislated or compulsory ones. However, a significant change in
his idea about the role of government took place during this period.
In fact, the change was foreshadowed in Mozhno li dopustit' in which

---

[628]Ibid., pp. 172-173.

[629]Nol'de, p. 82.

Samarin implied that the government must legislate the completion of landlord-peasant agreements if necessary. It was clearly spelled out in a note which was probably written in September under the title, Programma svedeniy, neobkhodimykh dlya opredeleniya zakonodatel'nym poryadkom otnosheniy pomeshchikov k krest'yanam (A programme of information, necessary for the determination by legislation of relationships between landlords and peasants). His point was that it was no longer possible to achieve a satisfactory reform by the path of voluntary agreements, and that it would, therefore, be necessary to resort to legislative action:

> Acknowledging the necessity, justice and advantage of a decree, having the aim of easing and encouraging the completion of voluntary agreements, it is essential to accept [the fact] that Russia will not escape from serfdom by this route.... Therefore, it is now necessary to prepare another form of action by legislation.[630]

As the record demonstrates, Samarin rooted his investigation of problems, and ultimately his solutions to them, in historical analysis. It is hardly surprising, therefore, that part of the research he did in confronting the peasant problem involved a study of the abolition of serfdom in Prussia. The article, Uprazdnenie krepostnogo prava i ustroystvo otnosheniy mezhdu pomeshchikami i krest'yanami v Prussii (The abolition of serfdom and the organization of relationships between landlords and peasants in Prussia), which he wrote as a result of these investigations, contains two or three ideas which are important for what they indicate about the source of Samarin's commitment to reform,

---

[630]Sochineniya, II, 428.

on the one hand, and about Samarin the practical politician, on the
other.

Samarin concluded that Prussia had collapsed under Napoleon's
attack in 1806 for two reasons: her "domestic disorder" coupled with
"stagnation," and her shameful and vacillating foreign policy.[631]
That these twin deficiencies were a recipe for a humiliating national
defeat and could not, therefore, be tolerated, was driven home to
Samarin by the outcome of the Crimean War to which "domestic disorder
and weakness" had so greatly contributed.[632] He found the antidote
in the reform initiatives of Stein and Hardenberg, which were pushed to
a successful conclusion in the face of stiff opposition from "a party,
which had enticed Prussia into a hopeless policy and consoled itself
with the hope of buying a shameful peace by unconditional submissive-
ness in foreign affairs and the systematic maintenance of stagnation
inside the state."[633] Thus Samarin concluded that there was much to
be learned from the reform process in Prussia, and emerged from his
Prussion studies more firmly committed to reform.

Samarin also drew an important political precept from his Prussian
studies. Rejecting the thought that the Stein-Hardenberg formula might
be applied to Russia in the present crisis, he said: "In practical work
there is not a [generally applicable] formula. The task of legislation lies

---

[631]"Uprazdnenie krepostnogo prave...v Prussii," Ibid., pp.
242-243.

[632]"O krepostnom sostoyanii," Ibid., p. 17.

[633]"Uprazdnenie krepostnogo prava...v Prussii," Ibid., p. 271.

in a hunt for the best measures for a given epoch, for a given locality, under given conditions."[634] Therefore Samarin was a politician who, in spite of his ideological persuasion, was prepared to make realistic compromises in the search for practicable solutions to difficult problems.

The first phase of Samarin's work on the great peasant reform came to an end 20 November 1857, when the first "Imperial Rescript," sometimes referred to as the "Nazimov Rescript," was sent to V.I. Nazimov the governor-general of Vilnius. From this time Samarin was directly involved in the practical work of negotiating and preparing the reform. But, what was the first "Imperial or Nazimov Rescript," and why did it alter the character of Samarin's reform work?

By September 1857 Alexander II's government had begun to seek the assistance of the nobility for its reform initiatives. Thinking that the peasants of the western provinces should be liberated first, because at least a portion of the nobility there favoured abolition, the government ordered Governor-General Nazimov to form provincial gentry committees comprising "district marshals of the nobility and 'respected' seigniors [sic] ... to review the inventories of landowner estates."[635] Although these committees were properly convened, no useful proposals came from them, so that Nazimov had little to offer to St. Petersburg, when he made his personal report at the end of October.

---

[634]Ibid., p. 324.

[635]Zaionchkovsky, p. 54.

However, by this time the Ministry of Internal Affairs had worked out "General Principles for Organizing Peasant Conditions, and these after being considered along with Nazimov's report, provided a basis for the first "Imperial Rescript."[636]

The "General Principles" specified that all land belonged to the landlords; that serfdom had to be abolished slowly over eight to twelve years; that "in the interest of preventing harmful mobility and vagrancy in the rural population, the release of peasants from personal dependency must entail the conversion into property of the farmsteads they use and small parcels of garden pasture land, one half to one desyatin in all per household;"[637] and that farmsteads must be redeemed over a period of eight to twelve years.[638]

Thus these "General Principles" appeared as a part of the "Imperial Rescript," which was sent to Nazimov 20 November 1857. This decree required Lithuanian noblemen to begin compiling projects "for the organization and betterment of the life of gentry serfs." It also stipulated that this work of project development had to go forward under the agency of provincial committees comprised of one elected nobleman from each district, plus two landowners from each province appointed by the governor. The chairman of each provincial committee, it was stipulated, had to be the provincial marshall of the nobility.

---

[636]Ibid.

[637]As quoted in Zaionchkovsky, Ibid.

[638]Ibid.

It also enunciated the parameters within which these provincial committees had to work, and this is where the "General Principles" came into play:

1. The landlords retain ownership of all land. Peasants keep their homestead plots which they acquire as property by means of repayment over a certain time period. Moreover, the peasants are granted the use of an amount of land suiting local conditions to maintain themselves and to satisfy their obligations to the government and the gentry for which they pay obrok or perform work for the landowner.
2. Peasants must be organized into rural communities; the landlords maintain patrimonial police powers.
3. When establishing the future ties between masters and peasants, the punctual payment of state and local duties and monetary levies must be guaranteed in a suitable manner.[639]

The terms of this decree served as the official programme of the peasant reform. They proposed to grant personal freedom to the peasants, although in a way which would keep them partially dependent on their landlords. And they specified in a supplementary passage that "the peasants would pass through a 'transitional stage' not to exceed twelve years" by the end of which time they would be expected to redeem their farmsteads and could expect to have the size of their allotments and obligations fixed.[640]

The "Nazimov Rescript" proved to be a politically important move, because it provoked a series of events, some calculated by reactionaries to circumvent the reforms, and others calculated by liberals to advance them, which gave the government an opportunity to establish

---

[639]As quoted in Zaionchkovsky, p. 55.

[640]Ibid.

provincial committees throughout all of Russia by late 1858. Most

noblemen were opposed to the government's reform initiatives. One

specific example of this fact was provided by the chief of gendarmes in

a report describing nobility class reaction to the rescripts:

> The first imperial rescripts...made a sorrowful and alarming
> impression. Although, thanks to early rumours, everyone ex-
> pected this arrangement, as expressed officially, it worried
> even those who formerly approved this measure. Most land-
> lords viewed this act as an inequitable appropriation of
> their property and their future ruin. It was not the general
> desire expressed in the addresses, but the insistence of
> local authorities and the cooperation of a few chosen land-
> lords that moved the Lithuanian nobles and afterwards the
> nobles of St. Petersburg and Nizhnii Novgorod to request the
> formation of provincial committees.[641]

Another such example is contained in a letter which Ivan Turgenev wrote

to Alexander Herzen 26 December 1857:

> Two rescripts and a third on the same matter to Ignatiev
> produced unheard-of anxiety among our noblemen; under
> ostensible compliance is hidden the most narrow-minded
> stubbornness, and fear and niggardly stinginess.[642]

By contrast, Samarin's reaction was strikingly liberal and progressive.

Samarin's reform work from 20 November 1858 when the "Nazimov

Rescript" was issued, and June 1859 when he joined the Editing Com-

missions, falls into two categories.[643] In the first, he served as

---

[641]Ibid., pp. 56-57.

[642]Ibid., p. 57.

[643]The Secret Committee was renamed the Main Committee 16
February 1858 after the rescripts had been published. On 4 March 1858
Editing Commissions were formed to function as sub-committees of the
Main Committee for the purpose of assessing materials being submitted
by the provincial committees, and to draft a plan for reform. At the
outset two commissions were planned, one to draft a general overall
statute, and one to draft local regional statutes. Although only one
commission was ever formed, the name continued to be used in the
plural. Zaionchkovsky, p. 72.

a writer and contributor to A. I Koshelev's journal Sel'skoe blagoustr-oystvo (Rural Management): in the second he served as the government's appointed representative on the Samara provincial committee.

Of the articles published in Sel'skoe blagoustroystvo, perhaps the most important were those written in support of continued land owner-ship by the traditional peasant commune (obshchina). These articles are polemical in tone and were written to rebut the arguments being advanced by those who wanted the peasant reform to establish indepen-dent land ownership as the organizing principle of Russian agriculture. In this debate Samarin wrote, as did his editor A.I. Koshelev, as a spokesman of the Slavophil school.[644]

The principles defended by Samarin in his articles on the Obshchina (commune), and especially in O pozemel'nom obshchinnom vladenii (On communal land ownership), are an expanded version of the very same principles which he advanced to Grand Duke Konstantin in his memorandum Chto vygodnee.[645] To start with, Samarin declared that the obshchina was a vital organization which had evolved out of Russia's unique socio-economic experience. As such it simultaneously combined three forms of land utilization: "communal land ownership, joint land use, and personal land use."[646] The obshchina as a collective unit owned all of the land and determined how it would be

---

[644]Sochineniya, III, VIII.

[645]Ibid., III, pp. 3-18. See above, p. 246. See also, p. 228 above.

[646]O pozemel'nom obshchinnom vladenii," Sochineniya, III, 6.

used; part of the land, pasture lands, woodlands, etc., were set aside
for joint use; and the remainder, (plowlands or fields) were set aside
for personal use. On this part of the communal land every peasant was
an independent landholder with an equal opportunity to provide for his
needs by his own personal efforts. The tyaglo system, which Samarin
described as "the fullest and most characteristic manifestation of our
rural economic life,"[647] guaranteed fair and equitable devision and redivision of the plowlands.

The tyaglo was a quantitative unit devised by the agricultural
community to resolve the anomaly existing between "physical needs"
(fizicheskie potrebnosti) and "productive power" (rabochie cily) among
its members. On the one hand, it proved to be inequitable to divide
the land between active workers only, because it left many members of
the obshchina without sustenance: on the other hand, it proved to be
wasteful to allot equal shares of land to every member of the obshchina
because it left much of the land unused. Thus the tyaglo was devised
as a unit to "define quantitatively the productive power and needs of
each household in relation to the productive power and needs of the
whole obshchina."[648] In practice, the tyaglo was a unit comprising
a group of workers and consumers, varying between 2½ and 3 individuals,
which was used to divide all of the communal land set aside for
individual use as well as all of the obligations of the obshchina

---

647Ibid., p. 7.

648Ibid., pp. 7-8.

between its members.[649] Each peasant household received as much

land as it possessed tyaglos. And so Samarin concluded:

> The proportionality of the allotment of raw materials and
> the land, to productive power, to needs and burdens, satis-
> fied the demands of justice and guaranteed the general well-
> being.

> Without infringing on the products of free labour, this
> system, in an indirect way, prevented harmful extremes in
> the division of social wealth.

> The land cannot remain in the hands of those who do not need
> it or are not able to use it, and vice versa: those, who
> need it, and possess means and demands on its productivity,
> cannot be compelled to spend their capital on obtaining
> rights to the land or to take on themselves heavy, frequent-
> ly unredeemable debts.

> This is why our people value communal land ownership so
> much; and why they are right; for these very reasons, I
> consider any infringement on its ancient practises, at
> least, arbitrary and untimely.[650]

In other words, the tyaglo system was an intelligent and advantageous

system still capable of making a positive contribution to a reformed

Russian agricultural economy.

However, Samarin's eyes were not closed to the disadvantages of

communal land ownership and he was very careful to point them out in

this article. He well knew that periodic redivision of the land slowed

down and perhaps even blocked agricultural progress. Moreover he knew

that "prosperous and industrious" peasants opposed the obshchina. Still

---

[649]Ibid. For reasons of comparison it is useful to note that
Zaionchkovsky defines a tyaglo as "the total amount of obligations owed
by the peasant, the peasant's ability to pay them, and the unit used
for assessing obligations (generally an adult serf couple)." Zaionchkovsky, p. 8.

[650]"O pozemel'nom obshchinnom vladenii," Sochineniya, III, 12.

he was convinced by his investigations that a clear majority of peasants preferred communal land ownership:

> ...in the conceptions of our peasants, at this time, the inconvenience of reallotment is significantly outweighed by the advantages of proportional allotment of the land...[651]

Therefore he concluded that the reforms "must not disturb these customs which were valued by the people."[652]

These words sound very unequivocal, implying that Samarin was a one hundred percent defender of the obshchina and its tyaglo system of land allotment. However, the penultimate paragraph of O pozemel'nom obshchinnom vladennii gives pause for reconsideration. A fairer reading of his opinion is that the social advantages of the obshchina were too great to ignore, that it was too early to decide its fate for once and for all, and that a final decision on its future must be left to the Russian people:

> What will happen in the future - I do not know. Will the Russian people sacrifice the equilization of the tyaglo allotment system, and at the same time the economic foundation of communal life, with which its convictions, faith and customs are so tightly knit? Will it, for the sake of preserving communal land ownership, reject the rapid development of our basic industry (promyshlennost'), which demands the greatest possible concentration of productive power and the daring expenditure of capital, or will it find for us a novel escape from the economic dilemma which we are in no position to resolve, - about this it is only possible to guess....[653]

In addition the Sel'skoe blagoustroystvo publications contained a series of articles under the general heading "O tepershnem i budushchem

---

[651]Ibid., p. 18.

[652]Ibid.

[653]Ibid.

ustroystve pomeshchich'ikh krest'yan v otnosheniyakh yuridicheskom i khozyaystvennom" (On the present and future arrangement of the juridical and economic relationships of landlord and peasants). In this series Samarin planned to discuss all of the problems raised in the government's general reform programme. Unfortunately, censorship practices were tightened up in the spring, so that only three of eight projected articles were written and published.[654]

These articles parallel very closely the memoranda written prior to "Nazimov's Rescript" or the "First Imperial Rescript." However, the second article of the series, "O neizbezhnosti perekhodnogo sostoyan-iya," (On the unavoidability of a transitional state) deserves special attention because "it was essential for the development of Samarin's opinions and for the determination of the basic direction of his future practical work."[655]

The government programme of reform as expounded in the rescripts called for a gradual liberation of the peasants over a period in which inventories were to be completed. Samarin agreed with this general scheme of emancipation and he defended the necessity of a transitional period in this article. His defence was characteristically pro-peasant and quite consistent with his theory of peasant rights to the land. In brief he argued that a transitional period would best protect their rights, because it would minimize the pressure to reduce their claims on

---

[654]Ibid., pp. VIII-IX

[655]Nol'de, p. 94.

the land in exchange for civil freedom. During this period peasant land
allotments, accompanied by obligations to correspond, would be determined on the basis of current use, in a way which would ensure an improvement in the quality of peasant life as demanded by the rescripts.
On one point, Samarin was most emphatic - the peasant's lot could not be
improved if the amount of land presently at his disposal was reduced.
He also maintained that the heavy burdens of this transitional period
should be borne, first of all, by the landlords on whom "lay a heavy
debt to help the serfs to become citizens with full rights."[656] This
conviction of Samarin's had more significance for his practical reform
work than did more technical problems like the difficulties of developing a redemption system or adequate guarantees for individual landlord
economies after _barshchina_ or _obrok_ payments had been removed.[657]

Thus Samarin had formulated a positive emancipation programme
before he began to serve as a government appointee on the Samara provincial committee 25 September 1858. Already in May he spelled out the
important particulars of that programme in a precisely worded letter to
the provincial Marshal of the Nobility, P.A. Bestushev. Of course, it
assumed the abolition of serfdom and the establishment of a period of
temporary obligations for the peasantry and a firm commitment to im-
proving their lot. Firstly, only the land should be evaluated on peasant
farmsteads as all structures had been built by the peasants at their own

---

[656]_Ibid._, pp. 94-95.

[657]_Ibid._, p. 95.

expense. Secondly, the size of all allotments should be determined as a
factor of the number of peasants attached to a normal allotment. In
those cases where the peasants held more land than the norm they should
be allowed to retain it in exchange for proportionately higher obligations. Thirdly, the number of tyaglos comprising every estate should be
determined once and for all on the basis of 2-1/4 - 2-1/2 peasants per
tyaglo. Fourthly, the basic obligation owed for a normal allotment
should be two days work by a man and two days work for a woman per
tyaglo. Fifthly, the value of barshchina and obrok should be reduced
from present levels and permanently fixed in relation to one another.
Peasants should be allowed to pay their obligations by obrok instead of
barshchina on condition that they paid one year in advance. Sixthly, in
the event that most tyaglos transfer to obrok payments, the landlords
should have the right to demand a mutual guarantee of payment from the
whole community. Seventhly, when all tyaglos have been transferred to
obrok, the whole peasant community should be able to redeem all of the
property set aside for it including farmsteads and land by capitalizing
the obrok at six percent. Finally, the position of small landowners
required special consideration.[658] The most significant point of
Samarin's programme, and the clearest mark of his progressiveness, was
its provision for the transfer of all land being worked by the peasants
to their full ownership.

In the second category of his work during this period, that is in

---

[658]Sochineniya, II, 72-75.

his role as a government appointee on the Samara provincial committee, Samarin tried with great energy and exceptional persistence to implement the programme summarized above. Every article which was written by him during this period, as even a cursory glance at the table of contents of volume three of his _Sochineniya_ will reveal, was an expression of opinion or a statutory proposal relative to questions under discussion by the committee. Moreover, in every case he defended peasant interests in the face of determined opposition from the landlord class. His principal objective in the face of this opposition, the key to an understanding of all of his work, was "to guarantee the material well-being and in particular, the economic future of the peasantry."[659] About the other two closely-related questions of personal and social rights, he was less concerned, believing that the obstacles to their expansion, "omissions, evasions and mistakes," could be easily "improved and corrected by the government" without having to challenge "inviolable rights."[660] For this reason he could argue in favour of "the temporary limitation of personal freedom, gradualness in completing the reform, and postponement of a final solution of the question in order to save the principle for which he firmly stood - a guarantee of the economic future of the peasantry."[661]

Samarin's position on the very difficult question of obligations

---

[659]_Ibid._, p. XI.

[660]_Ibid._, p. 440.

[661]_Ibid._, pp. XII-XIII.

was also based on this principle. Initially, he accepted the widely-
held view that no obligations should be imposed on the peasants as the
price for their personal freedom. At first, he also accepted the
companion argument that compensation in the form of rent should be paid
by the peasants for the land which they received from their landlords
during the emancipation process. As Samarin put it:

> The right to peasant obligations is a <u>votchina</u> or land right
> deriving from the transfer of landlord land to the peasants.
> Redemption of an indiviudal, independently of redemption of
> the land, contradicts the views of the government and the
> principles, which have been accepted by the committee....
> Compensation for a financial or natural obligation, exceed-
> ing the value of the land, which has been transferred to the
> peasants, would be equivalent to redemption of a worker's
> power or an individual, and for that very reason cannot be
> allowed.[662]

But later as the practical difficulties of drafting a law on obligations
were manifested, he began to argue quite a different position on this
important question. Characteristically his arguments favoured the
peasants, even while taking the interests of the landlords into account.

Essentially Samarin repudiated the principle of obligations,
determined by the real value of land transferred, and paid in the form
of rent, in preference for the principle of obligations determined on
the basis of mutual landlord-peasant needs. In his words, "to determine
their obligatory relationships one to another...by subjecting arithmetic
conclusions to conditions of social agreement acceptable to both
sides."[663]

---

[662]<u>Ibid</u>., p. 207.

[663]<u>Ibid</u>., p. 458.

The reasons he advanced in support of this principle are interesting to contemplate, especially the historical argument about current landlord-peasant relationships. These two classes had become mutually dependent over centuries of living together. As a result their present interests were inextricably linked. Like Siamese twins they could not be separated. Establishing the problem's measure, he said: "An arithmetic problem of regulation does not stand in front of us now, but a social question of the first magnitude: to improve the life of the peasants, without ruining the landlords."[664]

Samarin's economic argument against determining obligations, as a form of rent equated with land values, was as follows: it would make periodic re-evaluation inevitable and legitimate to the detriment of both landlords and peasants. For the landlords the equilization of values would mean a catastrophic drop in the level of obligations: for the peasants, periodic re-evaluation, as land values increased and wages decreased under the impact of population growth, would mean increased obligations and gradual impoverishment. [665] And so, Samarin concluded, linking the economic cost of periodic re-evaluation with the historical argument advanced above:

> Re-evaluation, with all its ruinous results for the agricultural class, is still possible in those lands where, for example, in many parts of Germany, the peasants are not conscious of their immemorial rights to the land; but here, where this consciousness is so deep and vital, the introduc-

---

[664]Ibid., pp. 457-458.

[665]Ibid., p. 458.

tion of re-evaluation would have the same effect as periodi-
cally raising the question of serfdom.[666]

On the question of what form obligations should take, Samarin
argued that they should be paid as either obligatory work (barshchina)
or money payments (obrok), obrok being preferable, and transfer to obrok
being made possible by law.[667]

One very important final point must be made about Samarin's work
on the peasant question at the provincial committee level. It is, that
he demanded sufficient sacrifices from the landlord class to produce a
visible improvement in the material level of peasant life:

> An improvement in the economic life of the peasants assumes
> immediately a sacrifice on the part of the landlords, and
> precisely, a lightening of obligations especially of obliga-
> tory work or barshchina. Naturally, this means that in
> making a concession in obligations, the landlords must make
> it honestly, without any thought of compensating themselves
> by taking back part of the peasants' land. On the contrary,
> if having given up a third or quarter share of obligatory
> work, the landlords reduce the land allotment by that much,
> there will be no sacrifice on their part, and the life of
> the peasants will not improve in the present, and will be-
> come worse in the near future.[668]

Samarin as an expert on the peasant question, was invited to
participate in the work of the Editing Commissions in the spring of
1859. However, it was June 3, three months after the Commissions had
begun to sit, before he reached St. Petersburg. By this time a majority
of the Commissions' members had reached agreement on how to resolve the

---

[666]Ibid., pp. 413-414.

[667]Ibid., p. 460.

[668]Ibid., pp. 256-257.

important questions facing them. Although these principles uniting them had not been officially approved, they determined the subsequent course of the Commissions' deliberations.[669]

Samarin was opposed to a number of these principles. The majority favoured "compuslory cutoffs (<u>otrezki</u>)," that is, the idea that if a peasant's allotment was larger than the norm established by statute it should be reduced in size. Samarin argued that a peasant's allotment should contain all of the land which he had had the use of, with an appropriate increase in obligations if his allotment was larger than the norm. The Majority favoured the idea of determining the size of peasant allotments on the basis of "audited souls (<u>revizskie dushi</u>). Samarin argued for allotment by <u>tyaglo</u>. The majority favoured reforming Russian agriculture on the basis of individual land ownership. Samarin argued for preserving communal land ownership. The majority rejected compulsory redemption in favour of voluntary agreements between the landlord and his peasants, or redemption by the landlord's demand. Samarin argued against compulsory redemption in favour of voluntary agreements between the landlord and his peasants, redemption by the landlord's demand, or, redemption by the wishes of the peasants. This latter difference is explained by the fact that the majority accepted the law giving full land ownership to the landlords, whereas Samarin, in contrast, held to his view that the peasants had an historical right to the land. Finally, the majority favoured the idea of separating the

---

[669]<u>Sochineniya</u>, IV, X-XI.

commune's function as an economic unit from its function as a rural
administrative unit. Samarin, on the other hand, argued for preserving
the commune as both an economic and administrative unit in the country-
side, at least, until a single social unit combining landlord, state and
appenage peasants could be established.[670]

These differences were so great and the possibility of negotiating
a change so small that Samarin was about to resign. However, he was
persuaded by Prince V.A. Cherkassky and N.A. Miliutin[671] to stay even
though this meant turning away from ideas which he considered essential
to a successful reform. Presumably, he stayed because the Editing
Commissions were firmly committed to abolishing serfdom and granting the
peasants substantial allotments (achieving at least the main objectives
of the reform) in the face of powerful opposition from "the big landlords, who wanted to free the peasants without land or with very small
allotments.[672]

Having agreed to stay on the Editing Commisssions, Samarin carefully concealed his disagreements with other committee members from the
public; however, he argued strenuously in committee against those
measures which he disapproved of:

> So, he spoke out against compulsory cutoffs from peasant
> allotments, against the delimitation of administrative units
> from economic units in the rural social structure, and,
> finally, against decisions, which were directed at the
> destruction of communal land ownership, for example, against

---

[670]Ibid., pp. XI-XII.

[671]See p. 26, fn. 37.

[672]Sochineniya, IV, XIII.

giving each householder the right to demand a piece of the communal land.... It is not groundless to say, that if the norms for peasant allotments were not further reduced by the Editing Commissions, then it was to a significant degree because of Samarin; his influence, it must be thought, prevented the Editing Commissions from undertaking too decisive measures for the destruction of the commune.[673]

One question in relation to which Samarin played a particularly important role was the question of obligations. He and P.P. Semenov, who had also been appointed to the Commissions as an expert,[674] were assigned the task of preparing a recommendation on this question. Samarin demonstrated that obligations should be determined by using as a base "the existing obligation, and reducing it as much as possible without ruining the landlord."[675] This proposal was accepted by the Editing Commissions, and was subsequenty used as the basis for establishing barshchina and obrok payments. Samarin also convinced the Commissions that the size of a peasant's obligations should be decided once, and once only. He convinced them, in other words, that re-evaluation should be prohibited. However, this regulation was later modified. Samarin also convinced the Commissions, that obligations should never be raised above existing levels, and that they should never be raised either in cases where they were lower than the norm established under

---

[673]Ibid., p. XIV.

[674]P.P. Semenov was a brother of the Editing Commissions chronicler, N.P. Semenov. Cf. Osvobozhdenie krest'yan v tsarstvovanie Imparatora Aleksandra II. Khronika Deyatel'nosti Komissiy po krest'-yanskomu delu. 3 toma (posledniy v dvukh chastyakh). St. Petersburg, 1889-1892. See Sochineniya, IV, XLVIII, and Zaionchkovsky, p. 72.

[675]Sochineniya, IV, XIV.

the forthcoming statute.[676]

Later as the work of the Editing Commissions was coming to an end, Samarin wrote two works of some importance. One was an investigation of the size of allotments in Samara province, and the other was a short explanatory note to the statute project. The latter provides an insight into Samarin's view of the peasant question at this stage. Of course, it must be remembered that he was writing as a member of a committee, and that he had already made significant compromises with his own programme in the search for an agreement. However, several of his basic ideas had survived the committeee stage and were expounded once again. Thus, he repeated his argument that the personal freedom of the peasantry had to be guaranteed by giving them a satisfactory land allotment, and that this basic requirement of the reform was "a necessary consequence of the whole historical development of the peasantry's land relationships." Thus, he described the need for an immediate resolution of the most important economic questions of the reform. Thus, he once again proved the "impossibility of compulsory redemption and the necessity of a transitional state."[677] This report was accepted by the Commissions without alteration.

In addition to preparing special reports, Samarin took part in discussions on questions for which he had no special responsibility. The positions he took on some of these questions have special relevance for

---

[676]Ibid., p. XV.

[677]Ibid., pp. XVIII-XIX.

this study. For instance, he argued, that the peasants should be allowed, in order to win their confidence, to elect their own arbitrators
(mirovye posredniki). Although his position on this point was accepted
by the Commissions it was rejected by the government.[678] He also
argued that landlords should be allowed to impose disciplinary penalties
on peasants who fell into arrears. He was for such penalties in order
to preserve the concept of a transitional state, which, in his view, provided the best way to secure larger allotments for the peasants.[679]
And at a later stage he defended the communal structure in the face of
powerful attacks from those who wanted to preserve "patrimonial or
votchina jurisdiction."[680]

After the Editing Commissions were adjourned 10 October 1860,
Samarin remained in St. Petersburg to help defend its recommendations,
which were then tabled before the Main Committee. In this function, he
served as an unofficial advisor, available for consultation as well as
for compiling reference materials and memoranda for Grand Duke Konstantin, who was chairman of the Committee. His colleagues in this important defensive work were N.A. Miliutin and Prince V.A. Cherkassky.

The Emancipation Statute was proclaimed 19 February 1861. At this
point, Samarin could have abandoned peasant work without either back
thoughts or qualms of conscience. However, as a practical politician he

---

678Ibid., p. XIX.

679Ibid., p. XX.

680Ibid.

understood that implementing the reform laws properly was essential for
a successful transition to the new social, economic and political order.
And so, he became a "Member (chlen)" of the Office of Peasant Affairs in
Samara province. Because his enthusiasm and commitment to change went
far beyond ordinary limits, the reform work of that Office was soon
concentrated in his hands.[681]

During the next two and a half years he accomplished an impressive
amount of work. As secretary (deloproizvodital') of the Office, he kept
minutes of all meetings, and wrote reports as well as all important
papers.[682] He devised a form for the working documents or land charters (ustavnye gramoty) and performed a host of other tasks. For instance, he prepared instructions for completing land charters and redemption agreements. From the very beginning he checked and verified all
land charters and later before he left Samara he established procedures
for collecting statistical data on them. As he reported in a letter
to Cherkassky:

> We checked and corrected in the provincial Office, all 587
> land charters, without exception. Of 100 charters which
> were received only 5 were accepted for safe keeping without
> corrections. In truth, this work is fairly exhausting and
> tedious, but I have become absorbed in it. The advantage is
> obvious. Except for the correction of a multitude of volun-
> tary and involuntary mistakes, of many fairly essential mi-
> tigations, which have been given to the peasants, I observe,
> that the credit of the Provincial Office has risen consider-
> ably, - this circumstance also has its importance, - media-
> tors, leaders, members, Office staff, are becoming accus-

---

[681]ibid., p. XXVII.

[682]100 pages of such reports are included in Sochineniya, IV,
419-516.

tomed little by little to consistent and precise work. You will understand and appreciate this, knowing well our aristocratic provincial life.[683]

If Samarin was buoyed up by these positive developments, he was correspondingly depressed by the peasantry's negative reaction to the Emancipation Statute. In general the peasantry rejected its authenticity and responded to its measures with a "stubborn...passive opposition, which threatened to slow the reform's progress."[684] Samarin knew in advance that the peasantry's needs and aspirations would not be fully satisfied by the Emancipation Statute, but he did not anticipate their rejection of the principles upon which the reform had been built to the point where "compromise" or "benevolent influence" was impossible.[685] He was especially dumbfounded by the peasantry's response to land holding, for his whole reform programme was built on the assumption that the peasants would insist on holding all of the land which they had used under serfdom. Therefore, he had consistently opposed all measures to expropriate or to reduce these lands, and was even prepared to accept higher obligations and an extended transitional period in order to secure their attachment to the peasants. Mistakes of the latter type could be corrected he maintained, if only the principle was secured.[686]

---

[683]Ibid., p. XXVIII.

[684]Ibid., p. XXIX.

[685]Ibid.

[686]Ibid., p. XXX.

The peasantry's opposition was "general, in all places, and systematic."[687] Samarin noticed this instantly. As early as 23 March 1861 in a letter to Prince Cherkassky, he remarked that the peasants showed no interest in acquiring extra land, and were even prepared to accept reductions: "I confess," he said, "I did not expect that the peasants would accept a smaller allotment."[688] He also found that the peasants were not prepared to accept obligations. Instead they demanded an immediate end to serfdom without obligations and were prepared to accept as little as a quarter of an allotment. This attitude expressed their conviction that compulsory labour was inconsistent with freedom, and that the land was theirs outright for services rendered in the past. In any case, they were convinced they should not have to pay obligations to the landlords. As Samarin described the situation in his letter to Cherkassky: "In general the people do not understand and do not recognize the reasonableness of indefinite obligations, as payment for the land; they are in a position to submit to the law and to work off obligations, but deep down they are convinced, that they have already earned the land which the landlords hold."[689]

Nevertheless, Samarin still worked to implement the Statute. Even with its defects, he felt the basic principles of the reform were correct, and believed its results would ultimately prove beneficial. Con-

---

[687]Ibid.

[688]Ibid., p. XXXI.

[689]Ibid., p. XXXII.

vinced that premature alterations to the Statute would do harm to the long term prospects of the reform, he continued to work for its proper and effective implementation. Political considerations seemed to be uppermost in his mind for he was most emphatic in saying that changes to the act at such an early stage would undermine the peasantry's faith in the government, while at the same time encouraging doubt about the reform's permanency. Moreover, he questioned the wisdom of embarking on new changes based on "hasty untested impressions." Therefore, he worked for reform in accordance with the terms of the Statute in spite of its inadequacies.[690]

When this work was finally completed in the spring of 1863, Samarin resigned from his position as a "Member" of the Samara Provincial Office. And so his five year involvement in the work of preparing and implementing the "Great Peasant Reform" came to an end. According to Kliuchevsky, that reform, which Samarin so labouriously and selflessly helped to shape, "resolved the most difficult problem ever faced by the Russian people in the whole course of their history."[691]

---

[690]Ibid., p. xxxiii.

[691]Klyuchevsky, "Krepostnoy vopros," p. 114.

CONCLUSION

The preceding comprehensive summarization of Samarin's writings
has yielded up a rich harvest of political statements. Varied as the
subjects and circumstances eliciting these statements were, it is
possible to organize them into generally relevant political categories,
and to compile, thereby, a coherent statement of Samarin's political
thought.

Considering the definition of political thought advanced in the
introduction,[692] and the fact that political theorists have tradi-
tionally focused their attention on "institutions, government, justice,
liberty, equality, and - more basic perhaps than all others - cause and
effect, consequences, risks, possibility and impossibility, and universal human features;"[693] as well as the fact that the subjects
which have "attracted the most attention up to the beginning of this
century" have probably been "the ends of the state and the proper goals
and the best form of government;"[694] the following categorization
has been adopted for Samarin's political statements: Government,
Church, Nation, Epistemology, Tradition, Liberty, Change, Broad Principles, and Political Practice.

Government

Russia's State principle was the monarchical principle (autocracy). It was a just and reasonable principle. Firmly rooted in the

[692]Above, pp. 5-8.

[693]Arnold Brecht, "Political Theory-Approaches," *International
Encyclopedia of the Social Sciences*, Vol. 12, p. 314.

[694]Ibid., p. 319.

nation's experience, its development and elaboration was the main accomplishment of her history. Because of popular support it had survived the challenge of "aristocratic constitutionalism" in the eighteenth century and the Decembrist "plot" in the nineteenth century.[695]

The ideal at the heart of autocracy "presupposed the full independence of the individual and his full union in a free society." Laws and compulsion, as well as moral strengths were necessary to maintain the social and political good.[696] The power of the Tsar (in general supreme temporal power) is derived from God and not from the people. The Tsar-autocrat served two functions, as "the impartial representative of personality," on the one hand; and as "the acknowledged defender and mediator before [the community] of every one of its members," on the other.[697]

The commune had played an important role in the past and was a vital force in the present. "The communal principle constitutes the foundation, the ground of all Russian history, past, present and future...." The commune was a positive force, "the embryo of life and consciousness." It had the capacity to renew itself in different forms, and its most recent manifestation was in the form of the all-Russian unified state commune. Communal life "was not founded on personality... but presupposed the highest act of personal freedom and consciousness - self-denial." The communal principle was expressed at every stage of the evolution of the Russian political system in two mutually interdependent

---

[695]Above, pp. 38, 41, 124 and 38.

[696]Above, pp. 162, 164, and 169.

[697]Above, pp. 118 and 179.

"manifestations:" as an assembly (vyeche) uniting the community, and as a leader (prince) representing personality. Finally, the prince (tsar) manifested the superior Christian notion of individual responsibility, the idea that a "free individual" has "moral obligations."[698]

The State is "a vital union of all classes in a free communion." "The first condition of the existence of a State union is the submission of all rights and private interests, both local and class, to social uses, and to the right of the supreme power, no matter in what form it is expressed, to decide without appeal all questions related to social use and to implement those decisions." "A strong political and State organization is the guarantee of a peoples' internal strength."[699] The failure of a people "to give political definition to their national life or form an independent State" was a "moral evil." For a State to take form the people had to reach beyond considerations of "self-preservation and class interest," to the idea of "self-sacrifice" on behalf of the larger community or "fatherland." The responsibility of "the supreme power" was to provide "administrative unity, the social well-being of all, and the rule of law." Moral imperatives are binding on everyone in the State - tsar, officials and peasants alike.[700] Rights and obligations went hand in hand. Unselfish service had its source in commitment to country. Among Russians, commmitment to country was exemplified in

---

[698]Above, pp. 177, 178, 179, and 180.

[699]Above, pp. 202, 216, and 196.

[700]Above, pp. 202, 203, and 183.

love for their "best possessions - people, language and Orthodoxy."
These provided the real strength of the Russian government and the
raison de' etre of the Tsar, who was "the first man of the Russian land
and the first son of the Orthodox Church." "The idea of service and its
meaning is derived from the idea of the relationship of private individuals to the supreme power;" Russians with their high commitment to
country served as a matter of duty. In every State the laws had to be
numerous enough to allow for the successful adjudication "of all existing relationships and juridical questions," and had to be "accessible
to all." A government had to be a neutral arbitrator, and had to serve
the interests of all the people irrespective of the needs or advantages
of a particular class.[701]

A formal constitution was a legislative device for protecting
narrow class interests and privilege. The moral regeneration of society
was the best guarantee of security and justice in the State.[702]

The Russian State was "organically formed." Therefore, its
institutions and relationships had been synthesized from traditional
practices and current needs. The relationship between Church and State

---

[701]Above, pp. 209, and 215.

[702]Above, pp. 120, 163 and 212-214. Samarin felt that Russia
with its illiterate peasantry had little prospect of benefiting from
constitutional forms in the 1860's. At this point he had more faith in
reforming Tsars, education and the steady development of a firm foundation of local institutions. He believed the latter two elements were
essential before liberal constitutional ideas could be profitably
applied in Russia. See R. Wortman, "Koshelev, Samarin and Cherkassky
and the Fate of Liberal Slavophilism," Slavic Review, (June 1962), vol.
XXI, no. 2, pp. 277-279, where letters between Koshelev, Cherkassky and
Samarin are compared. "We are not yet ready for a people's constitution,
and a constitution that is not truly popular, that is, the rule of the
minority acting without the consent of the majority, is but a lie and a
deceit." Samarin writing in 1862. As quoted in Florinsky, Russia, II,
1068.

reflected this fact. The State's temporal authority extended over the civil side of Church life, but not over its spiritual side. The Church's function was "to cultivate in man a sense of spiritual love," and to teach him the difference between good and evil, so that he would obey the law as a matter of conscience.[703]

The government had the responsibility of initiating reforms, it had the responsibility of guaranteeing justice to all, and it had to rule in the interests of the people as a whole. "The government does not create life, but it can suppress it consciously or unconsciously, and it can also help its development."[704]

Samarin's theoretical perceptions did not blind him to the deficiencies of autocracy. Government paper work was filled with "unconscionable calculated lies," and it was done with "offensive carelessness." "To serve Petersburg was to betray Russia...." Petersburg's work was like a "comedy" about which it was ridiculous to speak either in terms of "duty to the fatherland" or "duty as a Christian." In 1848 he described the government as being "inconsistent and powerless" because of "an inner flaw" best described as "inner emptiness or...senselessness."[705] He was no uncritical defender of autocracy and after 1860 worked for its gradual reform by assisting in the construction of strong institutions of local government as the essential first step towards the

---

[703]Above, pp. 124, 125, and 120.

[704]Above, pp. 158, 159, 214, 215, and 219.

[705]Above, pp. 151, 152, 222, and 223.

introduction of a national legislative assembly.[706]

Church

Samarin's theology comprised at least these points. The Orthodox Church invested authority in ecumenical councils. Its role in Russian history had been moral because it made no claim to temporal power. The Christianization of Russia was an event of "great significance [proceeding] without war, without force, by the unanimous consent of all the people...." The Church unites the individual and the holy spirit. The "embryo" of dogma reaches consciousness through life in the Church. Clashes of interpretation of dogma are reconciled by ecumenical councils. There is no truth which the Church cannot perceive. "The Church was humanity recreated through the incarnation of Christ as God-man." "Without incarnation...there could be no growth in knowledge of the Holy Spirit." The Orthodox Church is superior to the Catholic Church. The Church was "an incarnation of the divine in the human." "The Spirit of God lives constantly in the Church, i.e., in the vital collectivity of her members, and not in one of them in particular." The Orthodox Church was inherently progressive.[707]

---

[706]Koshelev said in a letter to Cherkassky: "Samarin says that it is necessary to begin the construction of the building from the bottom, from the basis, local society." Cherkassky said in his reply: "In many respects, and in the real essentials I wholly share Samarin's opinion. Thus I do not see the gain in convening a Zemskaya Duma at the present time, and I am convinced that now time should be devoted to more essential and beneficial concerns, ... I repeat with Samarin from deep conviction: if Russia wants to be happy she must begin by placing beneath her a firm foundation of local institutions, and then later, think of the luxury of public life and the consolidation and ornamentation of political forms." R. Wortman, "Koshelev, Samarin and Cherkassky and the Fate of Liberal Slavophilism", Slavic Review (June, 1962), vol. XXI, no. 2, p.272.

[707]Above, pp. 40, 41, 44, 49, 50, 52, 54, 110, 95, and 107.

Samarin's theology was a powerful shaping force in his political thought. The Orthodox Church never tried to exist as a State. Her sphere was the "pure-spiritual sphere and she never tried to step beyond it. She saw the State as "a separate independent sphere [with] its own justification." Out of these facts Samarin elaborated the following set of relationships. The State recognizes the "spiritual" power of the Church and her clerical representatives. Clergymen have dual status - as representatives of the Church they exercise spiritual power and are not subject to State authority - as citizens of the State they are subject to State authority in the same way other citizens are. The normal relationship of Church and State in the Orthodox world is one of mutual recognition and full reconciliation. The Church gives supreme State power religious significance.... The State in its turn, defends the Church from external attacks, helps her in the eradication of abuses, protects the interests of ... her representatives." Focusing on the regenerative powers of "the Word" the Orthodox Church never had recourse to external methods of compulsion.[708]

The supreme temporal authority had the right to limit clerical privileges when they infringed upon the rights of good government. "The spirit of the Orthodox Church" required a Church-State relationship in which the Church existed in a recognized nation state and voluntarily accepted the supreme power of the duly established authority in all matters except those relating to the exercise of spiritual power. The

---

[708]Above, pp. 118, 119, and 120.

Church plays a constructive role in the State. It makes possible a
"strong, true, lasting premeditated penetration of the national life by
Christian morality; that man devoted to himself alone, torn away from
the Church is necessarily separated from God and his neighbours; that
the absence of a positive faith and authority leads to arbitrariness in
opinions and from there to arbitrariness in affairs...." Samarin was
absolutely convinced that any State - past, present or future - is
dependent on the objective Church for the establishment of that minimum
standard of behavior based on ethical principles which is so necessary
for the development and maintenance of a reliable, just, social and
political order.[709]

   "The positive side of Christianity...imposed a real obligation,...
a blessed burden on man in the very act of liberating him." Christianity "defined" a man's personality for him as well as introducing him to
the idea "of repudiating his personality...and subjecting himself unconditionally to the whole. This self-denial of each to the advantage of
all is the beginning of a free, but at the same time unconditionally
obligatory, union of people between themselves. This union, this commune
(obshchina), consecrated by the eternal presence of the Holy Spirit, is
the Church."[710] This perception Samarin carried into the political
sphere.

---

[709]Above, pp. 126, and 132.

[710]Above, p. 171. Samarin approved Gogal's statement that
"Society will only be righted when every private person...will live like
a Christian." Sochineniya, XII, 216.

Nation

Patriotism was an enduring feature of Samarin's thought. "The two principles of [Russian] nationality [were] Orthodoxy and autocracy." Russia's historical development had passed through three stages: "exclusive nationality, imitation and intelligent nationality." Russia survived the first two periods unscathed, i.e., her two principles Orthodoxy and autocracy, survived. In the third period Russia had come into her own. A glorious future based on "the fruit of her past" lay ahead. She would influence "the West through her ideas." Her development would be independent. She would "borrow only the material results of Western civilization as, for example, industrialization." Russia was not interested in territorial expansion. Her duty was to listen "to the word of the Creator," and to reject material wealth, imperial power and haughty pride.[711]

Russia's "national principle" survived the "centripetal" pressure of the appanage period because of Orthodoxy. Moscow emerged from the appanage period as the nation's "first and only capital." "Centrifugal" pressures compelled Russia to search for "a state idea, a vital centre, a Tsar." "The principle of autocracy" proved to be that idea. Samarin summarized his view of the nationality question as follows: "We did not have either conquest, or feudalism or aristocracy (in the sense of an independent principle) and there was no agreement (social contract) between the Tsar and the people. Unlimited power, indivisible and national,

---

[711]Above, pp. 36, 37, and 39.

acting in the name of all, going at the head of our civilization and completing without the horrors of revolution, that which in the West was the result of internecine war, religious discord and social upheavals - such is the form of government created for themselves by the Russian people; it is the holy inheritance of our history...any other would be tyranny." He summarized his view of Russia's future in this way: "We believe in the calling of the Slavic tribes to the great task of renewal; this task, we know, we will have to complete ourselves without the help of anyone; the people of the West will not sympathize with us in this task, and for a long time we will have to reconcile ourselves to the thought that in their eyes we are no more than objects of contempt and fear."[712]

Slavic life was free and splendid, Russia had achieved an exemplary "wholeness of self-consciousness conditioned by self-negation." Progress and fulfillment for the other Slav tribes lay through becoming "conscious of themselves in Russia."[713]

Russia's conversion to Orthodoxy was unanimous and spontaneous. The Russian people joined the Church "trustfully, co-operatively, uncontradictingly and were unusually Church-centred in their understanding of Christianity." The Moscow orientation (Slavophil) was marked by "a shared love of the past, a deep faith in Russian Orthodoxy and a profound respect for the Russian people." Slavophils respected "old Russia,

---

[712]Above, pp. 45, and 46.

[713]Above, pp. 60-61.

not because it was old or because it was Russian, but because it expressed those principles which they considered human or true."[714]

For Samarin, love of country was a powerful shaping force. He responded with humiliation, anger and vigor when Russia's character was impugned and her rights challenged. When Russia's national interests needed defending his idealism was conditioned by tough-minded practical power politics. "The systematic repression of the Russians by the Germans, the hourly insult to Russian nationality in the face of its relatively small number of representatives stirs my blood,..." "The union of the Baltic provinces to Russia was...an historically necessary event" made inevitable "by the fate of both lands and by their geographical positions." Historically, Russia's claim to the region rested on the fact of "first occupation," economically, it rested on the fact of providing the region's "source of wealth," and geopolitically, it rested on the fact of the region being Russia's "natural frontier." Moreover, the Baltic German's had deliberately and systematically obstructed Russia's access to West European knowledge and technique.[715]

For Samarin, love of country made unselfish service possible. It was the source of dutiful commitment. He was dumbfounded that "a Russian graduating from school would stand at the same point at which he entered life, disencumbered of all religious notion, of all respect for the family, and of all national instinct."[716]

---

[714]Above, pp. 106, 152, and 193.

[715]Above, pp. 200, 204, 205.

[716]Above, pp. 209, and 226.

Epistemology

Early in hs career, Samarin, who placed great store in reason and logical consistency of thought, tried to validate Orthodoxy and the Orthodox Church on the basis of Hegel's philosophical rationalism. "Orthodoxy will achieve fruition and will only triumph when science justifies it, the question of the Church depends on the question of philosophy, and the fate of the Church is tightly, inseparably bound to the fate of Hegel."[717]

Finally despairing of validating Orthodoxy through Hegel, Samarin adopted the epistemological foundations of Khomiakov. Knowledge is not only a function of intellect, but also of feeling and will. "Logical knowledge has nothing in common with knowledge of good and evil. Truly we know only that in which we live and by which we live." The inconsequentiality of reason brought Khomiakov to the conclusion that religion was the sole source of knowledge and understanding. For Khomiakov "divine truth" had been revealed and provided "the solution to all problems." His theology and philosophy were rooted in his faith. Khomiakov's basic idea was the idea that "the source of all theology and philosophy must be the whole life of the spirit." Central to the "wholeness of the spirit" idea was the conviction that faith and reason were not in "struggle and conflict" with one another, but in "agreement and harmony." Faith was first in importance. Reason was second, having the special function of attaining to "the level of sympathetic agreement

---

[717]Above, pp. 80, 79, 141, and 61.

with faith." Reason itself could not discover eternal truth without

assistance from the whole battery of man's cognitive faculties including

"sentiment" and "aesthetic sense" acting in concert and "inspired and

illuminated by faith." "The whole life of the spirit" was an "organic"

phenomenon accessible only to those who lived a vigorous religious life

focussed on the Orthodox Church. The Orthodox Church was "love" and

"freedom" and the source of Russia's uniqueness and messianic promise

for the future.[718]

These are the epistemological foundations which Samarin accepted.

He summarized them as follows: "The living vitalizing truth is never

revealed to simple curiosity, but is always given in accordance with

the demand of conscience, which is seeking understanding, and that in

this circumstance the act of intellectual comprehension demands an

achievement of will; that there is no kind of scientific truth,

which would not agree or would not definitely coincide with revealed

truth; that there is no such sense or aspiration, in the moral sense

irreproachable, no such rational demand of no matter what kind, from

which we must refrain, in spite of our consciousness and our conscience,

in order to buy peace in the bosom of the Church...it is possible to

believe honestly, conscientiously, and freely."[719]

Tradition

Samarin had enormous respect for both the formative power and the

cement of tradition. The two principles of Russian nationality - Ortho-

---

[718]Above, pp. 83, 86, and 87.

[719]Above, pp. 44, 45, 53, 157, 178, 179, and 182.

doxy and autocracy - were manifestly traditional institutions, dating
from the tenth century in the former case, and from the fifteenth century in the latter. The reality of institutions as well as their
validity was determined in large part by tradition. The Church's consciousness of itself as expressed in dogma was the product of development sanctioned by ecumenical councils. The communal principle, "the
embryo of life and consciousness," had developed through successive
stages of political sophistication from village assembly/tribal chief to
national assembly/tsar. In Novgorod the prince's role was defined on the
negative side by charter and on the positive side by tradition.[720]

His respect for tradition and its product, the organic growth of
relationships, institutions and practice, is manifest in his comments on
the Baltic provinces and the Ukraine. Russia had historical and natural
rights to the Baltic region. Privileges included "any agreement, regulation, decree, legal decision, in general, all written acts, serving to
define the juridical position of a province, city, class or person,
supplemented necessarily by the addition of custom or antiquity." "The
present organization of the Baltic provinces contradicts the basic
political and social principles evolved by recent history." The
Ostzeytsy claim to privileges was invalidated by the historical record.
"Let the Ukrainian people preserve their language, their customs, their
songs, their traditions; let them in brotherly cooperation, hand in hand
with the Great Russian people, develop in the field of science and art,

---

[720]Above, pp. 44, 45, 53, 157, 178, 179, and 182.

for which nature has so liberally endowed them, and develop their spiritual uniqueness in all of its natural originality; and let the institutions, which have been created for them, be adapted more and more to their local needs. But let them remember, that their historical role is within the limits of Russia."[721]

Finally, when it came to resolving the problem of serfdom, Samarin originated an historically based juridical argument to prove the peasantry's right to land. Why? Because his convictions about the role of tradition compelled him to root his investigation of problems, and ultimately his solution to them, in historical analysis.[722]

Liberty

The conflict between political authority and individual rights was a matter of serious concern to Samarin. His ideal was freedom limited only by obligations and the moral imperatives of Christianity. Freedom of conscience was a fundamental necessity of human fulfillment. It was available to all within the bosom of the Orthodox Church, and the State was powerless to prevent it. "The calling of the Orthodox Church was not to force its members to fulfill the religious laws; but to nourish within man himself a sense of spiritual love, force him to understand and to hate evil, so that the law loses for him the character of an outside obstacle and penetrates his whole life as a freely accepted fruitful principle." This high aim cannot be achieved by "compulsion" or by "temporal power," but only by "a spiritual implement the

---

[721]Above, pp. 205, 206, 212, 215, and 231.
[722]Above, pp. 238 and 248.

Word."[723]

Samarin's administrative ideal was exemplified in the Orthodox Church. Her administration was as open and democratic as the above principle of freedom implies. It was an independent council - "organic, free, fixed from inside the Church" - which was responsible to "a loose council, a vital union of all believers," or the Church.[724]

No enemy of personal freedom, Samarin accepted that "the normal relationships [understood in the idea of the prince] existing as a law...presupposes the full independence of the individual and his full union in a free society." The best guarantee of these freedoms was not a formal constitution which perverted justice in the interest of narrow class privilege, but moral uplift and regeneration inspired and guided by the Church.[725]

Samarin favoured voluntary mutually binding agreements. Formal voting procedures designed to resolve a problem by majority "marked the division of society...and a decay of the communal principle." The best decisions were consensus decisions based on the unanimity principle. He favoured free opinion and popular participation in the decision making process. Finally, he favoured cultural and religious autonomy for all nations.[726]

---

[723]Above, pp. 117, and 120. Sochineniya, V, 181.

[724]Above, p. 136.

[725]Above, pp. 162, and 132.

[726]Above, pp. 248, 182, and 231. On the question of free opinion and popular participation, consider his record as a publicist, and as an advocate and organizer of peasant reform. Above, pp. 236-273.

Change

Samarin had a progressive point of view on this critical question.
He held the view that change was necessary, even essential to preserve
the general well-being, social order and stability. Russia must not go
back to the social arrangements of Great Novgorod or Alexis Romanov.
Russia has exhausted, outlived Peter's reforms and must develop independently from within herself. Changing historical conditions required
that both the law and legal administrative practice be updated. The
whole "unnatural" situation in the Baltic Provinces demanded urgent
reform, because the government's stature and credibility was daily being
undermined by lies and abuses, and because the future prospects of both
Russians and Ostzeytsy were being threatened. "The hunger or eviction of
the masses," which was "inevitable" under contemporary capitalist conditions could only be resolved by a basic reform to establish "a lawful
order." Communism could only be conquered by reform. "If the demand
for the organization of agriculture and industry is natural and necessary, then it is realizable. As the development of law eventually became a matter of state, so with the passage of time, trade, agriculture,
and industrial production will assume the character of a social activity." Political development in the Baltic provinces had never grown
beyond the stage of "medieval anarchy." The hallmark of their history
was "continuous opposition to the spirit of the times, stubborn rejection of historical demands in the name of an obsolete past, and a battle
of provincialism and the class principle of separation with state and
national principles." Prussia had collapsed under Napoleon's attack for

two reasons: her "domestic disorder" coupled with "stagnation," and her shameful and vacillating foreign policy.[727]

Successful change required the following elements: government resolve to act with legislative and administrative measures; at least sympathetic support for the government's measures from the people; moderation in order to reconcile the various elements in society; thorough investigation of the historical roots of a problem coupled with careful factual analysis of present realities, including relevant theories; appropriate theory such as his juridical formula explaining Russian serfdom; active personal involvement by committed people with experience and training; and lastly, careful consideration of the possible: "In practical work there is not a [generally applicable] formula. The task of legislation lies in a hunt for the best measures for a given epoch, for a given locality, under given conditions."[728]

General Ideas

Political sense required that a people (nation) have the realism and strength of character "to submit to a just fate." "Tribal pride and unjustified boastfulness" were unworthy, destructive attitudes for a people to cultivate. "The spirit of class and national exclusiveness was...negative and fruitless."[729]

"Loyalty only had value when it was freely given by autonomous individuals." "If the foundation of the inner and outer life of a whole

---

[727]Above, pp. 191, 214, 218, 225, 203, and 249.

[728]Above, pp. 218, 243, passim, 233, 223, 158, and 250. See above, pp. 278, and 280. Note especially fns. 702, and 706.

[729]Above, p. 208.

society is not love, but egoism and disunity, if long service to class self-interest has dried up its soul and made it incapable of free sympathy and uncalculating enthusiasm it is possible and one must be sorry for it, but it is impossible to blame private individuals or a generation for the historical crime of a whole society."[730]

The condition of "legality" required "the existence of laws: (1) sufficient for the successful adjudication "of all existing relationships and juridical questions;" (2) applicable to current needs; (3) clearly separated into active and inactive categories; and (4) "accessible to all." A privilege was "an act of free favour" granted by "the supreme power" and subject to alteration or abrogation by that power as changing circumstances dictated.[731]

Political Economy was a "necessary, perhaps useful" science with the potential of helping Russia if it was studied as a method for examining important aspects of the national life and not as a system of directives. The criticism which French and English economists levelled at the general socialist "idea that man works according to need and desire" was a devastating criticism of Russian serfdom. Confronting the Political Economists' claim that society should provide for "The participation of the greatest number possible in the benefits of the territorial property" and "the use of methods of cultivation on a grand scale," he posed the question: "Is not the desired reconciliation found

---

[730]Above, p. 213.

[731]Above, pp. 214, and 215.

in communal ownership?"[732]

The "ailment of contemporary society is course, conscious materialism" and the only cure is "the spiritual principle."[733]

"An elected power is not strong enough, to defend the people, to put an end to the battle between classes and to bridle the nobility, because it is timid before those who have elected it." Accepting limits on personal and class freedom "constitutes a necessary condition for the existence of any State."[734]

Under the _tyaglo_ system "the proportionality of the allotment of raw materials and the land, to productive power, to needs and burdens, satisfied the demands of justice and guaranteed the general well-being. Without infringing on the products of free labour, this system in an indirect way, prevented harmful extremes in the division of social wealth."[735]

Political Practice

Sound political practice required factual knowledge and experience. "Our general insufficiency is poverty of factual knowledge." Civil service work provided valuable training: "It was necessary that one of us possesses a knowledge of our official reality." A political point of view had "to be supported with comprehensive and carefully tested fac-

---

[732]Above, pp. 227, 228.

[733]Above, p. 228.

[734]Above, p. 230.

[735]Above, p. 256.

tual information."[736]

Sound political practice required that people be approached with "prudence and calculation" in order to win their acceptance and support: "I act with an aim, prudently pressing more on that in which we are in agreement.... I am convinced that, speaking with and for another, we are obliged to speak his language, a language accessible not only to his understanding, but to his heart; all of this presupposes aim, calculation, prudence."[737]

Bold confrontationism only produces harsh countermeasures, thereby ending all hope of a peaceful, just accommodation of conflicting interests. A political position had to be defended with sound, clear statements of policy and position: "Recognition is compelled, a place is taken by storm, it is never given up voluntarily, it counts for little that there are rights, it is necessary to declare them."[738]

Private individuals had a critical reform role to play: "All the important questions, which occupy the government, will be resolved...by private people, acquainted with those spheres of life, with which they join their free sympathy or interests, i.e., by scholars, merchants, landlords, etc., ... Positive ideas and programmes adopted by the government should be supported. To do otherwise would be purely systematic opposition...I will accept the hate and injuries of society, and

---

[736]Above, pp. 146, 144, and 149.

[737]Above, p. 153.

[738]Above, p. 154.

give myself truly to the government."[739]

Reality, made complex by the interaction of factors like personal accident, the confrontation of contradictory principles, and the spirit of indifference made absolute judgements impossible. Prejudice, arbitrariness and passion were obstacles to sound political action. Policy had to be based on principles with an "embryo" for the future in them.[740]

Theory expounded in a scientific way was an important adjunct to practice. "[Russian serfdom] comprised the existence of two equally firm and sacred rights: the [peasant's] right of inheritance to property, and exactly the same [landlords'] rights of inheritance to use." "The proportionality of the allotment of raw materials and the land, to productive power, to needs and burdens, satisfied the demands of justice and guaranteed the general well-being."[741]

Full discussion involving all the parties involved or affected by a problem was an essential requirement of a just solution to it: "This memorandum has been prepared with the sole aim of calling all sides to a calm sincere discussion." Moderation and compromise were essential ingredients of successful political practice. "Far reaching radical demands" provoke opposition. Voluntary agreements guarantee "applicable and mutually satisfactory" terms of agreement. "The task of legislation

---

[739]Above, p. 158, and 222.

[740]Above, p. 159, 161, and 207.

[741]Above, pp. 220, 233, 238, 256, and passim.

es in a hunt for the measures for a given epoch, for a given locality,
der given conditions." "Involuntarily you become thoughtful, meeting
every step the necessary results, into which a system of administra-
on, founded on compulsory and not on voluntary submission leads."[742]

There is no doubt that Samarin was an original Salvophil, for he
lped to formulate and articulate Slavophil doctrine and publically
poused it. The preceding categorization has established that he was a
rious political thinker. It is even fair to say, considering the
oroughness of his scholarship and the range and depth of his state-
nts concerning political issues: authority and the individual, values,
e ends of government and society, freedom, security and stability,
ange, and the structure and function of government, that he was a very
mpetent political thinker.

Granting this much, however, how should his political orientation
defined? Was he a reactionary, a conservative, a liberal, a communist,
a revolutionary? The concatination of ideas in the preceding cate-
rization indicates a fairly clear answer to this question, but perhaps
s own statements, supplemented by a few from his mentor and friend, Khomiakov,
ll provide the best answer to this question. In 1849, commenting on the
trashevsky group conspiracy, he chose the word "lunacy" to describe
e event and characterized "the communist idea as a revolting absurdity."[743]
1844, writing from St. Petersburg he denounced the perceived revolutionism
f his Moscow confreres, and in writing about the commune during the peasant

---

[742]Above, pp.241, 243, 250, and Sochineniya, XII, 349.
[743]Above, pp.226.

reform period be likened revolution to a scourge.[744] While Zaionch-

kovsky repeatedly refers to Samarin as a liberal, Samarin himself spoke

disparagingly of "sour liberals, atoning for some innocent sins of first

youth" in one of his letters of 1851.[745] In 1857, while writing about

the commune he provided a clear indication of how he described his own

political orientation in the following statement:

> Intelligent conservatism demanded that we restrain ourselves
> from the premature transference of the question of land own-
> ership from the province of national custom to the province
> of legislation and administration.[746]

"Intelligent conservatism" is the key phrase in this quotation, bringing

to mind as it does three comments by Khomiakov, who referred to himself

as a "conservative reformer."

> We must show everyone that our [Slavophil principles] are
> just as far from conservatism in its absurd onesidedness, as
> from revolutionism in its immoral and passionate self-assur-
> edness; that they, finally constitute the beginning of ra-
> tional progress, and not senseless fermentation.

> "...true enlightenment has for the most part the character
> of conservatism which is constant betterment, always resting
> upon antiquity in the process of purification. A complete
> standstill is impossible, a rupture is fatal.

> "...only that is conservative which moves forward, and only
> that is progressive which does not break with the past."[747]

And so it seems fair to say that Samarin aspired to be an "enlightened

conservative" or, to use Khomiakov's phrase, a "conservative reformer."

---

[744]Above, pp. 155, and 246.

[745]Sochineniya, XII, 235.

[746]Above, p. 246.

[747]Above, p. 159, and Christoff, Xomjakov, p. 104.

As such he was a Christian statesman. As such he believed in the
organic development of society, and loved what was essential in Russia's
traditional institutions, the autocratic monarchy and the Orthodox
Church. As such he believed in justice for all, freedom of conscience,
freedom of opinion, popular participation in decision making processes,
and the orderly evolution of political, economic and social forms of
relationship.

APPENDICES

This Samarin critique of Hegel was written as a part of a more
general criticism of K.Aksakov's magistral dissertation when it was printed
in 1846 under the title, Lomonosov v istorii Russkoy literatury i Russkogo yazyka (Lomonosov in the History of Russian Literature and Language). *

In my opinion the principle (hachalo) itself of Hegelian logic
is false. The general (obshchee), as the general, exists (you
understand what I want to say). The law of dual negation of
troichnosti is realized in the closed circle of divine existence
and departure to the world of finite phenomena is in any case not
an act of logical necessity, but an act of moral freedom, not a
development, but a creation. You understand the formula of dual
negation in a purely formal way, that is abstractly, as an elastic
schema, and therefore your whole application is completely arbitrary and has no value in a philosophical sense. Having grasped
any conception it is possible to say, that it, as an abstraction
of the general, does not exist, that it, as its negation, presupposes a whole multitude of appearances, and, at last, that one
appearance must embody in itself the conception. For example:
individuality as individuality, does not exist; under the conception of individuality is an infinite number of manifestations
of individuality: finally, a single individuality must appear, as
a worthy expression of the general conception. The conception of
a tree - a multitude of trees - the ideal tree, etc. That nationality corresponds to Besonderheit - is entirely arbitrary: as a
conception, it is general, as a manifestation it is single.

In 1875 Samarin wrote the following introduction to the second
volume of K. Aksakov's collected works.**

The generation to which Konstantin Aksakov belonged,...could not help
but experience the influence of the Hegelian system, because as the
last word in German idealism, it ruled in Germany long and autocratically,.... There only Schopenhauer, who stood alone throughout
the course of his life, who was looked upon as a strange fellow, and
who has been valued by his compatriots only...after his death, did
not submit to it, and here Khomiakov, whose convictions and views
had definitely formed before Hegelian doctrine penetrated into Russia.

---

*Sochineniya, XII, 187-188.

**Sochineniya, V, XCI-XCII.

Still one external circumstance helped its rapid spread among us, besides its logical connection with the preceding teachings, which had also found their echo here. A group of gifted young scholars, who had been very successfully chosen by Count Uvarov for refreshing our universities and who had been sent abroad by him, completed their education, returned to Russia and were placed in various chairs during the very best period of the Hegelian school, before its division into various parties, before the internal contradictions hidden within it were discovered, when the system of the great thinker really seemed to be the last word in human wisdom and when all science, so to speak, had been fitted to it and had summed up its content under its formulas. So, for example, a whole school of publicists proved, in the forties, that the Prussian state structure of that time feature by feature coincided with the idea of the state, without foreseeing certainly what answer had been prepared to this glorification in the closest historical events.

A completely parallel manifestation had been completed among us. Original principles, which had been seen by us in the historical monuments of ancient Russia and, finally, identified by us in the contemporary life of the Russian people, were met with philosophical formulas which had been imported, and this meeting was solved by a series of long forgotten attempts at agreement. Among them the construction of Russian history on the basis of the Hegelian law of dual negation, occupies far from first place by its strangeness. At the very time when Konstantin Aksakov derived in this way and justified the appearance of Peter I, one of his closest friends worked on a composition in which it was proven that Hegel, so to speak, divined the Orthodox Church and a priori placed her, having called religion one of the moments (middle, but not last) in the logical development of the absolute spirit, striving towards the fullness of self-knowledge. All this, certainly, did not survive criticism, was later thrown aside by the inventors of this airy construction and, as the Germans say, was conquered (uberwunden), but conquered by the very same weapons which the Hegelian system had put into their hands, conquered by the exposure of inner contradictions which were seen, thanks to the fact that our intellectual vision had been sharpened passing through this strict school.

Let us not be too harsh towards the innocent enthusiasm of long past years. Speaking the language of that time: they were not without significance, as moments in the development of our social self-consciousness.

BIBLIOGRAPHY

BIBLIOGRAPHY

1. General Reference Works

2. General English Bibliographies

3. Bibliographies of Bibliographies

4. Bibliographies

5. Biographical Collections and Dictionaries

6. Historiographies

7. Samarin

    a) Sochineniya Yu. F. Samarina

    b) Works not included in the Collected Edition

    c) Books Edited by Samarin

    d) Letters not included in the Collected Edition

    e) Obituaries and Articles dedicated to
        Samarin at the Time of his Death

    f) Articles, Books, and Commentaries
        on Samarin and His Works

8. General Literature

9. Addendum

1. General Reference Works

Bol'shaya entsiklopediya. Slovar' obshchedostupnykh svedenii po vsem
    otraslyam znaniya. ed. S. N. Yuzhakov. 4th ed. 22 vols.
    St. Petersburg, 1896.

Bol'shaya sovetskaya entsiklopediya. 1st ed. 65 vols. Moscow, 1926-47.

Bol'shaya sovetskaya entsiklopediya. ed. S. L. Vavilov, and later, V. A.
    Vvedenskii. 2nd ed. 51 vols. Moscow, 1955.

Dictionary of Russian Historical Terms from the Eleventh Century to 1917.
    Compiled by S. G. Pushkarev. ed. by G. Vernadsky and R. T. Fisher Jr.
    New Haven and London: Yale University Press, 1970.
Dictionary of Russian Literature, W. E. Harkins. New York, 1956.
Encyclopaedia Britannica. 11th ed. 29 vols. Cambridge, England, 1910.

Encyclopaedia Britannica. A survey of universal knowledge. 24 vols.
    Chicago, London, Toronto, 1958.

Encyclopaedia of the Social Sciences. ed. Edwin R. A. Seligman.
    New York, 1935.

Entsiklopedicheskii slovar'. ed. Professor I. E. Andreyevsky, and later
    K. K. Arsen'yev. Pub. F. A. Brokgauz and I. A. Efron. 82 vols.
    St. Petersburg, 1890-1904.

Russkiy biograficheskiy slovar', 25 vols. St. Petersburg, 1896-1918.

2. General English Bibliographies

Besterman, Theodore. A World Bibliography of Bibliographical Catalogues,
    Calendars, Abstracts, Digests, Indexes, and the like. 2 vols. plus
    index. London, 1947-49.

Book Review Digest. Cumulated. New York, 1905-

The British National Bibliography. Cumulated Subject Catalogue. General ed.
    A. J. Wells. London, 1950-June, 1959.

Caron, Pierre and M. Jaryc. World List of Historical Periodicals and
    Bibliographies. Oxford, 1939.

The English Catalogue of Books. London, 1801-1950.

Heyl, Lawrence. Current National Bibliographies: A List of Sources of Information Concerning Current Books of all Countries. Chicago, 1933.

International Index to Periodical Literature. A quarterly guide to periodical literature in the Social Sciences and Humanities. (cumulated). New York, 1907-

Kaplan, Louis. Research Materials in the Social Sciences. An annotated guide for graduate students. Madison, 1939.

Mudge, Isadore G. Guide to Reference Books. Chicago, 1939.

Nineteenth Century Readers' Guide to Periodical Literature. 1890-1900. ed. H. G. Cushing and A. V. Morris. New York, 1944.

Poole's Index to Periodical Literature. London, 1802-1907.

Readers' Guide to Periodical Literature. Cumulated. New York, 1900-

Subject Index to periodicals. London, 1905.

Times, London. Official Index. London, 1906-
　　　　-Palmer's Index to the Times. London, 1805-

3. Bibliographies of Bibliographies

A Bibliography of Slavic Bibliography in English. New York Public Library, Slavic Division, New York, 1947.

Akhun, M. I. "Obzor russkoy istoricheskoy bibliograffi," Vspomogatel'nye istoricheskie distsipliny. Moscow-Leningrad, 1937, 373-398.

Bibliografiya russkoy bibliografii po istorii SSSR. Annotiorvannyi perechen' bibliograficheskikh ukazatele izdannykh do 1917 goda. Moscow, 1957,

Dorosh, John T. Guide to Soviet Bibliographies "A Selected List of References." Washington, 1950.

Lisovsky, N. Bibliografiya, obzor trudov bibliograficheskogo soderzhaniya. St. Petersburg, 1900.

Morley, Charles. Guide to Research in Russian History. Syracuse, 1951.

4. Bibliographies

The American Historical Association's Guide to Historical Literature.
New York: The Macmillan Company, 1961.

Anderson, V. M. Vol'haya russkaya pechat' v Rossiyskoy Publichnoy
Biblioteke. Petrograd, 1920.

Andrews, T. A. The Eastern Orthodox Church: A Bibliography.
New York: Greek Archdiocese-Publication Department, 1953.

Artsimovich, E. V. Ukazatel' knig po istorii i obshchestvennym
voprosam. St. Petersburg, 1909.

Bibliograf, zhurnal istorichesko-literaturnyi i bibliograficheskii.
14 vols. St. Petersburg, 1885-1900.

Cherepakhov, M. S., and Fingerit, E. M. Russkaya periodicheskaya
pechat' (1895-oktyabr' 1917) "Spravochnik." Moscow, 1957.

Doronin, I. P. Istoriya SSSR. Ukazatel' sovetskoy literatury za
1917-1952gg. Istoriya SSSR s drevneyshikh vremyon do
vstupleniya Rossii v period kapitalizma. Moscow, 1956.

Gosudarstvennye arkhivy. Kratkii spravochnik. eds. G. A. Belov,
A. I. Loginovaya, I. N. Firsov. Moscow, 1956.

Grimsted, P. K. Archives and Manuscript Repositories in the USSR:
Moscow and Leningrad. Princeton: Princeton University Press, 1972.

Internal History of Russia 1796-1894 (1796-1917.) Selected reading
list. Cambridge, 1949.

Kerner, Robert J. Foundations of Slavic Bibliography. Chicago, 1916.

_____ Slavic Europe. A selected bibliography in the western
European languages, comprising history, languages and literature.
Cambridge, 1918.

Knizhnaya letopis'. St. Petersburg and Moscow, 1907-

Lambin, Petr P. Russkaya istoricheskaya bibliografiya, 1855-1864.
10 vols. St. Petersburg, 1861-84.

Letopis' zhurhal'nykh statey. Moscow, 1926-

Lisovsky, N. Bibliografiya russkoy periodicheskoy pechati, 1703-1900
gg. Materialy dlya istorii russkoi zhurnalistiki. Petrograd, 1915.

Mashkova, M. V., Sokurova, M. V. Obshchie bibliografii russkikh periodicheskikh izdanii 1793-1954 i materialy po statistike russkoy periodicheskoy pechati. Annotirovannyi ukazatel'. Leningrad, 1956.

Materialy dlya bibliografii russkikh nauchnykh trudov za rubezhom (1920-1930). Izdanie Russkogo Nauchnogo Instituta v Belgrade. Belgrade, 1931.

Mezhov, Vladimir I. Krest'yanskii vopros v Rossii. Polnoe sobrannie materialov dlya istorii krest'yanskogo voprosa na yazykakh russkom i inostrannykh, napechatannykh v Rossii i za granitsey. St. Petersburg, 1865.

_____. Russkaya istoricheskaya bibliografiya. Ukazatel' knig i statey po russkoy i vseobshchey istorii i vspomogatel'nym haukam za 1800-1854 vkl. 3 vols. St. Petersburg, 1892-1893.

_____. Russkaya istoricheskaya bibliografiya za 1865-1876 vkl. 8 vols. St. Petersburg, 1882-90.

_____. Zemskiy i krest'yanskiy voprosy. Bibliograficheskiy ykazatel' knig i statey, vyshedshikh po pervomu voprosu s samogo nachala vvedeniya v deystvie zemskikh uchrezhdeniy i ranee, po vtoromu --ş 1865 g. vplot' do 1871 g. St. Petersburg, 1873.

Mez'er. A. V. Ukazatel' istoricheskikh romanov, original'nykh i perevodnykh, raspolozhennykh po stranam i epokham. St. Petersburg,1902.

Mintslov, S. R. Obzor zapisok, dnevnikov, vospominaniy pisem i puteshestviy, otnosyashchikhsya k istorii Rosii i napechatannykh na russkom yazyke. Novgorod, 1921.

Morokhovets, Yevgeny A. "Opyt bibliograficheskogo ukazatelya po istorii krest'yanskogo dvizheniya v Rossii," Vestnik Kommunisticheskoy Akademii, nos. 3-7, 12, 2- (1923-27).

Popov, V. Sistematicheskiy ukazatel' statey pomeshchyonnykh v perio-dicheskikh izdaniyakh s 1830 po 1884 god. St. Petersburg, 1885.

Rose, William John. Book List 136 - Poland. A selected list of books compiled by W. J. Rose. London, 1941.

Rozanov, Ya. S. Istoricheskiy materializm. Bibliografiya knizhnoy i zhuranl'noy literatury za 1865-1924 gg. Kiev, 1925.

Rubakin, N. A. Sredi knig. 3 vols. Moscow, 1911-15.

Shilov, A. A. Chto chitat' po istorii russkogo revolyutsionnogo
dvizheniya. Ukazatel' vazhneyshikh knig, broshyur i
zhurnal'nykh statey. Petrograd, 1922.

Shvedova, O.I. Istoriki SSSR. Ykazatel' pechatnykh spiskov ikh trudov.
Moscow, 1941

_____ Istoriya SSSR s drevneyshikh vremyon do kontsa XIX v.
Spisok rekomenduemoy literatury i osnovnykh posobiy.
Moscow, 1941.

Sokurova, M.V. Obschie bibliografii russkikh knig grazhdanskoy
pechati 1708-1955. Annotirovannyy ukazatel'. Leningrad, 1956.

Somov, N.M. Bibliografiya russkoy obshchestvennosti k vopros ob
intelligentsii. Moscow, 1927-31.

Ukazatel' russkikh knig i broshyur po bogoslovskim naukam, vyshedshikh
s 1801-1889 gg. 2 vols. Moscow, 1891.

Ukazatel' sotsial-demokraticheskoy literatury na russkom yazyke,
1883-1905 gg. Paris, 1913.

Ukazatel' vospominaniy, dnevnikov i putevykh zapisok XVIII-XIX vv.
(iz fondov Otdela Rukopisey). ed. P. A. Zayonchkovsky
and E. N. Konshina. comp. S. V. Zhitomirskaya, K. P.
Kamenetskaya, I. V. Koz'menko, and E. N. Konshina. Moscow,1951.

Vladislavlev, I. B. Russkie pisateli. Opyt bibliograficheskogo
posobiya po russkoy literature XIX-XX st. Moscow-
Leningrad, 1924.

Voznesensky, S. V. Materialy dlya bibliografii po istorii narodov
SSSR, XVI-XVII vv. Leningrad, 1933.

_____ Programma chteniya po russkoy istorii. Ukazatel'
literatury. Petrograd, 1923.

_____ Russkaya literatura o slavyanstve. Opyt bibliograficheskogo ukazatelya. Petrograd, 1915.

Zabielska, Janina. Bibliography of Books in Polish or Relating to
Poland Published Outside Poland Since September 1, 1939.
Vol. I, 1939-1951. London, 1953.

Zabelin, Ivan E., and Belokurov, S. Spisok i ukazatel' trudov,
issledovaniy i materialov, napechatnnykh v sovremennykh
izdaniyakh Imperatorskogo; obshchestva istorii i drevnostey
rossiyskikh za 1815-1894 gg. 3 vols. Moscow, 1883-94.

5. Biographical Collections and Dictionaries

Avtobiografii revolyutsionnykh deyateley russkogo sotsialisticheskogo dvizheniya 70-80-kh gg. Moscow.

Azbuchnyy ukazatel' imyon russkikh deyateley dlya russkogo biograficheskogo slovarya. St. Petersburg, 1887-8. 2 vols.

Bantysh-Kamensky, D. N. Slovar' dostopamyatnykh lyudey russkoy zemli. 8 vols. Moscow, 1836-47.

Biograficheskiy slovar' professorov i prepodavateley imperatorskogo moskovskogo universiteta, za istekayushchee stoletie. 2 vols. Moscow, 1855.

Deutsch, Lev G. Russkaya revolyutsionnaya emigratsiya. 70-kh godov. Petrograd, 1920.

Deyateli revolyutsionnogo dvizheniya v Rossii. Biobibliograficheskiy slovar' ot predshestvennikov dekabristov do padeniya tsarizma. Vols. 1-3, 5. Moscow, 1927-33.

Dolgoroukov, Pyotr V. A Handbook of the Princtpal Families in Russia. Trans. F.Z. London, 1858.

Eckardt, Julius W. A. Distinguished Persons in Russian Society. London, 1873.

Gennadi, G. N. Spravochnyy slovar' o russkikh pisatelyakh i uchenykh, umershikh v XVIII-XIX stoletiyakh, i spisok russkikh knig s 1725 po 1825 g. 3 vols. Berlin, Moscow, 1876-1906.

Kaufman, I. M. Russkie biograficheskie i biobibliograficheskie slovari. Moscow, 1955.

Kritiko-biograficheskiy slovar' russkikh pisateley i uchyonykh, ot nachala russkoy obrazovannosti do nashikh dney. 6 vols. St. Petersburg, 1889-1904.

Kostomarov, N.I. Russkaya istoriya v zhizneopisaniyakh eyo glavneyshik deyateley. 2 vols. St. Petersburg, 1873-1886.

Nashi deyateli. Galleryea zamechatel'nykh lyudey Rossii v portretakh i biografiyakh. pub. A. O. Bauman. Vols. 5-8. St. Petersburg, 1879-1880.

Nicholas, Grand Duke of Russia. Portraits russes des XVIIIe et XIXe siècles. 5 vols. St. Petersburg, 1905-1909.

Petrov, Pyotr N. Istoriya rodov russkogo dvoryanstva. St. Petersburg, 1886.

Russkiy biograficheskiy slovar'. 25 vols. Moscow-St. Petersburg-
    Petrograd, 1896-1918.

Skal'kovsky, Konstantin A. Nashi gosudarstvennye i obshchestvennye
    deyatali. St. Petersburg, 1891.

Slovar' chlenov Obshchestva Lyubiteley Rossiyskoy Slovesnosti pri
    Moskovskom Universitete, 1811-1911. Moscow, 1911.

Velikaya reforma. Osvobozhdenie krest'yan. Deyateli reformy.
    Vol. 5. Moscow, 1911.

Velikie Lyudi. Biograficheskaya biblioteka. ed. Wilhelm Bittner.
    6 vols. St. Petersburg, 1912-1913.

Vengerov, S. A. Glavnye deyateli osvobozhdeniya krest'yan.
    St. Petersburg, 1903.

Vlavovic, V. S. Slavic Personalities (past and Present).
    New York, 1940.

Historiographies.

Ikonnikov, Vladimir S. Opyt russkoy istoriografii. 2 vols. Kiev,
    1891-1908.

Mazour, Anatole G. An Outline of Modern Russian Historiography.
    Berkley, 1939.

Picheta, Vladimir I. Vvedenie v russkuyu istoriyu. Istochniki i
    istoriografiya. Moscow, 1922.

Rubinshteyn, N. L. Russkaya istoriografiya. Moscow, 1941.

Tikhomirov, M.N., and Nikitin, S.A. Kurs istochnikovedeniya istorii
    SSSR. 2 vols. Moscow, 1940.

Valk, S.N. Sovetskaya arkheografiya. Moscow, 1948.

Samarin
A. Sochineniya Yu. F. Samarina.

    Volume I Stat'i raznorodnogo soderzhaniya i po pol'skomu voprosu.
        pub. D. Samarin. Moscow, 1877. pp. X,403.

    Contents:

    A. Stat'i raznorodnogo soderzhaniya
        1. Tarantas, putevyya vpechatleniya Sochinenie Grafa V.A.
            Solloguba, 1-27.
        2. O mneniyakh "Sovremennika" istoricheskikh i literaturnykh, 28-108.

7. Poezdka po negotorym mestnostyam Tsarstva Pol'skogo v oktyabre 1863 goda, 353-394.

C Prilozheniya

1. Nachertanie zhitiya i deyaniy Nikona. Sochinenie arkhimandrita Apolloca, 395-401.

2. Po povody knigi: L'ancien regime et la revolution par Tocqueville, 402-403.

Volume II Krest'yanskoe delo do Vysochayshego Reskripta 20 noyabrya 1857 goda. pub. D. Samarin. Moscow, 1878. pp. XI, 444.

Contents:

1. Zamechaniya ob inventaryakh, vvedyonnykh v 1847 i 1848 g. v pomeshchich*ikh imeniyakh kievskoy, volynskoy i posol'skoy guberniy, i o krepostnom prave v Malorossii, 1-16.

2. O krepostnom sostoyanii i o perekhode iz nego k grazhdanskoy svobode, 17-136.

3. Zametka o proektakh osvobozhdeniya krest'yan, 137-138.

4. Ob uchrezhdenii pri Vol'nom Ekonomicheskom Obshhestve i pri Moskovskom Obshchestve Sel'skogo Khozyaystva otdeleniy sel'skogo upravleniya, 139-143.

5. Chetyre zapiski po krest'yanskomu delu, napisannyya v avguste 1857 goda:

a) O prave krest'yan na zemlyu, 144-161.
b) Chto vygodnee: obshchinnoe mirskoe vladenie zemley ili lichnoe?, 162-170.
c) Mozhno li dopustit' srochnye dogovory?, 171-175.
d) Proekt ukaza o polyubovnykh sdelkakh mezhdu pomeshchikami i pripisannymi k ikh imeniyam krepostnymi lyud'mi, 176-190.

6. Uprazdnenie krepostnogo prava i ustroystvo otnosheniy mezhdu pomeshchikami i krest'yanami v Prussii, 191-400.

7. O merakh dlya smyagcheniya i oblegcheniya krepostnogo sostoyaniya, 401-425.

8. Programma svedeniy, neobkhodimykh dlya opredeleniya zakonodatel'nym poryadkom otnosheniy pomeshchikov k krest'yanam, 426-432.

9. Zaklyuchenie k istoricheskomu obozreniyu unichtozheniya
   krepostnogo sostoyaniya v Liflyandii, 433-438.

10. Zametki i nedokonchennyya stat'i po krest'yanskomu delu, 439-444.

Volume III   Krest'yanskoe delo s 20 noyabrya 1857 po iyun' 1859 goda.

pub. D. Samarin. Moscow, 1885, pp. XXXII, 495.

Contents:

A. Stat'i, napisannyya do otkrytiya samarskogo gubernskogo komiteta
   25 sentyabrya 1858 goda.

   1. O pozemel'nom obshchinnom vladenii, 3-18.

   2. O tepereshnem i budushchem ustroystve pomeshchich'ikh krest'yan
      v otnosheniyakh yuridicheskom i khozyaystvennom:

      a) O krest'yanskoy zemle, 19-31.
      b) O neizbezhnosti perekhodnogo sostoyaniya, 32-44.
      c) Ob usad'bakh, 45-54.

   3. Zamechaniya na proekt plana rabot, predstoyashchikh Dvoryanskim
      Gubernskim Komitetam po ustroystvu krest'yanskogo byta, 56-71.

   4. Pis'mo Samarskomu Uezdnomu Predvoditel'yu Dvoryanstva, 72-75.

   5. Obshchinnoe vladenie i sobstvennost'. Sochinenie A. N. Butovskogo,
      76-112.

   6. Pozemel'naya sobstvennost' i obshchinnoe vladenie. Sochinenie S.
      Ivanova, 113-170.

B. Trudy po sostavleniyu proekta polozheniya ob uluchshenii byta
   pomeshchich'ikh krest'yan v Samarskom Gubernskom Komitete s 25 sentyabrya
   1858 goda po iyun' 1859 goda.

   1. Mneniya i predlozheniya:

      a) Ob otmene prava pomeshchika otdavat' krepostnykh lyudey v
         usluzhenie, v rabotu i vo vremennoe vladenie, 173-178.
      b) O predostavlenii krepostnym lyudyam prava vstupat' v mnoshestvo
         i v voennyyu sluzhby bez soglasiya pomeshchika, 179-182.
      c) Ob otmene prava pomeshchika perevodit dvorovykh, bez soglasiya
         v krest'yane, 183-194.
      d) O prave krest'yanina trebovat' uvol'neniya iz obshchestva, pri
         uslovii vykupa im chasti obroka, prevyshayushchey nayomnuyu
         tsennost' nadel'noy zemli, 195-208.

Volume IV <u>Krest'yanskoe delo s iyunya 1859 po aprel' 1864 goda.</u>

pub. F. Samarin. Moscow, 1911. pp. LVI, 559.

Contents:

3. Stat'ya II, 500-515.

4. Stat'ya III, 516-526.

E. Melkiya i neokonchennyya stat'i.

    1. Geschichte der Russischen Kirche. Periode des Patriarchats 1588-1720, 527-535.

    2. O kurgessenskoy tserkvi, 536-539.

    3. Pis'ma o materializme, 540-554.

    4. Ob otnoshenii tserkvi k svobode, 555-562.

Volume VII <u>Pis'ma iz Rigi i istoriya Rigi</u>. pub. D. Samarin. Moscow,

1889. pp. CXXXV, 658.

A. <u>Pis'ma iz Rigi</u>.

    1. Pis'mo I-oe. Istoricheskoe razvitie gosudarstvennogo nachala v ostzeyskom krae, 3-19.

    2. Pis'mo II-oe. Istoricheskoe razvitie protivodeystviya sosloviy gosudarstvennomu nachalu, 20-31.

    3. Pis'mo III-ie. Sovremennoe otnoshenie ostzeyskogo kraya k Rossii i k pravitel'stvu, 32-57.

    4. Pis'mo IV-oe. Polozhenie Russkikh v ostzeyskom krae, 58-105

    5. Pis'mo V-oe. Vernost', zakonnost' i obyazatel' privilegiy v ostzeyskom krae, 106-133.

    6. Pis'mo VI-oe. Rasprostranenie pravoslaviya v ostzeyskom krae, 134-158.

    7. Pis'mo VII-oe. Obshchee zaklyuchenie, 159-162.

B. <u>Istoriya Rigi</u>.

    1. Otdel pervyy. Istoricheskoe obozrenie otnosheniy goroda Rigi k prestavitelyam verkhovnoy vlasti, 1200-1796.

        a) Period I, ot osnovaniya Rigi do podchineniya eyo Pol'she, 1200-1581 g., 165-216.

        b) Period II, ot podchineniya Rigi Pol'she do podchineniya eyo Shvetsii, 1581-1621, 217-238.

Volume VIII Okrainy Rossii. pub. D. Samarin. Moscow, 1890

pp. XXVII, 622.

Contents:

A. Vsepoddanneyshee pis'mo k Imperatoru Aleksandru II-mu, IX-XXVII.

B. Okrainy Rossii.

1. Vypusk pervyy. Russkoe baltiyskoe pomor'e v nastoyashchuyu minutu, 1-176.

2. Vypusk vtoroy. Zapiski pravoslavnogo Latysha Indrika Straumita, 1840-1845 g.

    a) Ot izdatelya, 181-184.

    b) Bolezn' i pervyya sudorogi liflyandskogo rasslablennogo, 185-247.

    c) Vtoroy krizis, 248-290.

    d) Posleslovie, 291-300.

3. Vypusk tretiy. Pravoslavnye Latyshi.

    a) K chtatelyam, 423-454.

    b) Period pervyy 1841 i 1842, 455-622.

C. Reponse a une Lettre Anonyme de Baden-Baden. pp. 301-314.

D. Otbet gg. Boku i Shirrenu po Povodu "Okrain Rossii." pp. 315-418.

Volume IX Okrainy Rossii. pub. D. Samarin. Moscow, 1898. pp. XXXIV,485

Contents:

A. Biograficheskiy ocherk Yu. F. Samarina, IX-XXXIV.

B. Okrainy Rossii.

1. Vypusk chetvyortyy. Protsess russkogo pravitel'stva s evangelicheskim soyuzom.

    a) K chitatelyam, 5-6.

    b) Pervyy opros, 7-34.

    c) Vtoroy opros, 35-49.

    d) Doznanie na mestakh, 50-106.

Contents:

d) Pristup k ispolneniyu. Protivodeystvie dvoryanstva, volhenie v narode, 171-198.

e) Glava IV. Izmerenie i gradatsiya krest'yanskikh zemel'. Vopros ob otsenke bushlanda i pokosov, 199-226.

f) Glava V. Predsedatel' rizhskoy kommissii A.I.Arsen'ev. Vopros o datrakakh, 227-285.

g) Zagovor protiv siversa i vendenskoy komissii. Delo o sostavlenii vakenbukhov v nemezhevannykh imeniyakh. Dopolnitel'nyya pravila 28 fevralya 1809 goda, 285-346.

2. Pravoslavnye Latyshi.

a) Period vtoroy 1845-1848 g., 409-480.

Volume XII Pis'ma, 1840-1853. pub. P. Samarin. Moscow, 1911. pp.XII, 477.

Contents:

A. Otdel pervyy (1840-1844).

1. K Konstantinu Sergeyevichu Aksakovu, 7-52 (62 letters)

2. K Ivanu Sergeyevichu Gagarinu, 53-58 (4 letters).

3. K Kn. Varvare Mikhaylovne Gagarinoy, 50 (1 letter)

4. K Chlenu Kamery Deputatov g. Mogenu, 60-69 (1 letter)

5. K Kn. Dmitriyu Aleksandrovichu Obolenskomu, 70-74 (2 letters)

6. K Mikhailu Petrovichu Pogodinu, 75-79 (9 letters).

7. K Aliksandru Nikolaevichu Popovu, 80-100 (8 letters)

8. K roditelyam, 101-129 (26 letters).

9. K Aleksey Stepanovichu Khomiakovu, 130-131 (1 letter).

B. Otdel vtoroy (1844-1853).

1. K Konstantinu Sergeyevichu Aksakovu, 141-222 (29 letters)

2. K Ivanu Sergeyevichu Aksakovu, 223-227 (2 letters)

3. K Sergey Timofeyevichu Aksakovu, 228-239 (4 letters).

4. K Nikolayu Vasil'evichu Gogolyu, 240-249 (2 letters)

5. K Fedoru Ivanovichu Ienikhenu 249 (1 letter).

6. K Mikhailu Petrovichu Pogodinu, 250-268 (9 letters)

7. K Aleksandru Nikolayevichu Popovu, 269-308 (29 letters).

8. K roditelyam, 309-344 (26 letters).

9. K Vladimiru Fedorovichu Samarinu, 345-350 (5 letters).

10. K Mikhailu F. Samarinu, 351-353 (2 letters).

11. K Nikolayu F. Samarinu, 354-357 (2 letters).

12. K Aleksandre Osipovne Smirnovoy, 358-395 (17 letters).

13. K Mitropolitu Filaretu, 396-397 (1 letter).

14. K Yakovu Vladimirovuchu Khanykovu, 398-410 (3 letters).

15. K Aleksey Stepanovichu Khomiakovu 411-437 (8 letters).

16. K Stepanu Petrovichu Shevyrevu, 438-443 (2 letters).

C Prilozheniya.

1. Perevod pis'ma Yu. F. Samarinu k Chlenu Kamery Deputatov g. Mogenu, 447-457.

2. Pis'ma A. N. Popova k Yu. F. Samarinu po voprosu o razvitii tserkvi, 458-471.

3. Pis'mo Professora Kryukova k Yu. F. Samarinu, 472.

4. Iz otchyotov Moskovskogo Universiteta. P. Popova, 473.

5. Pis'mo N. V. Gogolya k Yu. F. Samarinu, 476-477.

B. Works Not Included in the Collected Edition.

Samarin, Yu. F. "Adres Gosudaryu", in Barsukov, H. Zhizn' i trudy M. P. Pogodina, vol. 14, (St. Petersburg, 1899), 17-18.

_____ "Doklad Moskovskoy Gubernskoy Zemskoy Komissii po voprosu ob izmenenii sistemy podushnykh sborov," Sovremennaya letopis', povoskresnoe pribavlenie k Moskovskim vedomostyam, no. 21 (June 16, 1871), 2-11.

326

Samarin Yu. F. "Dva slova v otvet na stat'yu 'Sovremennoy letopisi' (No. 22, June), po voprosu: polezno li bylo by dlya Rossii, esli by Russkie, prozhivayushchie za granitseyu, vozvratilis' v svoyo otechestvo?" <u>Den'</u>, no. 31 (1863) 4-6.

——————————."Finansovyya reformy v Prussii v nachale nyneshnyago stoletiya," <u>Sbornik gosudarstvennykh znaniy.</u> ed. V. P. Bezobrazov. (1878), 6, 257-326.

——————————."Iz dnevnika vedyonnago Iu. F. Samarina v kieve v 1850 gody", <u>Russkiy Arkhiv</u>, bk. 2, 15, 229-232.

——————————."Iz Samary," <u>Den'</u> no. 27 (April 17, 1862) 7-8.

——————————."Iz Vladimira," <u>Den'</u> no. 24 (1861), 10-11.

——————————."Iz vospominaniy ob universitete 1834-1838," <u>Rus'</u>, no. 1 (November 15, 1880), 18-19.

——————————K Serbam poslanie iz Moskvy. Signed Aleksey Khomyakov, Mikhail Pogodin, Aleksey Koshelev, Ivan Belyaev, Nikolai Elagin, Yuriy Samarin, Pyotr Bezsonov, Konstantin Aksakov, Pyotr Bartenev, Fyodor Chizhov, Ivan Aksakov. Leipsig, 1860.

——————————"O proekte zemskikh khozyaystvennykh uchrezhdeniy," <u>Den'</u> no. 29, 30, and 35 (July 20, July 27, and August 31, 1863) 4-8, 5-11, 4-9.

——————————"Ob-yasnenie, po povodu stat'i gazety "Fur Stadt Und Land,' ob avtore k kasayushchego uchastiya v krest'yanstskom voprose v Pribaltiyskikh guberniy," <u>Moskovskiya vedomosti</u> no. 69 (1869)

——————————."Otryvok iz zapisok Yu. F. Samarina," <u>Tatevskiy sbornik.</u> ed. S. A. Rachinskiy. 1899, 128-133.

——————————"Po povodu tolkov o konstitutsii v Rossii," <u>Rus'</u>, no. 29 (May 30, 1881), 13-14.

——————————"Predislovie, primechanya i posleslovie" k knige, <u>Russkiy administrator noveyshey shkoly, zapiska Pskovskogo Gubernatora B. Obukhova i otvet na heyo.</u> Berlin, 1868.

——————————"Protest gg. Chlenov ot Zemstva Yu. F. Samarina i khyazya Shcherbatova 22 noyabrya 1874 g.," <u>Zhurnaly Moskovskogo Gubernskogo Uchilishchogo Soveta za 1874 g.</u> Moscow, 1890.

——————————Revolyutsionnyy konservatizm. Berlin, 1875.

C. Books Edited by Samarin

Khomiakov, A. S. Sochineniya bogoslovskiya. Prague, 1867.

Russkiy Administrator Noveyshey Shkoly. Zapiska Pskovskago
Gubernatora B. Obvkhova I Otvet Na Heyo. Berlin, 1868.

Zapiski, mneniya i perepiska Admirala A. S. Shishkova. ed.
    N. Kiselev, and Yu. Samarin. 2 vols. Berlin, 1870.

D. Letters Not Included in the Collected Edition.

Letters to:

Alexander II, in Baron B. E. Nol'de, Yuriy Samarin i ego vremya
(Paris, 1926) pp. 147-148.

Aksakov, I. S. Rus',

Aksakov, S. T. Rus', no. 7 (1880): also in Barsukov, vol. 12,
    pp. 165-167.

Arapetov, I. P., in Baron B. E. Nol'de, Yuriy Samarin i ego
    vremya, (Paris, 1926), pp. 147-148. (1 letter).

Bartenev,   Russkiy arkhiv, bk. 2 (1912), p.472.

Chaadayev, P. Ya., in Sochineniya i pis'ma P. Ya. Chaadayeva,
    ed. M. Gershenson, (Moscow, 1913), vol. 1, 402-403. (1 letter).

Cherkasskaya, Knyaginya E. A. "Pis'mo iz Drezdena," Rus',
    no. 11 (1881). (1 letter - probably to Knyaginya Cherkasskaya).

Cherkasskaya, Knyaginya E. A. Rus',nos. 43 and 45 (1881),
    (2 letters).

Cherkaskiy, V. A., in O. N. Trubetskaya, Materialy dlya biografii
    Kn. V. A. Cherkasskogo, (Moscow, 1901-4), vols. 1 and 2,
    passim. (Many letters).

Galagan, Ezhegodnik Kollegii Pavla Galagana, 1897-1898, (1898),
    p. 270; god 8, 1902-1903, p. 64. (2 letters).

Gogol, N. V. Russkaya starina, vol. 63 (1889), 163-176. (4 letters).

Golovnin, A. V. Russkaya starina, vol. 93 (1898). 92. (1 letter).

Herzen, A. I. Rus' nos. 1 and 2 (3 January and 17 January) 1883),
    30-42; 23-30.

Khanykov,N. V., in Baron B. E. Nol'de, Yuri Samarin i ego vremya, (Paris, 1926), pp. 189-190 (1 letter).

Khomiakov, A. S. Russkaya starina, vol. 92 (1897), 19-20. (1 letter).

Meschcherskiy, Knyaz' I. A. Russkiy arkhiv, bk. 2 (1887), 103-107. (5 letters).

Milyutin, N.A., in Anatole Leroy-Beaulieu, L'Empire des Tsars et les Russes, (Paris, 1881-2), vol. 1, 408, 409, 410,414, 416, 429, 448, and 470. (8 letters).

Milyutin, N. A., in Anatole Leroy Beaulieu, Un Homme D'Etat Russe (Nicolas Milutine), Paris,1884, pp. 47, 86-90, 96-97, 179, and 193-5. (5 letters).

Milyutin, N. A., and Milyutina, M. A. Russkaya starina, vol. 97 (1899), 270, 271, 282, 284, 286, 287, 594, and 601.

Obolensky,Knyaz' D. A., in B. E. Nol'de, Ibid., pp. 212-213.

Panin, Count V. N., in B. E. Nol'de, Yuri Samarin and His Time, Paris, 1926, pp. 136-138.

Pis'mo v redaktsiyu, po povodu stat'i v 8 i 10 nos. "Vesti" o Samarskom Gubernskom Zemskom sobranii. Russkiy invalid, no. 47 (1866).

Pogodin, M. P., in N. Barsukov, Zhizn' i trudy M. P. Pogodina, (St. Petersburg, 1888-1907), 11 vols., passim.

Rahden, Baroness E. F. Perepiska Yu. F. Samarina s Baronessoy E. F. Rahden, 1861-1876 g. pub. D. Samarin. Moscow, 1893.

Rahden, Baroness E. F. The Correspondence of Iu. Samarin and Baroness Rahden 1861-1876, ed. L. Calder, trans. T. Scully, H. Swediuk-Cheyne and L. Calder (Waterloo, 1974).

Sverbyeeva, E. A., in B. E. Nol'de, Ibid., pp. 199-200.

Tatarinov, Russkiy mysl',bk. 3 (1911), 113.

Zhikharev, M. E., in Sochineniya i pis'ma P. Ya. Chaadayeva, ed. M. Gershenson, (Moscow, 1913), vol. 1, 403. (1 letter).

Zhiznevskiy, Russkiy arkhiv, bk. 2 (1906), p. 276.

E. Obituaries and Articles Dedicated to Samarin at the Time
of His Death.

"Yu F. Samarin (nekrolog)," Birzhevyya vedomosti, no. 82 (1876).

"Nekrolog. Yu. F. Samarin i bibliograficheskiya zametki o
ego trudakh," by Dmitriy Yazykov, Gazeta A. Gattsuka,
nos. 12 and 13 (1876): portret, no. 15.

"Pamyati Yuriya Fyodorovicha Samarina," Golos, no. 84 (1876).

"O Yu. F. Samarine," v fel'etone Gammy, Golos, no. 88 (1876).

"Panikhida Pribaltiyskogo Bratstva po Yu. F. Samarine," Golos,
no. 90 (1876): also in "Pamyati Yuriya Fyodorovicha
Samarina," Pravoslavnoe obozrenie, (1876), pp. 700-1.

"Pamyati Yu. F. Samarina. Pis'mo iz Rigi," Golos, no. 92 (1876):
also in "Pamyati Yuriya Fyodorovicha Samarina," Pravoslavnoe obozrenie, (1876), pp. 701-2.

"Vospominanie g. Koyalovicha o Samarina," Golos, no. 93 (1876).

"Yu. F. Samarin," Grazhdanin, no. 13 (1876).

"Yu. F. Samarin (s portretom), 1819-1876" Gramotey, no. 4 (1876),
20-39.

"Nekrolog. Yuriy Fyodorovich Samarin," Domashnyaya beseda,
no. 15 (1876).

"V pamyat' Yuriya Fyodorovicha Samarina," by Protoierey V. Nechayev,
Dushepoleznoe chtenie, no. 5 (1876), 103-5: also in "Pamyati
Yuriya Fyodorovicha Samarina," Pravoslavnoe obozrenie, (1876),
pp. 691-693.

"Yu. F. Samarin," Zhivopisnoe obozrenie, no. 18 (1876).

"Nekrolog. Yuriy Fyodorovich Samarin," Illyustrirovannaya
nedelya, no. 14 (1876).

"Vzglyad pokoynogo Yu. F. Samarina na administrativnyya zadachi
nashego kraya (Peredovaya stat'ya)," Kievlyanin, no. 39 (1876).

"Zapiska N. P. Zaderatskogo i N. A. Rigel'mana o Yu. F. Samarine,"
Kievlyanin, no. 44 (1876).

"Rech' I. S. Aksakov o Yu. F. Samarine," Kievlyanin,
no. 50 (1876): also in "Pamyati Yuriya Fyodorovicha
Samarina," Pravoslavnoe obozrenie, (1876), pp. 709-14.

"Yu. F. Samarin," Kievskaya eparkhial'naya vedomost', no. 11
(1876), pp. 393-395.

"Pamyati Yu. F. Samarina," Molva, no. 13 (1876).

"O Yu. F. Samarina. Rech'Knyazya Shcherbatova v Moskovskoy
Gorodskoy Dume," Moskovskiya vedomosti, no. 80 (1876):
also in "Pamyati Yuriya Fyodorovicha Samarina," Pravoslavnoe
obozrenie, (1876), pp. 707-709.

"Slovo pri pogrebenii Yu. F. Samarina, priznesyonnaya
A. Klyucharevym," Moskovskiya vedomosti, no. 83, (1876): also
in "Pamyati Yuriya Fyodorovicha Sam-rina," Pravoslavnoe
obozrenie, (1876), pp. 685-690.

"Pis'mo N. Vinogradskogo (o bolezni Yu. F. Samarina),"
Moskovskiya vedomosti, no. 88 (1876).

"Nekrolog. Yuriy Fyodorovich Samarin," Narodnaya shkola,
no. 4 (1876), pp. 10-12.

"Nekrolog. Yu. F. Samarin," Nedelya, no. 3 and 5 (1876).

"Yu. F. Samarin. Opyt kharakteristiki," by O. Miller, Nedelya,
nos. 19, 23, and 26 (1876): also in Slavyanstvo i evropa,
stat'i i rechi, (St. Petersburg, 1877), pp. 414-417.

"Yuriy Fyodorovich Samarin," Niva, no. 28 (1876).

"Nekrolog. Yu. F. Samarin," Novoe vremya, no. 23 (1876).

"V pamyat' Yu. F. Samarina," Novoe vremya, no. 30 (1876).

"Yu. F. Samarin (s portretom)." Pchela, no. 29 (1876).

"Nekrolog Yu. F. Samarina," Peterburgskiy listok, no. 58 (1876).

"Pamyati Yu. F. Samarina i A. P. Shuvalova. Stikhotvorenie
klassika," Petdrburgskiy listok, no. 76 (1876).

"Pamyati Yuriya Fyodorovicha Samarina," Pravoslavnoe obozrenie
vol. 1, no. 4 (1876), 673-729.

"Pokhval'noe slovo pochivshemu v boze Yuriyu Fyodorovichu Samarinu,
proiznesyonnoe Tikhonom, episkopom Saratovskim i Tsarit-
synskim," Pravoslavnoe obozrenie, vol. 2, no. 6 (1876), 367-
371: also in Saratovskiy spravochnyy listok, no. 86 (1876).

"Nekrolog. Yu. F. Samarin," Rizhskiy vestnik, no. 67 (1876).

"O deyatel'nosti Yu. F. Samarina v pribaltiyskom krae," Rizheskiy vestnik, no. 68 (1876).

"Nekrolog. Yu. F. Samarin. +19-go marta 1876 g.," Russkaya starina, vol. 15, no. 4 (1876), 877-878.

"Nekrolog. Yu. F. Samarin," Russkiy mir, no. 81 (1876).

"Nekrolog. Yu. F. Samarin. Stat'ya F. Dmitrieva," Russkiya vedomosti, no. 73 (1876).

"Nekrolog. Yu. F. Samarin," S. Peterburgskiya vedomosti, no. 81 (1876).

"Nekrolog. Yu. F. Samarin," Samarskiya gubernskiya vedomosti, no. 28 (1876).

"Nekrolog. Yu. F. Samarina." Sovremmennyya izvestiya, no. 78 (1876).

"Nekrolog. Yu. F. Samarin. Stat'ya A. L--na," Tserkovnyy vestnik, no. 14 (1876): also in Pravoslavnoe obozrenie, vol. 1, no. 4 (1876) 717-722.

"Nekrolog. Yuriy Fyodorovich Samarin," Tserkovno-obshchestvennyy vestnik, nos. 35, 37, 38, and 40 (1876).

V pamyat' Yuriya Fyodorovicha Samarina, rechi, proiznesyonnyya v Peterburge i v Moskve po povodu ego konchiny. ed. T. I. Filippov. St. Petersburg, 1876.

"Nekrolog. Yu. F. Samarin. Stat'ya K. D. Kavelina," Vestnik evropy, vol. 2, no. 4 (1876), 906-190: also in Sobranie sochineniy K. D. Kavelina, vol. 2 (St. Petersburg, 1898), 1228-33. ("Po povodu zametki g. Kavelina o Yu. F. Samarine. Stat'ya L.," Golos, no. 103 (1876).

"Yuriy Fyodorovich Samarin," Vsemirnaya illyustratsiya, no. 82 (1876).

F. Articles, Books and Commentaries on Samarin and His Works.

Aksakov, I. S., "Po povodu predisloviya Yu. F. Samarina k bogoslovskim sochineniyam Khomiakova," Sochineniya I. S. Aksakova, vol. 4 (Moscow, 1886), 159-174.

Aksakov, I.S. "Po povodu zapiski Yu. F. Samarina o Konstitutsii,"
Teoriya Gosudarstva u Slavyanofilov. Sbornik stat'ey I.S.
Aksakova, K. S. Aksakova, A. V. Vasil'eva, A. D. Gradovskago,
Yu F. Samarina i S.F. Sharapova. ed. S. Sharapov.
(St. Petersburg), pp.61-65.

Aksakov, K. S. "O russkom vozzrenii," Russkaya Beseda (1856) I, 84-86.

_____ "Eshchyo neskol'ko slov o russkom vozzrenii," Russkaya
Beseda (1856) II, 139-147.

Belinsky, Vissarion G. "Otvet Moskvityaniny", Polnoe Sobranie
Sochinyeniy, vol. 10 (Moscow, 1956), pp.221-269.

Bochkarev, V. N. "Yuriy Fyodorovich Samarin," Velikaya reforma,
vol. 5 (Moscow, 1911), 92-107.

Bock, W.von. Russisch Bekenrungen wie sie...G. von Samarin
enthüllt und bekennt. Von einem stillen Beobachter.
Leipzig, 1874.

Bol'shaya entsiklopediya. Slovar' obshchedostupnykh svendenii po
vsem otraslyam znaniya, vol. 17 (St. Petersburg), 9-10.

Bol'shaya sovetskaya entsiklopediya 2nd ed., vol. 37 (Moscow, 1955),
648.

Borozdin, A. K. "Yuriy Fyodorovich Samarin i osvobozhdenie
krest'yan," Literaturnyya kharakteristiki, vol. 2
(St. Petersburg, 1911), 333-345.

Boutourlin, P.P. Les Jesuites et Leurs Rapports avec La Russie
par M. G. Samarine traduit du Russe. Paris, 1867.

Chicherin, B.N., "O narodnosti v nauke," Russkiy vestnik,
bk. I (May 1856), 62-71; bk. 1 (September, 1856), 8-27.

Davydov, Vasiliy . "Samarin--opolchenets (iz vospominaniy ego
druzhinnogo nachal'nika po opolcheniyy 1855 g.,"
Russkiy arkhiv, bk. 2 (1877), 42-49.

Diederichs, H. "Briefwechsel Yuri Samarins mit ber Baronesse Ebith
Radden. Moscow, 1893 (Perepiska Yu. F. Samarina s Baronessoyu
E. F. Raden. 1861-1876. Moskva)," Baltische Monatsschrift,
(Revel, 1893), pp.368-380.

Dostoyevsky, F.M. "O Yurii Samarine", Dnevnik pisatelya za 1876 god,
I (Paris, 1951) 143-144.

E. K. "Vzglyad na zadachi sovremennoy kritiki," Ateney, pt. 1 (1858),
61-69.

Eckardt, Julius. J. Samarin's Anklage gegen die Ostsee provinzen Russlands...Eingeleitet...von J. E. 1869.

Encyclopaedia of the Social Sciences, vol. 13 (New York, 1935), 527.

Gershenzon, M. O. "Uchenie o prirode soznaniya (Yu. F. Samarin)," Istoricheskiya zapiski, (Moscow, 1910), pp. 41-86. 2nd edition (Berlin, 1923), pp. 119-162.

Gradovsky, A. D. "Pamyati Yuriya Fyodorovicha Samarina (1876 g.)," Sobranie sochineniy A. D. Gradovskogo, vol. 9 (St. Petersburg, 1904), CXLIV-CLIII.

Grot, K. Ya. "Pamyati Yu. F. Samarina," Istoricheskiy vestnik, (November, 1916), pp. 427-453.

Hare, Richard. Pioneers of Russian Social Thought. Studies of Non-Marxian Formation in Nineteenth-Century Russia and of its Partial Revival in the Soviet Union, (London,1952), pp. 162-170.

Harkins, W. E. Dictionary of Russian Literature, (Moscow,1924), p. 345.

Herzen, A. I. "Moskovskiy panslavizm i russkiy evropeizm", O razvitii revolyutsionnykh idei v Rossiy, in A. I. Herzen, Sobranie sochinenii v tridtsati tomakh, Vol. 7 (Moscow 1956), pp. 244-248.

_____ "Pis'ma k protivniku",.Kolokol numbers 191, 193, 194. Also in Alexander Herzen, Selected Philosophical Works (Moscow, 1956), pp. 546-570. Also in "Perepiska Yu. F. Samarina S A. I. Herzen" Rus' (Moscow 1882), no. 1, pp. 30-43, and no. 2, pp. 22-30.

Ivantsov-Platonov, A. M. "Predislovie," Sochineniya Yu. F. Samarina, vol. 5 (Moscow, 1880), VII-XXXIV.

Katkov, M. "Russkaya beseda i tak nazyvayemoe slavyanofilskoe napravlenie," Russkiy vestnik, bk. 1 (June, 1856), 219-223.

_____ "Vopros o narodnosti v nauke," Russkiy vestnik, bk. 2 (June, 1856), 312-319.

Kavelin, K. D. "Moskovskie slavyanofily sorokovykh godov (Sochineniya Yu. F. Samarina. Tom pervyy. Izd. D Samarina)," Sobranie sochineniy K. D. Kavelina, vol. 3 (Moscow, 1899) pp. 1134-1166.

Kavelin, K. D. "Otvet'Moskvityaninu²," Sobranie sochineniy
K. D. Kavelina, vol. 1 (Moscow, 1897), pp. 67-96.

Klevensky, M.M. "Herzen-izdatel' i ego sotrudniki,"
Literaturnoe nasledstvo, vols. 41 and 42 (Moscow, 1941),
572-620.

Klyuchevsky, V.O. "Krepostnoy vopros nakanune ego zakonodatel'-
nogo vozbuzhdeniya. Razbor vtorogo toma Sochineniy
Yu. F. Samarina," Otzyvy i otvety, (Moscow, 1914),
pp. 297-320; also in Klyuchevsky, V.O. Sochineniya,
vol. VII (Moscow, 1959) pp. 106-125.

Kolubovsky, Ya. N. "Materialy dlya istorii filosofii v Rossii
1855-1888: Slavyanofily," Voprosy filosofii i
psikhologii, year 2, no. 2, bk. 6 (Moscow, 1891),
appendix 1, 74-88.

Kornilov, A.A. Ocherki po istorii obshchestvennogo dvizheniya
i krest'yanskogo dela v Rossii, (St. Petersburg, 1905),
pp. 453-473.

Leythekker, E., and Meshcheryakova, N.L. "Arkhiv Samarinykh,"
Zapiski Otdela Rukopisey Vsesoyuznoy Biblioteki imeni
V. I. Lenina, issue 1 (Moscow, 1938), 42-48.

Lettre à Mr. J. Samarine sur ses Brochures: "Okrainy Rossii."
Berlin, 1869.

Lobov,   Pamyati I. Aksakov i Yu. Samarina. St. Petersburg, 1906.

Lossky, N.O. "K. Aksakov--Y. Samarin," History of Russian
Philosophy, (New York, 1951), pp. 41-46.

Masaryk, T. G. The Spirit of Russia. Studies in History,
Literature and Philosophy, trans. Eden and Cedar Paul,
vol. 1 (London, 1955), 285-287.

Mel'gunov. N. A. "Neskol'ko slov po povody stat'i: O mnyeniyakh
Sovremennika istoricheskikh i literaturnykh,"
Moskvityanin, no. 3 (Moscow, 1847).

Meshchersky, A. V. "Iz moey stariny," Russkiy arkhiv, bk. 1
(1901), 486-488.

Meshchersky, Knyaz' V.P. "Konchina Yu. F. Samarina - ego
kharakteristika," Moi vospominaniya, chast' vtoraya
(1865-1887 gg.), chapt. 24 (1976), 321-327.

335

Meyendorff, Baron F. von. Lettre à Mr. J. Samarine sur
ses Brochures: "Okrainy Rossii." Berlin, 1869.

Mikhaylovsky, N. K. "Pis'ma o pravde i nepravde," Sochineniya
N. K. Mikhaylovskogo, vol. 4 (St. Petersburg, 1897),
382-463.

Miller, O. F. "Yuri Feodorovich Samarin", Slavoyanstovo i
Europa. Stat'i i rechi (St. Petersburg, 1877), pp. 131-192.

Nashi deyateli. Gallereya zamechatel'nykh lyudey Rossii v
portretakh i biografiyakh, pub. A. O. Bauman, vol. 5
(St. Petersburg, 1879), pp. 120-137.

Nol'de, Baron B. E. Yuriy Samarin i ego vremya. Paris, 1926.

"Po povodu rechi g. Samarina v moskovskom gubernskom zemskom
sobranii," Nedelya, no. 1 (1867).

"Po povodu stat'i 'Rokovoy vopros'," Russkiy vestnik, vol. 45
(1863), 398-418.

Proudhon, P. J. "Pis'mo Proudhon k Yu. F. Samarinu," Rus',
no. 2 (Moscow: January 17, 1882).

"Russkiy bogoslov iz svetskikh lyudey sorokovykh godov.
Sochineniya Yu. F. Samarina. Tom pyatyy. Moskva,1880 g.,"
Pravoslavnoe obozrenie, (May, 1880), pp. 42-98.

Riasanovsky, Nicholas V. "Iurii Samarin," Russia and the West
in the Teaching of the Slavophiles. A Study of Romantic
Ideology, (Cambridge, Mass., 1952), pp. 55-59.

Samarin, D. F. "Biograficheskiy ocherk Yu. F. Samarina,"
Sochinyeniya, vol. 9 (Moscow, 1898) pp. ix-xxxiv.

_____ "Dannyya dlya biografii Yu. F. Samarina za
1840-1845 gg.," Sochineniya Yu. F. Samarina, vol. 5
(Moscow, 1880), XXXV-XCII.

_____ "Samarin, Yu. F.," Russkiy biograficheskiy slovar',
vol. 18 (St. Petersburg, 1904), 133-146.

Samarin, F. D., "Chto napisano Yu. F. Samarinym vo vremya ego v
Redaktsionnykh Komissiyakh?," Sochineniya Yu. F. Samarina,
vol. 4 (Moscow, 1900), 519-559.

Schirren, Carl Livländische Antwort an Herrn Juri Samarin.
Leipzig, 1869.

Semevskiy, V.I. "Otnoshenie slavyanofilov k krest'yanskomu voprosu: Khomiakova, I.V. I P. V. Kireyevskikh, Koshelyeva, Yu. F. Samarina, K. S. i I. S. Aksakovykh. - Kn. V. A. Cherkasskiy," Krest'yanskiy vopros v Rossii v XVIII i pervoy polovine XIX beka. Vol. II Krest'yanskiy vopros v tsarstvovanie Imperatora Nikolaya, (St. Petersburg, 1888) pp. 386-428.

Slovar' chlenov Obshchestva Lyubiteley Rossiyskoy Slovesnosti pri Moskovskom Universitete, 1811-1911, (Moscow, 1911).

Smirnova, A. 0. "Iz zapisok A. 0. Smirnovoy," Russkiy arkhiv, bk. 3 (1895) pp. 80-83.

Solov'yov, V. S. "Yu. F. Samarin v pis'me k Baronesse E. F. Raden," Sobranie sochineniy Vladimira Sergeyevicha Solov'yova, vol. 6 (1911), 401-410.

Sternberg, E. Die Livländischen Bekenrungen wie sie Herr Samarin erzählt: dem Russischen entnommen und erläutert E. von Sternberg. Leipzig, 1872.

Struve, P. B. "Yuriy Samarin. Opyt kharakteristiki i otsenki," Vozrozhdenie, No. 376 (June 13, 1926).

Stupperich, Robert. Die Anfänge der Bauernbefreiung in Rusland. Berlin, 1939.

Terner, F. G. Vospominaniya zhizni, (St. Petersburg, 1910).

Vengerov, S. A. Glavnye deyateli osvobozhdeniya krest'yan, (St. Petersburg, 1903).

Vinogradov, P. "A Prophetic Career," British Review, vol. 12, (October, 1915), 3-14.

Vvedensky, S. Osnovy filosofii Yu. F. Samarina. Kiev, 1899.

Wortman, R. "Koshelev, Samarin and Cherkassky and the Fate of Liberal Slavophilism," Slavic Review, (June 1962), vol. XXI, no. 2, pp. 261-279.

Zen'kovsky, V.V. Istoriya russkoy filosofii, vol. I (Paris,1948), 235-242.

General Literature

Acton, J. (Lord). Essays on Church and State. ed. D. Woodruff.
New York: Thomas Y. Crowell, 1968.

Aiken, H. D. The Age of Ideology: The Nineteenth Century Philosophers.
New York: The New American Library, 1956.

Aksakov, I. S. "Pis'mo k izdatelyu po povodu pred'idushchey stat' i,"
Russkiy arkhiv, (1873)pp. 2508-2529.

_____ Polnoe sobranie sochineniy. 7 vols. Moscow, 1886-7.

_____ Polnoe sobranie sochineniy. ed. I. S. Aksakov.
3 vols. Moscow, 1861-80.

Alzog, J. Manual of Universal Church History. Trans. Rev. F. J.
Pabisch and Rev. T. S. Byrne. 4 vols. Dublin: M. H. Gill
& Son, 1895.

Anderson T. Russian Political Thought: An Introduction. Ithaca,
N. Y., Cornell University Press, 1967.

Avrich, P. Russian Rebels 1600-1800. New York: Schocken Books, 1972.

Bakunin, M. The Confession of Michail Bakunin. Trans. R. C. Howes.
Intro. L. D. Orton. Ithaca and London: Cornell University
Press, 1977.

Barratt, G. The Rebel on the Bridge: A Life of the Decembrist
Baron Andrey Rozen 1800-84. London: Paul Elek, 1975.

Barsukov, N. P. Zhizh' i trudy M. P. Pogodina. 11 vols. St. Petersburg,
1888-1907.

Belinsky, Vissarion G. Polnoe sobranie sochineniy. 13 vols.
Moscow, 1956.

_____ Selected Philosophical Works, Moscow: Foreign Languages
Publishing House, 1948.

_____ Sobranie sochineniy V. G. Belinskogo v shesti tomakh.
ed. B. K. Fuks. Kiev, 1911.

_____ "Vzglyad na russkuyu literaturu 1846 goda," Sovremennik,
(1847), pp. 1-56; also in Sobranie sochineniy V. G.
Belinskogo, Vol. 5 (Kiev, 1911), pp. 246-278.

Belyaev, I. D. Sud'by zemshchiny i vybornogo nachala na Rusi. 1906.

Benz, E. The Eastern Orthodox Church: Its Thought and Life. Trans. Richard and Clara Winston. New York: Anchor Books, 1963.

Berdyaev, N. Aleksey Stepanovich Khomjakov. Moscow, 1912.

_____ Leontiev. London, 1940.

_____ The Russian Idea. Trans. R. M. French. London, 1947.

Berlin, I. The Hedgehog and the Fox. New York, 1957.

Bezsonov, P. "Knyaz' V. A. Cherkassky," Russkiy arkhiv, bk. 2 (1878), 203-227.

Bil'basov, V. A. "Samarin Gagarinu o Lermontove," Istoricheskiya monograffi, vol. 2, pp. 413-424.

Bilmanis, A. A History of Latvia. Princeton, New Jersey, 1951.

Bloom, A., with Jaffa, H. V. Shakespeare's Politics. New York: London: Basic Books Inc., 1964.

Blum, J. Lord and Peasant in Russia from the Ninth to the Nineteenth Century. New York: Atheneum Paperbacks. 1964.

Bock, W. von. Livlandische Beitrage...(Herausgegeben von W. von Bock) Zeite durchgeschene und vermehrte Auflage. Bd. 1-3, Berlin, 1869; pp. 67-71.

Bolshakoff, S. The Doctrine of the Unity of the Church in the Works of Khomyakov and Moehler. London: Society for Promoting Christian Knowledge, 1946.

Bowle, John. Politics and Opinion in the Nineteenth Century. An Historical Introduction. London, 1954.

Briantchaninoff, A. N. Ideological Foundations of Russian Slavonism. Trans. Madame Sophie de Bellegrade, London, 1916.

The Cambridge History of Poland--From Augustus II to Pilsudski, 1697-1935. ed. W. F. Reddaway and others, Cambridge,1941.

Catlin, G. E. G. A Study of the Principles of Politics: an Essay towards Political Rationalization. London, 1930.

_____ Systematic Politics: Elementa Politica et Sociologica. Toronto: University of Toronto Press, 1962.

Chadwick,Norah. The Beginnings of Russian History: an Inquiry into Sources. Cambridge, 1946.

Cherkassky, V. A. Materialy dlya biografii Kn. V. A. Cherkasskogo. Moscow, 1901.

Chernyshevsky, N. G. Selected Philosophical Essays. Moscow: Foreign Languages Publishing House, 1953.

Chicherin, B. N. O narodnom predstavitel'stve. 1867.

Chizhevsky, D. I. Gegel v Rossii. Paris, 1939.

Christoff, P. K. An Introduction to Nineteenth Century Russian Slavophilism. A Study in Ideas. Volume I: A. S. Xomjakov. The Hague: Mouton & Co., 1961. Volume II: I. V. Kireevskij. The Hague: Mouton & Co., 1972.

_____ The Third Heart: Some Intellectual-Ideological Currents and Cross Currents in Russia 1800-1830. The Hague: Mouton & Co., 1970.

The Chronicle of Novgorod 1016-1471. Trans. R. Michell and N. Forbes. Intro. C. R. Beazley. Account of text A. A. Shakhmatov. Camden Third Series vol. XXV. London, 1914. Reprinted New York: AMS Press. 1970.

Cross, S. H. The Russian Primary Chronicle. Cambridge: Harvard University Press, 1930.

Cummings, D. The Rudder. Chicago: The Orthodox Christian Educational Society, 1957.

Custine, A. Marquis de. Journey for Our Time. ed. and trans. P. O. Kohler. Chicago: Henry Regnery Company, 1951.

Durant, W. The Story of Philosophy. The Lives and Opinions of the Greater Philosophers. Toronto: Doubleday, Doran and Gundy, 1926.

Eckardt, Julius. Die Baltischen Provinzen Russlands. Politische aufsatze. Leipzig, 1868.

Eckardt, Julius. Modern Russia: Comprising Russia under Alexander II, Russian Communism, the Greek Orthodox Church and its Sects, and the Baltic Provinces of Russia. London, 1870.

Fadeyev, R. A. Opinion on the Eastern Question. trans. T. Michell. London, 1871.

_____ Russkoe obshchestvo v nastoyashchem i bydyshchem (chem ham byt') St. Petersburg, 1874.

Fedotov, G. F. The Russian Religious Mind. Cambridge, Massachusetts: Harvard University Press, 1966.

Field, G. C. Political Theory. London: Methuen & Co. Ltd., 1956.

Findlay, J. N. Hegel: A Reexamination. London: Allen & Unwin, 1958.

Fischer, George. Russian Liberalism: from Gentry to Intelligentsia. London, 1958.

Florinsky, Michael T. Russia. A History and an Interpretation. 2 vols. New York, 1953.

Garmiza, V. V. Podgotovka zemskoy reformy 1864 goda. Moscow, 1957

Gershenzon, M. O. Istoricheskiya zapiski. Moscow, 1910.

Gleason, A. European and Muscovite: Ivan Kireevsky and the Origins of Slavophilism. Cambridge, Massachusetts: Harvard University Press, 1972.

Gogol, N. V. Sochineniya i pis'ma N. V. Gogolya. ed. P. A. Kulish. vols. 5 and 6. St. Petersburg, 1857.

Gratieux, A. A. S. Khomiakov et le Mouvement Slavophile. 2 vols. Paris, 1939.

Grekov, B. C. Glavneishie etapy v istorii krepostnogo prava v Russii. Moscow, 1940.

Hailsham, Viscount. The Conservative Case. Harmondsworth, Middlesex, Penguin Books Ltd., 1959.

Halecki, O. Borderlands of Western Civilization. New York: Ronald Press, 1952.

_____ The Limits and Divisions of European History. London: Sheed and Ward, 1950.

Hammer, D. P.   Two Russian Liberals: The Political Thought of B. N. Chicherin and K. D. Kavelin. Ph.D. thesis Columbia University, 1962.

Hare, Richard   Maxim Gorky: Romantic Realist and Conservative Revolutionary. London: Oxford University Press, 1962.

——————   Pioneers of Russian Social Thought. Studies of Non-Marxian Formation in Nineteenth-Century Russia and of its Partial Revival in the Soviet Union. London, 1951.

——————   Russian Literature from Pushkin to the Present Day, London, 1947.

Haxthausen, Baron A.   The Russian Empire, its People, Institutions, and Resources. trans. Robert Farie. 2 vols. London, 1956.

Herzen, A. I.   Byloe i dumy. 2 vols. Moscow, 1963

——————   Selected Philosophical Works. Trans. L. Navrozov. Moscow, 1956.

——————   Sobraniye sochinyeniy v tridtsati tomakh. Moscow,1956.

Höffding, Harald.   A History of Modern Philosophy. A Sketch of the History of Philosophy from the Close of the Renaissance to our own Day. trans. B. E. Meyer. 2 vols. London, 1900.

Iswolsky, H.   Christ in Russia: The History, Tradition and Life of the Russian Church. Milwaukee: The Bruce Publishing Company, 1960.

Jackson, J. H.   Estonia. London: George Allen & Unwin, 1948.

Karamzin, N. M.   Memoir on Ancient and Modern Russia. ed. and trans. R. Pipes. Cambridge, Mass: Harvard University Press, 1959.

Katz, M.   Mikhail N. Katkov: A Political Biography 1818-1887. The Hague: Mouton & Co., 1966.

Kaufmann, W.   Hegel: Reinterpretation, Text and Commentary. New York: Doubleday, 1965.

Kavelin, K. D.   Sobranie sochineniy K. D. Kavelina, 4 vols. St. Petersburg, 1897-1900.

Khomiakov, A. S. "Pis'ma A. S. Khomiakova k Yu. F. Samarinu," Russkiy Arkhiv, (Moscow, 1879), pp. 301-353.

_____ Sochineniya A. S. Khomiakova. 2 vols. Prague, 1867.

Khrushchyev, D. P. Materialy dlya istorii uprazdneniya krepostnogo sostoyaniya pomeshchich'ikh krest'yan v Rossii v tsarstvovanie imperatora Aleksandra II. Berlin, 1860-62.

Kireyevsky, Ivan V. Polnoe sobranie sochinenii Ivana Vasil'evicha Kireyevskogo. pub. A. I. Koshelev (2 vols.); Moscow, 1861.

Klyuchevsky, V. Peter the Great. Trans. L. Archibald. New York: Vintage Russian Library, 1958.

Kohn, Hans. The Idea of Nationalism. A Study of its Origins and Background. New York, 1945.

_____ Pan-Slavism: Its History and Ideology. Notre Dame, Indiana, 1953.

Kolyupanov, N. Biografiya Aleksandra Ivanovicha Kosheleva. 2 vols. Moscow, 1889-1892.

Kornilov, A. A. Modern Russian History from the Age of Catherine the Great to the End of the Nineteenth Century. New York: Knopf, 1943

Koshelev, A. I. Konstitutsiya, samoderzhavie i zemskaya duma. Leipzig, 1862.

Kostyushko, I. I. Krest'yanskaya reforma 1864 goda v tsarstve pol'skom. Moscow, 1962.

Krest'yanskoye dvizheniye v Rossii v 1850-1856 gg. Moscow, 1962.

Langer, W. L. European Alliances and Alignments. New York, Knopf, 1931.

Laski, Harold J. English Political Thought from Locke to Bentham. New York, 1920.

_____ A Grammar of Politics. London, 1951.

_____ An Introduction to Politics. London, 1951.

Lasswell, H. D. Politics: Who Gets What, When, How. New York: Peter Smith, 1950.

Lentin, A. Shcherbatov: On the Corruption of Morals in Russia. New York: Macmillan and Company, 1968.

M. Yu. Lermontov v vospominaniyak sovremennikov. Penzenskoye
    izdatel'stvo, 1960.

Leroy-Beaulieu, Anatole. L'Empire Des Tsars et Les Russes.
    Paris, 1881-82. Eng. ed. trans. Z. A. Ragozin,
    3 vol. New York-London, 1893-96.

Leslie, R. F. Polish Politics and the Revolution of November,
    1830. London, 1956.

_____ Polish Society and the Rebellion of November, 1830.
    Ph.D. Thesis, University of London, 1951.

_____ Reform and Insurrection in Russian Poland, 1856-65.
    Oxford University Press, London, 1963.

List, Georg Friedrich The National System of Political Economy.
    Trans. S. S. Lloyd. ed. J. S. Nicholson. London: Longmans
    Green and Co., 1909.

Lossky, N. O. History of Russian Philosophy. New York, 1951.

Lukashevich, S. Ivan Aksakhov, 1823-1886: A Study in Russian
    Thought and Politics. Cambridge, Massachusetts:
    Harvard University Press, 1965.

Lyashchenko, Pyotr I. Istoriya narodnogo khozyaystva SSSR.
    2 vols. Moscow, 1952.

Mabbott, J. D. The State and the Citizen. London: Hutchinson
    University Library, 1948.

MacIntyre, D. Constantine Dimitrievich Kavelin (1818-1885):
    A Study of His Life and Thought. Ph.D. thesis: University
    of Iowa, 1966.

Macpherson, C. B. The Political Thought of Possessive Individualism
    Hobbes to Locke. London: Oxford University Press, 1962.

Mamanov, E. "Slavyanofily. Istoriko-kriticheskiy ocherk," Russkiy
    Arkhiv, Bk. 2, II (1873) pp. 2488-2529.

Masaryk,T. G. The Spirit of Russia. Studies in History, Literature
    and Philosophy. trans. Eden and Cedar Paul. 2 vols.
    London, 1955.

McNeill, W. H. Europe's Steppe Frontier 1500-1800. Chicago and
    London: The University of Chicago Press, 1964.

Medlin, W. I., and Patrinelis, C. K. Renaissance Influences and Religious Reforms in Russia. Geneva: Librairie Droz, 1971.

Meehan, E. J. The Theory and Method of Political Analysis. Homewood, Illinois: The Dorsey Press, 1965.

Menczer, B. Catholic Political Thought 1789-1848. London: University of Notre Dame Press, 1962.

Meyendorff, J. The Orthodox Church: Its Past and Its Role in the World Today. Trans. J. Chapin. New York: Pantheon Books, 1962.

_____ Orthodoxy and Catholicity. New York: Sheed and Ward, 1966.

Micklem, N. Politics and Religion. London: Pall Mall Press, 1960.

Mill, J. S. Autobiography. Preface H. J. Laski. London: Oxford University Press, 1928.

Miller, A. The Christian Significance of Karl Marx. London: S.C.M. Press, 1946.

Miller, O. F. Slavyanstvo i Evropa. Stat'i i rechi. St. Petersburg, 1877.

Mills, C. W. The Marxists. New York, 1962.

Milyukov, P. History of Russia: From the Beginnings to the Empire of Peter the Great. New York: Funk & Wagnalls, 1968.

_____ Ocherki po istorii russkoy kul'tury. 3 vols. St. Petersburg, 1900-2.

_____ "Slavyanofilstvo," Entsiklopedicheskiy slovar', ed. Brockhaus and Efron, vol. 30 (1900), 307-314.

Möhler, J. A. Symbolism: or Exposition of the Doctrinal Differences Between Catholics and Protestants. Trans. from the German by J. B. Robertson. 3rd ed. London: Catholic Publishing & Bookselling Co., 1843.

Moore, Barrington. Political Power and Social Theory: Six Studies. Cambridge, Mass., 1958.

Moskov, E. The Russian Philosopher Chaadayev, His Ideas and His Epoch. New York, 1937.

Medlin, W. I., and Patrinelis, C. K. Renaissance Influences and
   Religious Reforms in Russia. Geneva: Librairie Droz, 1971.

Meehan, E. J. The Theory and Method of Political Analysis. Homewood,
   Illinois: The Dorsey Press, 1965.

Menczer, B. Catholic Political Thought 1789-1848. London: University
   of Notre Dame Press, 1962.

Meyendorff, J. The Orthodox Church: Its Past and Its Role in the
   World Today. Trans. J. Chapin. New York: Pantheon
   Books, 1962.

_____ Orthodoxy and Catholicity. New York: Sheed and Ward, 1966.

Micklem, N. Politics and Religion. London: Pall Mall Press, 1960.

Mill, J. S. Autobiography. Preface H. J. Laski. London: Oxford
   University Press, 1928.

Miller, A. The Christian Significance of Karl Marx. London:
   S.C.M. Press, 1946.

Miller, O. F. Slavyanstvo i Evropa. Stat'i i rechi. St. Petersburg,1877.

Mills, C. W. The Marxists. New York, 1962.

Milyukov, P. History of Russia: From the Beginnings to the Empire
   of Peter the Great. New York: Funk & Wagnalls, 1968.

_____ Ocherki po istorii russkoy kul'tury. 3 vols.
   St. Petersburg, 1900-2.

_____ "Slavyanofilstvo," Entsiklopedicheskiy slovar', ed.
   Brockhaus and Efron, vol. 30 (1900), 307-314.

Möhler, J. A. Symbolism: or Exposition of the Doctrinal Differences
   Between Catholics and Protestants. Trans. from the German
   by J. B. Robertson. 3rd ed. London: Catholic Publishing
   & Bookselling Co., 1843.

Moore, Barrington. Political Power and Social Theory: Six Studies.
   Cambridge, Mass., 1958.

Moskov, E. The Russian Philosopher Chaadayev, His Ideas and His Epoch.
   New York, 1937.

Murray, A. R. M. An Introduction to Political Philosophy. London: Cohen and West Ltd., 1953.

Narveson, J. F.   Thinking About Ethics. University of Waterloo, 1967.

_____ Thinking About Politics. University of Waterloo, n.d.

Niesel, W. The Gospel and the Churches: A Comparison of Catholicism, Orthodoxy and Protestantism. Trans. D. Lewis. Philadelphia: The Westminster Press, 1962.

Nodol, E. Estonia. Nation on the Anvil. New York: Bookman Association, 1963.

Oakeshott, M. J. Rationalism in Politics and other essays. New York: Basic Books Publishing Co., 1962.

Obukhov, B. Russkiy administrator noveyshey shkoly. Zapiska Pskovskogo Gubernatora B. Obukhova i otvet na neyo. Berlin, 1868.

Pares, Bernard. A History of Russia. New York: Alfred A. Knopf, 1950.

_____ Russia and Reform. London, 1907.

Petrovich, M. B.   Emergence of Russian Panslavism, 1856-1870. New York: Columbia University Press, 1956.

Pipes, R. Russia Under the Old Regime. London: Weidenfeld and Nicolson, 1974.

Pisarev, D. Selected Philosophical, Social and Political Essays. Moscow: Foreign Languages Publishing House, 1958.

Plant, R. Hegel. London: George Allen & Unwin Ltd., 1973.

Plekhanov, G. Selected Philosophical Works. Vol. I. Moscow: Foreign Languages Publishing House, n.d.

Pobedonostsev, K. P. Reflections of a Russian Statesman. Forward M. Polner. Ann Arbor: University of Michigan Press, 1965.

Pokrovsky, M.N. Russkaya istoriya s drevneyshikh vremyon. 4 vols. Moscow, 1965.

Pyziur, E. The Doctrine of Anarchism of Michael A. Bakunin. Milwaukee, Wisconsin: The Marquette University Press, 1955.

Raeff, M. The Peasant Commune in the Political Thinking of
Russian Publicists. Ph.D. Dissertation, Harvard
University, 1950.

_____ "The Political Philosophy of Speranskii," The American
Slavic and East European Review, XII, (1953) 1-21.

_____ Russian Intellectual History: An Anthology. Intro.
I. Berlin. New York: Harcourt Brace & World, 1966.

_____ Michael Speransky, Statesman of Imperial Russia,
1772-1839. The Hague: M. Nijhoff, 1957.

Redekop, J. H. The American Far Right: A Case Study of Billy
Hargis and Christian Crusade. Grand Rapids, Michigan:
William F. Eardmans Publishing Company, 1968.

Riasanovsky, N. V. A History of Russia. London: Oxford University
Press 1969.

_____ Russia and the West in the Teaching of the Slavophiles.
A Study of Romantic Ideology. Cambridge, Mass. 1952.

Robinson, Geroid Tanquary. Rural Russia under the Old Regime. A
History of the Landlord-Peasant World and a Prologue of
the Peasant Revolution of 1917. London, 1932.

Rosen, Baron. Forty Years of Diplomacy. London: Allen and Unwin, 1922.

Runciman, S. The Orthodox Churches and the Secular State. Trentham,
New Zealand: Auckland University Press, 1971

Russell, Bertrand. Philosophy and Politics. London, 1947.

Russian Thought and Politics. ed. H. MacLean, M.G.Malia and
G. Fischer. The Hague, 1957.

Sabine, George H. A History of Political Theory. London, 1951.

Samarin, D. F. "Pobornik vselenskoy pravdy. Vozrazhenie V.S.
Solov'yovu na ego otzyvy o slavyanofilakh 40-kh qodov,"
Novoe vremya, nos. 5015, 5021, and 5029 (1890).

_____ Sobranie stat'i, rechey i dokladov. 2 vols. Moscow,
1903 and 1908.

Schapiro, L.   Rationalism and Nationalism in Russian 19th Century
              Political Thought. New Haven: Yale University Press,
              1967.

Schemann, A.   Eastern Orthodoxy. Trans. by L. W. Kesich. New York:
              Holt, Rinehart and Winston, 1963.

Semevsky, V. I.   Krest'yanskiy vopros v Rossii v XVIII i pervoy
              polovine XIX veka. 2 vols. St. Petersburg, 1888.

Seton-Watson, H.   The Decline of Imperial Russia 1855-1914.
              London: Methuen & Co., 1952.

Shakhmatov, A. A.   Skazanie o prizvanii Varyagov. St. Petersburg, 1904.

Sharapov, S. F. (ed.) Teoriya Gosydarstva y Slavyanofilov. Sbornik
              Stat'i I. S. Aksakova, K. S. Aksakova, "A. V. Vasil'eva
              A. D. Gradovskaro, Yu. F. Samarina i S. F. Sharapova.
              St. Petersburg, 1898.

Simmons, Ernest J. (ed.) Continuity and Change in Russian and Soviet
              Thought. Foreward Ernest J. Simmons, Cambridge,
              Mass., 1955.

Smirnova, A. O. "Iz zapisok A. O. Smirnovoy," Russkiy árkhiv,
              bk. 3 (1895), 77-90.

Soloviev, A. V.   Holy Russia: The History of a Religious-Social Idea
              The Hague: Mouton & Co., 1959.

The Spiritual Regulation of Peter the Great Trans. and ed., Alexander
              V. Muller, Seattle: University of Washington Press, 1972.

Stace, W. T. The Philosophy of Hegel: A Systematic Exposition.
              New York: Dover Publications, 1955.

Stein, L.   Der Socialismus und Kommunismus des Heutigen Frankreich.
              Leipzig, 1848.

Stojanovic, J.   "The First Slavophiles: Khomiakov and Kireyevsky,"
              The Slavonic Review, vol. 6 (March, 1928), 561-578.

Struve, P. B.   "Ivan Aksakov," Slavonic and East European Review
              vol. 2, no. 6 (March, 1924), 514-518.

_____   Obshchestvennoe dvizhenie pri Aleksandre II (1855-1881).
              Istoricheskie ocherki. Paris, 1905.

Taylor, C. Hegel. Cambridge: Cambridge University Press, 1975.

Terner, F. G. Vospominaniya zhizni F. G. Ternera. 2 parts.
St. Petersburg, 1910.

Thompson, Herbert M. Russian Politics. London, 1896.

Thomsen, V. The Relations between Ancient Russia and Scandinavia,
and the Origin of the Russian State. Oxford and
London, 1877.

Thomson, D.(ed.) Political Ideas. Harmondsworth, Middlesex:
Penguin Books Ltd., 1966.

Trubetskaya, O. N. Materialy dlya biografii Kn. V. A. Cherkasskogo.
2 vols. Moscow, 1901-04.

Uustalu, E. The History of the Estonian People. London: Boreas
Publishing Co. Ltd., 1952.

Valuyev. P. A. Dnevnik P. A. Valuyeva Ministra Vnutrennikh Del
1865-1876. 2 vols. Moscow, 1961.

Velikaya reforma. eds. A. K. Dzhivelegov, S. P. Mel'gunov, and
V. I. Picheta. 6 vols. Moscow, 1911.

Vereker, C. The Development of Political Theory. London:
Hutchinson University Library, 1957.

Vernadsky, George. Political and Diplomatic History of Russia.
Boston, 1936.

Wallace, Sir Donald MacKenzie. Russia. London and New York, 1912.

Windelband, W. A History of Philosophy. The Formation and Development
of its Problems and Conceptions. trans. James H. Tufts.
New York, 1893.

Yarmolinsky, Avrahm. Road to Revolution. A Century of Russian
Radicalism. London, 1957.

Zaionchkovsky, P. A. Provedenie v zhizn' krestianskoy reformy 1861 g.
Moscow, 1958.

Zapiski Otdela Rukopisey. Gosudarstvennaya Ordena Lenina Biblioteka
SSSR imeni V. I. Lenina. 19 issues. Moscow, 1938-57.

Zasedaniya Obshchestva Lyubiteley Rossiyskoy Slovesnosti pri
Imperatorskom Moskovskom Universitete 1858-1866.
Moscow, 1859-66.

Zen'kovsky, V. V. Istoriya russkoy filosofii.2 vols. Paris, 1948.

_____ Russkie mysliteli i Evropa. Kritika evropeyskoy
kul'tury u russkikh mysliteley. Paris, 1926. English
trans. S. Bodde. Ann Arbor: J. W. Edwards. 1953.

_____ "The Slavophil Idea Restated," Slavonic and East
European Review, vol. 6, no. 17 (December, 1927),
302-310.

Zernov, N. Eastern Christendom: A Study of the Origin and Development
of the Eastern Orthodox Church. London: Weidenfeld and
Nicolson, 1961.

_____ Three Russian Prophets Khomyakov, Dostoyevsky, Solov'yov.
London, 1944.

Zhurnaly Moskovskogo Gubernskogo Zemskogo Sobraniya. Yanvar' 1868
goda, (Moscow, 1868): Dekabr' 1868 goda.

ADDENDUM

Crick, Bernard. In Defence of Politics. Harmondsworth, Middlesex, England: Penguin Books, Ltd., 1976

Dahl, Robert A. Modern Political Analysis. New Jersey: Prentice Hall, Inc., 1976.

Easton, David. The Political System: An Enquiry into the State of Political Science. New York: Alfred A. Knopf, 1965

Nicolson, Harold. The Congress of Vienna: A Study in Allied Unity, 1812-1822. New York: The Viking Press, 1962.

Zaionchkovsky, P. A. The Abolition of Serfdom in Russia, ed. & trans. S. Wobst, Intro. Terence Emmons. Gulf Breeze, Florida: Academic International Press, 1978.